Violence, Law and the Impossibility of Transitional Justice

The field of transitional justice has expanded rapidly since the term first emerged in the late 1990s. Its intellectual development has, however, tended to follow practice rather than drive it. Addressing this gap, *Violence, Law and the Impossibility of Transitional Justice* pursues a comprehensive theoretical inquiry into the foundation and evolution of transitional justice. Presenting a detailed deconstruction of the role of law in transition, the book explores the reasons for resistance to transitional justice. It explores the ways in which law itself is complicit in perpetuating conflict, and asks whether a narrow vision of transitional justice – underpinned by a strictly normative or doctrinal concept of law – can undermine the promise of justice. Drawing on case material, as well as on perspectives from a range of disciplines including law, political science, anthropology and philosophy, this book will be of considerable interest to those concerned with the theory and practice of transitional justice.

Catherine Turner is a Lecturer at Durham Law School, Durham University, UK.

Transitional Justice
Series Editor: Kieran McEvoy
Queen's University Belfast

The study of justice in transition has emerged as one of the most diverse and intellectually exciting developments in the social sciences. From its origins in human rights activism and comparative political science, the field is increasingly characterised by its geographic and disciplinary breadth. This series aims to publish the most innovative scholarship from a range of disciplines working on transitional justice-related topics, including law, sociology, criminology, psychology, anthropology, political science, development studies and international relations.

Titles in this series:

The Concept of the Civilian
Legal Recognition, Adjudication and the Trials of International Criminal Justice
Claire Garbett (2014)

After Violence
Transitional Justice, Peace and Democracy
Elin Skaar, Camila Gianella and Trine Eide (2015)

Transitional Justice and Reconciliation
Lessons from the Balkans
Edited by Martina Fischer and Olivera Simić (2016)

Transitional Justice in Latin America
Elin Skaar, Jemima García-Godos and Cath Collins (2016)

Forthcoming titles in the series:

The Judiciary and the Politics of Transition
Police Brutality Cases in Chile, Northern Ireland and South Africa
Marny Requa

The Trouble with Truth
Dealing with the Past in Northern Ireland
Kieran McEvoy

Violence, Law and the Impossibility of Transitional Justice

Catherine Turner

Routledge
Taylor & Francis Group
LONDON AND NEW YORK

First published 2017
by Routledge
2 Park Square, Milton Park, Abingdon, Oxon, OX14 4RN

and by Routledge
711 Third Avenue, New York, NY 10017

First issued in paperback 2017

Routledge is an imprint of the Taylor & Francis Group, an informa business

British Library Cataloguing in Publication Data
A catalogue record for this book is available from the British Library

Library of Congress Cataloguing in Publication Data
Names: Turner, Catherine (Law teacher)
Title: Violence, law and the impossibility of transitional justice / Catherine Turner.
Description: Abingdon, Oxon; New York, NY : Routledge, 2016. |
Series: Transitional justice | Includes bibliographical references and index.
Identifiers: LCCN 2016001213| ISBN 9781138907560 (hbk) |
ISBN 9781315695044 (ebk) Subjects: LCSH: Transitional justice.
Classification: LCC JC580.T87 2016 | DDC 320.01/1–dc23
LC record available at https://lccn.loc.gov/2016001213

ISBN 13: 978-1-138-48187-9 (pbk)
ISBN 13: 978-1-138-90756-0 (hbk)

Typeset in Baskerville by
Out of House Publishing

Contents

Acknowledgements

This book is the product of a personal journey with the law. The journey began when I was an undergraduate student at Trinity College Dublin and has travelled via The Hague, London and Belfast. In the course of that journey I have met and been impressed by too many people to name individually, but each has played their part.

My professional journey in transitional justice began at the Transitional Justice Institute, Ulster University, where I worked with Professors Fionnuala Ní Aoláin and Colm Campbell. Under their guidance I learned to articulate the questions I had about transitional justice. The research I undertook with them initiated a critical engagement with the law that underpins this book. During my years at the Transitional Justice Institute I was also lucky enough to enjoy the friendship and support of my colleagues, including Catherine O'Rourke, Louise Mallinder, Monica McWilliams and Kirk Simpson, all of whom have read and commented on parts of this work at one stage or another. They have between them provided advice and support for the journey, and the occasional timely intervention at critical junctures. Thanks also go to Lisa Gormley for her friendship and her help over the years organising a research career, and to Elizabeth Super and Tim Cunningham, who I appreciate in too many ways to list. I have also benefited from advice and support from colleagues at Queen's University Belfast, where I undertook my doctoral research. Thanks are due to Kieran McEvoy for taking an interest in the project, and to Rory O'Connell and Bal Sohki-Bulley who have both provided helpful advice and comments along the way. Special thanks must go to Gordon Anthony and to Sara Ramshaw. Both have been so generous with their time and with their expertise, and both have helped me to make better sense of a number of aspects of this work.

My journey has not been exclusively academic. I have also had the privilege to work for a number of years with Mediation Northern Ireland, and to gain experience of peace-building in practice. During the course of this work I have met and worked with a number of truly inspirational people who are quietly making a very significant social impact in Northern Ireland. I am particularly indebted to Brendan McAllister, who gave me the opportunity to become involved in this work, and whose pioneering approach to mediation in Northern Ireland has profoundly shaped my outlook on questions of law and justice.

In latter years my journey has taken me out of Northern Ireland and into the academic community of Durham University. Completion of the manuscript was facilitated by a period of research leave granted by Durham University, and I am most grateful to have had the space to immerse myself fully in the project in its final months. At Durham my research has been supported through my membership of the Durham Global Security Institute and the Law and Global Justice research cluster in Durham Law School. The Senior Common Room at Hatfield College has also provided a convivial social and intellectual space in which to debate some of the ideas presented in the text. My thanks go to Anthony Bash for welcoming me into the Hatfield community, and for sharing his thoughts on Derrida with me.

Finally I would like to thank my family. My mother and father, Helen and Brian Turner, have supported me both practically and intellectually from my decision to study law at university through the many years of study that have culminated in this book. To them I am greatly indebted. I would also like to thank my husband Richard Ross, and the wider Ross family, whose support has allowed me to take opportunities that have arisen to progress in my career. Richard has selflessly dedicated himself to tasks ranging from proofreading large volumes of work on Derrida, to equine management and more than his fair share of childcare to facilitate the completion of this book, and I am very grateful to him for that. And last, but by no means least, our precious little daughter arrived in the middle of this project, bringing with her immense love and joy. I dedicate this work to her, in the hope that her future will not be held hostage to the past.

For Julia Helen Ross

Chapter 1

Introduction

1.1 What is 'transitional justice'?

> *Transitional Justice [n]*: the full range of processes and mechanisms associated with a society's attempts to come to terms with a legacy of large-scale past abuses, in order to ensure accountability, serve justice and achieve reconciliation.

This definition of transitional justice first appeared in a report published in 2004 by the Secretary General of the United Nations on the 'Rule of Law and Transitional Justice in Conflict and Post-Conflict Societies'.[1] For transitional justice scholars and activists, its publication represented a watershed.[2] It was the moment in which transitional justice – a concept that had emerged less than a decade previously[3] – became institutionalised and was given definite form in international policy. Since the publication of the Report, this definition has been cited extensively as the generally accepted definition of 'justice' in the aftermath of war, violence or repression. The effect of the codification of transitional justice in this, and subsequent, United Nations reports has been the emergence of an institutionalised model, with a clearly defined list of options for post-conflict states seeking to address an abusive past.[4] These include trials, truth commissions and reparations, which can all be used in pursuit of justice. The model is characterised by its use of law as a means of moving conflicted societies from a state of war, conflict or repression, towards peace and justice.[5] A normative model is intended

1 Report of the Secretary General on the Rule of Law and Transitional Justice in Conflict and Post Conflict Societies (UN Doc. S/2004/616, 2004), para. 8. The mechanisms may include individual prosecutions, reparations, truth-seeking, institutional reform, vetting and dismissals, or a combination thereof.

2 Jelena Subotić, 'The Transformation of International Transitional Justice Advocacy' (2012) 6 *International Journal of Transitional Justice* 106, 116.

3 See Paige Arthur, 'How "Transitions" Reshaped Human Rights: A Conceptual History of Transitional Justice' (2009) 31 *Human Rights Quarterly* 321.

4 See also United Nations, 'The Rule of Law and Transitional Justice in Conflict and Post-Conflict Societies: Report of the Secretary General to the Security Council' (UN Doc. S/2011/634, 2011).

5 See generally Ruti Teitel, *Transitional Justice* (Oxford University Press 2000).

to transcend politics, thereby ensuring that just outcomes are achieved through the application of objective standards that incorporate principles of justice.[6]

The study and practice of transitional justice has more recently been characterised as a 'field' of inquiry.[7] In drawing the distinction between a 'field' and a 'discipline', Bell defines transitional justice as comprising 'both a sphere of activity and a sphere of academic knowledge, with a praxis relationship between the two',[8] and a field of activity held together by a common claim to legitimacy rather than a more coherent 'discipline' with its own common procedures and methods.[9] The effect of the institutionalisation of transitional justice is therefore not limited to the evolution of academic discourse. In very practical terms the conceptualisation of transitional justice as a distinct field of endeavour has profoundly influenced the way in which it has developed in practice.[10] The model therefore engages a number of different levels, from academia to policy and practice. This looser definition of 'field' is intended to allow transitional justice to accommodate divergent disciplinary perspectives within a more or less common framework of understanding as to its purpose. This book argues that the effect of the institutionalisation of transitional justice at the international level has been to create a 'theatrical space' within which efforts at post-conflict peace-making must play out.[11] There is a clearly defined model of 'transitional justice' within which efforts are both designed and evaluated. In this context it asks whether, as a 'field', transitional justice continues to accommodate divergent perspectives, or whether the effect of this institution has been to create new sites of silence and exclusion.

1.2 Aim of the book

While the field of transitional justice has expanded rapidly since the term first emerged, its development has been largely reactive to practice. Theorising has tended to follow practice rather than drive it.[12] While research is now beginning to exert a more discernable impact on policy in some areas,[13] transitional justice

6 Ibid. Discussed in Chapter 2.

7 Christine Bell, 'Transitional Justice, Interdisciplinarity and the State of the "Field" or "Non-Field"' (2009) 3 *International Journal of Transitional Justice* 5.

8 Ibid. 7.

9 Ibid.

10 For a good overview, see Subotic (n. 2).

11 Jacques Derrida, *On Cosmopolitanism and Forgiveness*, Mark Dooley and Michael Hughes tr. (Routledge 2001) 29.

12 Good examples of the theorisation of practice include Diane Orentlicher, 'Settling Accounts: The Duty to Prosecute Human Rights Violations of Prior Regimes' (1991) 100 *Yale Law Journal* 2539, identifying a normative 'duty to prosecute' in international law, and Priscilla Hayner's extensive study of truth commissions that laid the groundwork for the inclusion of such commissions within the definition of transitional justice: Priscilla Hayner, 'Fifteen Truth Commissions – 1974–1994' (1994) 16 *Human Rights Quarterly* 597.

13 See, for example, Louise Mallinder, *Belfast Guidelines on Amnesty and Accountability* (Transitional Justice Institute 2014). See also UN Women, *A Window of Opportunity: Making Transitional Justice Work for Women*, 2nd edn (United Nations 2010).

remains a field in which theory has not managed to keep pace with practice.[14] This work seeks to address this gap by presenting a comprehensive theoretical inquiry into the foundations of the field of transitional justice and the way in which it has evolved. This does not take the form of a historical account or evaluation of the field,[15] but rather of a more focused deconstruction of how the ways in which transitional justice has been conceptualised have influenced its ability to deliver the underlying goal of establishing lasting peace. In particular, the book presents a detailed deconstruction of the role of law in transition. To do this, it addresses three key themes that underpin all work in and on transitional societies: violence, law and justice. Using these themes to illustrate underlying theoretical arguments, the book is structured around three key objectives. The first is to present a detailed analysis of the foundational assumptions of transitional justice and the ways in which these have shaped the field, focusing in particular on the role of law in transition. The second is to challenge the assumption of a linear progression from conflict to peace that underpins much of the theory and practice in this field. The final objective is to illustrate the ways in which a narrow vision of transitional justice, underpinned by a strictly normative concept of law, can undermine the promise of justice in transition. It therefore seeks to ask some of the big questions that have been absent from transitional justice research to date.[16]

These objectives are addressed by drawing on the work of Jacques Derrida, and in particular his approach of deconstruction,[17] to explore the dynamics of transitional justice. Deconstruction for these purposes is characterised as an ongoing process of questioning. Rather than searching for a solution to the dilemmas of transitional justice, deconstruction requires awareness of oppositions, of differences and divisions, and a willingness to work with difference rather than supress it.[18] The work therefore deconstructs some of the core assumptions upon which transitional justice is based, and in so doing generates new insights into some of the more persistent problems of transition. Throughout the book deconstruction is translated into a language that is familiar to transitional justice scholars generally, but also to lawyers in particular.[19] This requires a focused approach to the transitional justice

14 See Kieran McEvoy, 'Beyond Legalism: Towards a Thicker Understanding of Transitional Justice' (2007) 34 *Journal of Law and Society* 411; Harvey Weinstein, 'Editorial Note: The Myth of Closure, the Illusion of Reconciliation: Final Thoughts on Five Years as Co-Editor-in-Chief' (2011) 6 *International Journal of Transitional Justice* 1.

15 This has been done by Arthur (n. 3).

16 McEvoy (n. 14).

17 For a basic explanation of deconstruction see Jacques Derrida, 'Letter to a Japanese Friend' in Peggy Kamuf and Elizabeth G Rottenberg (eds), *Psyche: Interventions of the Other Volume III* (Stanford University Press 2008) 1.

18 This dynamic cannot be reduced to a single citation but is discussed in detail in Chapter 3.

19 In adopting this approach, inspiration is drawn from the work of Martii Koskenniemi, who in his text *From Apology to Utopia* seeks to 'defer the more "radical" consequences which such an outlook might produce in order to remain as close as possible to the style and problematique which international lawyers will recognise as theirs': Martii Koskenniemi, *From Apology to Utopia: The Structure of International Legal Argument* (Cambridge University Press 2005) 7.

literature. Although a relatively new field of inquiry, transitional justice has already generated a very significant volume of literature. Due to the scope of this work, and its aim to deconstruct fundamental assumptions, it has been necessary to be selective in the texts used. The texts that have been chosen are those that either define the field, or that subject it to substantial critique, thereby exposing its limits. Finally, in order to illustrate how deconstruction can further our understanding of transitional justice, the book draws on the example of the transition in Northern Ireland. Therefore, texts that specifically address that particular case have also been chosen. These are then used to illustrate broader trends in transitional justice. The aim is to set up a dialogue between the singular example of Northern Ireland and the general theoretical argument. The discussion of Northern Ireland is not a 'case study' that generates new empirical research on the Northern Ireland conflict, but rather presents a re-reading of existing literatures as a means of demonstrating how deconstruction can cast new light on seemingly intractable problems.

The book presents a highly contextualised engagement with post-structural theory. It seeks to demonstrate to transitional justice scholars and practitioners alike the benefits of critical engagement as a means of evaluating the field. It uses theory to explore the limitations of a normative concept of transitional justice that does not remain responsive to critique, and in so doing it interrogates the relationship between law and justice in a way that has not yet been undertaken. However, there is one final point to note – a point that arises directly from the choice of deconstruction as a means to interrogate the claims of transitional justice. The purpose of deconstructive analysis is to challenge the idea of a 'true' interpretation of the meaning of justice. The place of the writer within the field of transitional justice must therefore be acknowledged. A writer will always be inscribed within a determined system.[20] This book 'marks [one] reading and the writing of [one] interpretation' of transitional justice.[21] Any writer in the field works within the history of transitional justice. They draw upon a language that was already there, and operate within an existing network of understanding.[22] There will always be other interpretations, other views on the question of justice. The book makes no claim to be putting forward an authoritative understanding of the requirements of justice in transition. There is nothing to say that this interpretation is better than others. What is important, however, is that the existence and validity of alternatives is recognised. Therefore, this book is presented as one among many interpretations of the shape of the field, its constituent inclusions and exclusions and its ultimate aspirations.

1.3 Northern Ireland: a conflicted democracy

The book draws on the example of the 'transition' in Northern Ireland to illustrate some of the theoretical insights that Derrida's work brings to transitional justice.

20 Jacques Derrida, *Of Grammatology*, G Spivak tr. (Johns Hopkins University Press 1976) 160.
21 Ibid.
22 Ibid.

Northern Ireland is a relatively well-studied jurisdiction when it comes to transitional justice.[23] Despite having undergone a range of legal reforms pursuant to the 1998 peace agreement, including measures intended to address the legacy of the conflict,[24] the issue of how to 'deal with the past' continues to dominate political discourse. At the time of writing, political agreement has been reached on the creation of what are termed 'legacy mechanisms' to replace the existing 'piecemeal' approach for dealing with the past that has been adopted to date.[25] These mechanisms, if established, will include a Historical Investigation Unit (HIU), an International Commission for Information Retrieval (ICIR), an Oral History Archive and an Implementation and Reconciliation Group (IRG).[26] All of the mechanisms will be designed to satisfy transitional justice requirements in terms of truth and justice. The proposals are discussed in more detail in Chapter 6. Suffice to note that now, as the implementation of these mechanisms is debated, is an opportune moment to reflect on what 'justice' means in this context, and how these legacy mechanisms might best pursue it.

Since its establishment in 1920 Northern Ireland has been defined by division. The creation of a separate parliament for the six counties in the North of Ireland was a response to a long history of conflicted Anglo-Irish relations.[27] Increasingly militant demands for Irish independence from British rule in 1916 had led to Unionists, who wished to maintain a constitutional link with the United Kingdom, making demands for their own provisional government. These demands were met in the Government of Ireland Act of 1920.[28] The Act, which was to remain the

23 For a snapshot see: Colm Campbell, Fionnuala Ní Aoláin and Colin Harvey, 'The Frontiers of Analysis: Re-framing the Transition in Northern Ireland' (2003) 66 *Modern Law Review* 317; Colm Campbell and Catherine Turner, 'Utopia and the Doubters: Truth, Transition and the Law' (2008) 23 *Legal Studies* 374; Patricia Lundy and Bill Rolston, 'Redress for Past Harms? Official Apologies in Northern Ireland' (2015) *International Journal of Human Rights* http://dx.doi.org/10.1080/13642987.2015.1050235, accessed 19 October 2015; Marny Requa, 'Truth, Transition and the Inquiries Act 2005' (2007) 12(4) *European Human Rights Law Review* 404; Cheryl Lawther, *Truth, Denial and Transition: Northern Ireland and the Contested Past* (Routledge 2014).

24 These include the reform of the criminal justice system to ensure that it complies with Article 2 of the European Convention on Human Rights (ECHR). See Gordon Anthony and Paul Mageean, 'Habits of Mind and "Truth Telling": Article 2 ECHR in Post-Conflict Northern Ireland' in K McEvoy *et al.* (eds), *Judges, Transition and Human Rights* (Oxford University Press 2007) 181. This is discussed in Chapter 6.

25 Christine Bell, 'Dealing With the Past in Northern Ireland' (2002) 26 *Fordham International Law Journal* 1095.

26 Stormont House Agreement 2014.

27 The choice to focus on modern history is a pragmatic one. For some, the history of the conflict dates back as far as 1172 and the Norman conquest of Ireland. See, e.g., John Derby, 'Conflict in Northern Ireland: A Background Essay' in Seamus Dunn (ed.), *Facets of the Conflict in Northern Ireland* (Macmillan Press 1995).

28 Sinn Fein's refusal to take its seats at Westminster following the 1918 general election meant that Irish representation was by and large absent for the passage of the Government of Ireland Bill through the Commons. See Thomas Hennessy, *A History of Northern Ireland 1920–1996* (Gill and MacMillan 1997) 8.

de facto constitution of Northern Ireland for a further fifty years, created two separate jurisdictions in Ireland with two separate parliaments, one for the Irish Free State and one for Northern Ireland. Northern Ireland remained a part of the United Kingdom, but with its own parliament and law-making authority. The boundaries of Northern Ireland were, for the purposes of the Act, defined as the six counties of Ulster that comprised a Unionist majority.[29] Irish nationalists argued that the Act, and by definition partition, was unnatural and did not correspond with any existing sense of nation – indeed that it was set up specifically to pacify a section of a province within a nation.[30] Further, it was argued, the Act served to stereotype racial and religious differences by constituting an artificial political area under an ascendancy party.[31]

The division between Unionist and nationalist has been narrated as a result of a historic progression, originating with English conquest in Ireland and the Plantation of Ulster by English and Scottish settlers.[32] The effect of this history, it has been argued, has been the creation of two distinct groups in Ireland. This distinction was clearly visible in the years leading to partition, with Unionists viewing themselves as culturally distinct from nationalists.[33] The division between nationalists and Unionists that drove the decision to partition Ireland has had lasting consequences in terms of how the conflict has been analysed. In the years following partition, division was reinforced by the way in which the new legal order was interpreted by those on both sides.[34] This in turn has led to the conflict in Northern Ireland being characterised as an 'ethnic' conflict.[35] Distinction continues to be drawn along lines roughly equated with religious affiliation. Catholics are characterised as Irish nationalist or republican in their political views. This is contrasted with Protestants, who are most likely to be Unionist in their politics.[36] Since its creation Northern Ireland has suffered sporadic violence and, in recent years, it has also suffered significant and sustained levels of political violence. The reasons for the outbreak of this violence are discussed in Chapter 3. However, the common acceptance of the ethnic conflict paradigm presents a useful, if somewhat simplified, lexicon for understanding political divisions. It clearly demonstrates the oppositional nature of legal and political contestation and the way in which politics is represented as a clash

29 Government of Ireland Act 1920, Art. 1(2).

30 Hennessy (n. 28) 17.

31 Ibid. 9.

32 For a detailed analysis of the historical origins of the 'ethnic' division, see Brendan O'Leary and John McGarry, *The Politics of Antagonism: Understanding Northern Ireland* (Athlone Press 1993).

33 Nicholas Manseragh, 'The Influence of the Past' in David Watt (ed.), *The Constitution of Northern Ireland: Problems and Prospects* (Heinemann 1981) 5, 7.

34 This is discussed in more detail in Chapter 3.1.

35 O'Leary and McGarry (n. 32).

36 The existence of a Unionist political community means that analysis of violence and transition is not simply a calculation between actions of state and non-state actors, but is complicated by the existence of a non-state constituency that is nevertheless loyal to the state. Manseragh (n. 33).

between two distinct and clearly defined ethno-religious groups. Indeed, this division continues to be mirrored in attitudes towards transitional justice, as discussed in Chapter 5 and 6. It also represents one of many binaries, or oppositions, that underpin transitional justice discourse in Northern Ireland. In reading the case of Northern Ireland, as the book demonstrates, account must be taken of how analysing the conflict in terms of two competing 'sides' shapes the response thereto.

Since the outbreak of the most recent 'Troubles', as the violence in Northern Ireland is euphemistically known, 3,336 people have been killed, and thousands more injured.[37] It is this period of violence, from 1969 until the signing of the peace agreement in 1998, that defines, in transitional justice terminology, the 'war' from which it is in transition. The fact that Northern Ireland is part of a democratic state distinguishes it from what have been termed the 'paradigmatic' transitions upon which the field of transitional justice was constructed.[38] There was no complete breakdown of law and order. Indeed, many of the institutions of justice continue to exist post-transition, albeit in a reformed legal and political context. It also means that the boundaries between right and wrong are not so clearly drawn in the context of Northern Ireland as they may have been in other transitions. For example, in the Latin American transitions what was at issue was the extensive use of extra-legal or extra-judicial violence by the state against political opponents, in clear violation of international human rights law.[39] Similarly in the case of mass atrocity or genocide, such as occurred in Rwanda, while there may be debate over how justice is delivered,[40] there is little doubt as to the illegal nature of the violence. In contrast, in Northern Ireland the fact that the state was a democracy and ostensibly committed to the rule of law meant that there was, and still is, considerable contestation over the legitimacy of the use of political violence to challenge the state and its response to that violence.[41] As noted by Leebaw, transitional justice in this context 'condemns as shameful actions that may previously have been championed as a matter of duty to a particular political community'.[42] The existence of competing narratives over the causes of the conflict and the legitimacy of violence means that negotiating transition has been a rocky

37 For documentation of the victims of this violence, see D McKittrick *et al.*, *Lost Lives: The Stories of the Men, Women and Children Who Died as a Result of the Northern Ireland Troubles* (Mainstream Publishing 1999) 1474.

38 Colm Campbell and Fionnuala Ní Aoláin, 'The Paradox of Transitions in Liberal Democracies' (2005) 27 *Human Rights Quarterly* 172.

39 For an account of the place of the Latin American transitions in the evolution of the field, see Ruti Teitel, 'Transitional Justice Genealogy' (2003) 16 *Harvard Human Rights Law Journal* 69.

40 Rwanda is a paradigmatic example of the local vs global binary in transitional justice. See, e.g., Phil Clark, *The Gacaca Courts and Post-Genocide Justice and Reconciliation in Rwanda: Justice Without Lawyers* (Cambridge University Press 2010).

41 The challenges that this new direction in transitional justice poses for the model (as it originally emerged) is discussed in detail by Campbell and Ní Aoláin (n. 38).

42 Bronwyn Leebaw, 'The Irreconcilable Goals of Transitional Justice' (2008) 30 *Human Rights Quarterly* 95, 101.

road.[43] Seventeen years after the Agreement was signed there remains considerable division over the past. While the legal framework of transitional justice has helped to shape debate in this regard, it has not been able to effectively transcend difficult and divisive political issues.[44]

The timing of this book as a deconstruction of the model of transitional justice *per se* is therefore important. What will be demonstrated is that we cannot judge in the present whether a particular action or decision is just or unjust, legitimate or illegitimate.[45] Rather, our understanding of events depends on a continual process of negotiation between the past, the present and the future. Our understanding of the present depends not only on how it relates to the past, but also on how it is interpreted in the future. The 1998 Belfast Agreement and the period immediately following it required a re-evaluation of popular understandings of the violence of the Troubles. This was necessary in order to allow for prisoner release, for example, or for the inclusion of Sinn Fein in executive government. Similarly, understandings of the Agreement itself continue to be influenced by the way in which it is interpreted in the present day. The meaning ascribed to the Agreement was not fixed at the time of signing, but rather continues to be subject to an ongoing process of negotiation.[46] The lapse in time between the Agreement, its characterisation as having given rise to a 'transition' in Northern Ireland and the publication of this book allows for deconstruction of the Agreement and the application of the discourse of 'transition' to Northern Ireland that is only possible with the passage of time. Such analysis of the 'transition' would not have been possible ten years ago, as the language of transition was first applied to Northern Ireland.[47] Any contribution to the present debate must therefore be read in that context.

1.4 Outline of the book

The book comprises six substantive chapters. The first two chapters set the context for a deconstruction of transitional justice by exploring the way in which the

43 This is evidenced in the fact that since the original peace agreement was signed in 1998, there have been two more rounds of high-level talks aimed at resolving difficult conflict-related issues, both of which have led to new agreements. See St Andrews Agreement (November 2006) (and most recently the Stormont House Agreement (n. 26)).

44 This is reflected in the ongoing political controversy over issues such paramilitary violence that continue sporadically to threaten the stability of the new institutions. See Henry McDonald, 'Government Creates Northern Ireland Ceasefire Monitor After IRA Claims' *The Guardian* (London, 18 September 2015) www.theguardian.com/uk-news/2015/sep/18/government-northern-ireland-ceasefire-monitor-ira-claims, accessed 19 October 2015.

45 For discussion, see Chapter 3.1.3.

46 This is discussed in detail in Chapter 5.

47 This is resonant with Derrida's point that we can never tell at the moment that a new law or new legal order emerges whether it will be just or unjust. Jacques Derrida, 'Force of Law: The Mystical Foundation of Authority' in Drucilla Cornell *et al.* (eds), *Deconstruction and the Possibility of Justice* (Routledge 1992) 13 (hereinafter 'Force of Law').

field has been constituted and how post-structural theory brings a new perspective to the existing body of literature. They therefore lay the groundwork for the following three chapters that deconstruct the model of transitional justice as it is currently applied in the Northern Ireland context. Chapter 2 consists of a detailed overview of the field of transitional justice. It outlines the way in which the field of transitional justice has evolved to become the dominant language in which the move from war to peace is discussed, thereby creating a 'theatrical space' of transitional justice. To distinguish this account from existing histories or normative accounts of transitional justice, the chapter focuses on two key features of this development. The first is the way in which the field has come to be dominated by law. The second is the role that binary oppositions have played, and continue to play, in our understanding of transitional justice. The chapter argues that the field of transitional justice is founded on a series of binary distinctions, for example war versus peace and acknowledgement versus denial. It is argued in this chapter that transitional justice is firmly rooted in this oppositional model. Theorising often assumes a move from one form of being to another, from violence to rule of law, or from divisive politics to impartial legality.[48] Similarly, oppositions underlie our assessment of the legitimacy of certain forms of action. The distinction between victim and perpetrator dictates who is included in and excluded from the transitional phase.[49] The existence of an oppositional model facilitates a particular way of thinking about transitional justice initiatives, determining those deemed legitimate (trials, for example) and those deemed illegitimate (amnesties).[50] The chapter suggests that what has emerged is a mainstream of transitional justice – that reflected in international law and policy – and a margin that consists of critical reflection on the possibility of transitional justice. In surveying these critical approaches, this chapter locates the book both in the context of the mainstream and the critical margin.

Chapter 3 then proceeds to outline how a Derridean approach can contribute to the existing critical transitional justice literature. The primary aim of this chapter is to explore how deconstruction can contribute to our understanding of the significance of the creation of a 'theatrical space' of transitional justice. The chapter presents a clear and concise explanation of deconstruction, illustrated with reference to transitional justice. This takes the form of a detailed discussion of Derrida's work, focusing on his interpretation of how meaning is constructed. In particular, it introduces the concept of a violent hierarchy of meaning whereby seemingly oppositional concepts, such as violence and law, are locked in an ongoing process of negotiation in which each attempts to assert its dominance over the other. It further introduces the idea of metaphysical violence

48 See Leebaw (n. 42).

49 See Claire Moon, 'Narrating Political Reconciliation: Truth and Reconciliation in South Africa' (2006) 15 *Social and Legal Studies* 257.

50 See Louise Mallinder, *Amnesty, Human Rights and Political Transitions: Bridging the Peace and Justice Divide* (Hart 2008) for discussion.

that helps to conceptualise the effect of law when introduced into sharply contested political contexts. The theme of violence is central to Derrida's work. From his early work on language and linguistics to his more recent interventions in respect of law, politics and ethics, violence underpins Derrida's analysis of how we construct meaning. Through discussion of this work, it is suggested that post-structural theory can bring new insights into how we conceptualise transitional justice. Chapter 4 then begins a substantive engagement with transitional justice in Northern Ireland. Following on from the explanation of deconstruction in Chapter 3, this chapter develops Derrida's understanding of violence and explores it in the context of law and political conflict. Situations in which transitional justice arises are characterised by the presence of political violence that challenges the legitimacy of the state and its law-making authority. This anti-state violence will inevitably be met by a response from the state. This response can and should be legal, in that the state responds to the violence and its causes through the legal system. However, the response often involves the use of physical force by the state in defence of its authority. This element of violence and response gives rise to the oppositional rhetoric of legitimate versus illegitimate uses of force. The use of the separate terms of violence (illegitimate, illegal) and force (legitimate, legal) illustrates the way in which law and violence are cast as opposites, as two separate phenomena. But, for Derrida, revolutionary violence casts new light on the relationship between violence and law. Rather than accepting the two as separate phenomena, a Derridean analysis reveals the traces of violence within the law itself. The aim of this chapter is to question whether violence and law can ever be separated. It considers the position of the state in claiming a monopoly on the use of force, and the implications that this has for the ability of the state to justify life-and-death decisions.[51] In the case of Northern Ireland, the interplay between violence and law was made visible through the introduction and maintenance of a regime of emergency powers that defined the possibilities of legitimate challenge to the state. The necessity of a 'security' response to political violence dominated legal and political discourse during the Troubles, subordinating human rights arguments in respect of the actions of the state. Finally, the chapter discusses the possibility that, where anti-state violence is successful in overthrowing a regime, that violence will inevitably be legitimised as 'a means to the end of social and legal transformation'.[52] Indeed, this possibility of founding a new law or legal order may even be used to justify the recourse to violence.[53] This dynamic has clear resonance in the context of transitional justice. Deconstruction of the relationship between law and violence therefore offers critical insights into the way in which violent challenge to the state, and the response of the state to that challenge, are framed.

51 Jacques Derrida, *The Death Penalty, Volume 1*, Peggy Kamuf tr. (University of Chicago Press 2014).

52 Costas Douzinas and Adam Geary, *Critical Jurisprudence: The Political Philosophy of Justice* (Hart 2005) 73.

53 'Force of Law' (n. 47) 35.

Chapter 5 builds on the analysis of the relationship between violence and law presented in Chapter 4 to explore in more detail the nature of law itself. It considers the idea of the moment in which law is founded as a moment of metaphysical violence, and the way in which this violence is perpetuated through legal interpretation. This chapter draws out in more detail the relationship between political violence and the metaphysical violence of the law. Specifically, it considers how all efforts at interpreting and giving content to the law will be driven by the need to reinforce the legitimacy of the law, and in so doing to legitimate historical accounts that have given rise thereto. This raises the question of whether law can ever adequately respond to deep-rooted political violence. In the context of transitional justice, and of Northern Ireland, this dynamic is illustrated with reference to the Belfast (Good Friday) Agreement and the centrality of the human rights provisions it contains. What is suggested is that in the transitional phase the opposition between 'security' and 'human rights' that had characterised the Troubles was gradually revealed and inverted. Whereas human rights concerns had been subordinated to security concerns during the Troubles, human rights gradually came to dominate legal and political discourse in the years following the Agreement. This chapter suggests that the legal framework of 'transition' that has been applied to Northern Ireland is no less violent than the framework of 'emergency' that it replaced. However, 'violence' in this context refers to the metaphysical violence of the law. While the opposition between security and human rights may have been exposed, it has not been transcended. Rather, the legal discourse of transition remains trapped within an oppositional logic in which competing narratives vie for dominance. This chapter exposes the role of law in perpetuating this oppositional approach.

The final theme to be considered is that of justice and, more specifically, the relationship between law and justice. It has been noted that scholarship in the field of transitional justice has as its underlying purpose the quest for justice. Drawing on Derrida's characterisation of the relationship between law and justice, Chapter 6 builds on the discussion of legality presented in the previous chapter to explore the consequences of an approach that has tended to equate justice with law. In the context of transitional justice, the discourse of human rights and rule of law is often regarded as a means of mediating the division between law and justice. They are a means of accessing justice.[54] In this way, the theme of justice addresses the relationship between rights, law and justice that is central to transitional justice scholarship. This chapter specifically asks whether equating justice with law means that justice will also be tainted by violence. It explores the possibility of achieving justice in a context where the concepts of violence, law and justice are interdependent. This Derridean analysis diverges from the mainstream transitional justice literature in the way in which it characterises justice. While transitional justice scholars have tended to equate justice with law, or to

54 See Roberto Buonamono, 'The Economy of Violence: Derrida on Law and Justice' (1998) 11(2) *Ratio Juris* 168, 169–170.

view justice as something that can be achieved through law, for Derrida, justice is always and necessarily '*to come*'.[55] To the extent that justice can be present in law and (reformed) institutions, it is only as a possibility. It should not be treated as an identifiable endpoint such as a particular model of accountability or of governance. Justice, for Derrida, is only possible through the ongoing critique of the violence of law. The pursuit of justice should not, therefore, be the pursuit of certainty, of closure or absolute truth. Justice must be about the incapacity of law to do justice because of the endless particularity of each case.[56] The chapter therefore looks at the reasons why law has failed to resolve outstanding political issues in the Northern Ireland transition. It considers the existence of challenges to the narrative of 'transition' and explores how the oppositional structure of law contributes to these challenges. In so doing, it returns to Derrida's two-part structure of deconstruction whereby the reversal of binaries is not enough, but rather deeper questioning of structures is required. It suggests that in Northern Ireland a number of binaries have been reversed, but that the underlying structures of conflict remain unaddressed. For this reason, law has been unable to facilitate a move beyond current stalemates. While not aiming to propose an alternative model, this chapter concludes by considering how justice as a possibility, rather than as a determined outcome, might look in the Northern Ireland context.

The concluding chapter presents three key reflections on the aims of this book. It reflects on how critical engagement can advance thinking in the field, before drawing substantive conclusions on the relationship between violence, law and justice, and the extent to which justice is possible in transitional contexts. While Derrida remained sceptical about the possibility of achieving justice, this does not mean that he eschews the possibility of law as a means of improving lives, and this should be borne in mind when critiquing the capacity of law to deliver justice in transition.[57] The concluding chapter therefore outlines and assesses the significance of Derrida's view that, just because law is not the perfect solution to any given problem, it should not be disregarded altogether. Ultimately, the book proposes that any temptation to act in an unquestioning manner must be resisted – for this, no matter how progressively intended, can also result in injustice.[58] The value of this critical engagement therefore lies in the way in which it reveals, and thereby challenges, the way in which law defines transition, and in so doing sets limits on the possibility of justice.

55 'Force of Law' (n. 47).

56 Ibid. 17.

57 See ibid.

58 Ibid. 28 (referring to the idea of justice being appropriated for the most perverse calculation). See also John P McCormick, 'Derrida on Law: or, Poststructuralism Gets Serious' (2001) 29 *Political Theory* 395.

Chapter 2

Transitional justice

The constitution of the field

Transitional justice as a field has come a long way in the past 25 years. A term virtually unheard of before 1990, it is now widely accepted both in scholarship and practice as a 'field' of inquiry in its own right, as a 'self-conscious field of practice and study'.[1] While there are a number of different accounts of the origin and aims of transitional justice,[2] there is now broad consensus that as a field of inquiry the term refers to the 'conception of justice in periods of political transition'.[3] Since its inception, transitional justice has expanded well beyond its original modest aims.[4] It has been applied in divergent geographical and political contexts and has expanded to include a range of different means and ends.[5] While this has brought a number of different disciplinary perspectives to the question of how states deal with a legacy of violence and trauma, there has, until relatively recently, been remarkably little deeper questioning of the basic premise of transitional justice or the foundations upon which it is constructed.[6] This is consistent with the development of any field, where advocacy is consolidated by doctrinal consolidation, which is then followed by reflection on practice. In the case of transitional justice, lawyers have adopted a doctrinal approach that has provided normative standards for justice in transition.[7] Political scientists have adopted an empirical approach that seeks

1 Christine Bell, 'Transitional Justice, Interdisciplinarity and the State of the "Field" or "Non-Field"' (2009) 3 *International Journal of Transitional Justice* 5, 8.

2 Ruti Teitel, 'Transitional Justice Genealogy' (2003) 16 *Harvard Human Rights Law Journal* 69 (hereinafter 'Genealogy'); Paige Arthur, 'How "Transitions" Reshaped Human Rights: A Conceptual History of Transitional Justice' (2009) 31 *Human Rights Quarterly* 321; Bell (n. 1).

3 Bell (n. 1) 8.

4 Thomas Obel Hansen, 'The vertical and horizontal expansion of transitional justice: Explanations and implications for a contested field' in Susanne Buckley-Zistel *et al.* (eds), *Transitional Justice Theories* (Routledge 2014) 105.

5 See, for example, United Nations, 'Mandate of the UN Rapporteur on the Promotion of Truth, Justice, Reparation and Guarantees of Non-Recurrence' (UN Doc. A/HRC/RES/18.7, United Nations 2011).

6 See Kieran McEvoy, 'Beyond Legalism: Towards a Thicker Understanding of Transitional Justice' (2007) 34 *Journal of Law and Society* 411 on the dominance of legalism and the need to ask bigger questions.

7 On the success of this project see Jelena Subotić, 'The Transformation of International Transitional Justice Advocacy' (2012) 6 *International Journal of Transitional Justice* 106.

to measure the extent to which the normative standards set by the lawyers have been achieved.[8] This literature has focused on the ability to provide quantitative measurements of the impact of transitional justice, thus demonstrating 'real world' impact to substantiate some of the foundational claims of transitional justice.[9] Seen in this light, transitional justice has become a field of practice subject to normative benchmarks and impact assessment that has come to dominate the post-conflict environment. The centrality of law to the definition of transitional justice is therefore the underpinning foundation of the analysis presented. However, the focus on law and normative approaches to transitional justice does not seek to deny that alternative disciplinary approaches to transitional justice exist. These alternative approaches have provided valuable critical contributions to the field, as outlined in section 2.3 of this chapter. It is suggested, however, that among the competing voices of transitional justice scholarship and practice it is law that has shouted the loudest,[10] with the result that it is law that now dominates the policy landscape in respect of transitional justice. What has been largely absent is any deeper philosophical questioning of what transitional justice is for.[11]

This chapter explores the way in which transitional justice has evolved from being just one among many different options for dealing with the past to being the dominant language in which the move from war to peace is discussed in the early twenty-first century.[12] In so doing, it reveals some of the key underlying assumptions on which the field is founded. The chapter is divided into three sections. Section 2.1 outlines the way in which law has come to dominate transitional justice literature and discourse. It highlights the increasing trend towards formulaic approaches to transition that include the production of toolkits and expert guides to transition. This approach to transitional justice, it is argued, allows for the setting of normative benchmarks, the existence of which then facilitates evaluation of the 'impact' or otherwise of transitional justice mechanisms. Section 2.2 considers the effect of this dominance of law in terms of how transitional justice is conceived both in theory and practice. It outlines the way in which this model has instilled a binary approach to questions of justice in transition and the effect that this way of thinking has on our ability to adequately assess the value of transitional justice. Finally, section 2.3 provides an overview of where critique of transitional justice has emerged in the literature. This section outlines the ways in which critical scholars

8 Geoff Dancy, 'Impact Assessment, not Evaluation: Defining a Limited Role for Positivism in the Study of Transitional Justice' (2010) 4 *International Journal of Transitional Justice* 355.

9 See Tricia D Olsen, Leigh Payne and Andrew Reiter, *Transitional Justice in Balance: Comparing Processes, Weighing Efficacy* (United States Institute of Peace 2010) as an example of this type of scholarship, much more common in the US academy than in Europe.

10 See McEvoy (n. 6) for a detailed analysis of how loud law has shouted. In a way, it could also be argued that it is inevitable that law will come to dominate, given its disciplinary preference for drawing normative conclusions, which can be contrasted with, for example, the approach of anthropologists who resist the push to make judgment on what they observe.

11 Ibid. 433.

12 Bell (n. 1).

have sought to highlight the blind spots created by the legal frameworks of transition and the limitations of foundational goals such as truth and reconciliation. It therefore provides a concise overview of the state of the field of transitional justice, its advocates and its discontents. A brief survey of this literature provides both a context and a starting point for the deconstruction of transitional justice.

2.1 Establishing the 'field'

Transitional justice as a concept was unheard of in international law prior to the end of the Cold War. While retrospective claims are often made about the genesis of transitional justice in the trials at Nuremberg in the 1940s, the term itself was not applied until the 1990s.[13] Efforts at achieving what is now termed transitional justice during the 1970s and 1980s had been subject to political wrangling, and therefore subject to whatever concession on human rights could be secured politically, rather than rooted in a normative (let alone international) obligation to pursue a particular course of action.[14] Work in the field in the early years consisted primarily of the documentation of efforts that were already being made by states to deal with former abusive governments. Dancy describes this phase as the 'cataloguing of those structural realities within political transitions that harness the possibilities for victims' justice'.[15] With the end of the Cold War and the apparent triumph of liberalism, however, a newly found confidence allowed normative conclusions to begin to be drawn from this documentary work, and for those conclusions to be drawn internationally as a means for dealing with past human rights abuse.[16] This laid the foundation for a new normative model of transitional justice.

2.1.1 The law and politics of transition

Although operating within distinct legal and political frameworks at the time, each of the regimes of post-conflict reconstruction, human rights and international criminal law contributed to the emergence of an overarching conceptual field of transitional justice[17] – one which sought to reconcile the key aims of each of these disciplines or endeavours within a coherent conceptual framework. It was in this immediate post-Cold War period that a distinctive normative concept began to emerge.[18] Transitional justice was initially narrowly defined, dealing with judicial responses to human rights abuse and operating alongside other regimes of post-conflict reconstruction, such as state-building and democratisation, which

13 Arthur (n. 2).
14 'Genealogy' (n. 2).
15 Dancy (n. 8) 357.
16 See, for example, Diane Orentlicher, 'Settling Accounts: The Duty to Prosecute Human Rights Violations of Prior Regimes' (1991) 100 *Yale Law Journal* 2539.
17 McEvoy (n. 6).
18 'Genealogy' (n. 2).

operated in a less legal and more politically oriented framework. It emerged as an international criminal law response to human rights abuse, entailing an understanding of 'justice' as 'criminal justice'.[19] Transitional 'justice', in the form of prosecution for past human rights abuse, was simply one among many divergent tools that could be used to move a state from conflict to peace, as evidenced in the separate frameworks for action. Gradually, however, the scope of transitional justice expanded. What had initially been seen as mutually incompatible courses of action, such as pursuing peace at the expense of justice or vice versa, gradually became subsumed into a broader framework of justice.[20] Criminal prosecutions came to be seen as a means to address more broadly defined ideas of political and social transformation.[21] Gradually, and largely due to the international prominence of the South African Truth and Reconciliation Commission, the pursuit of 'truth' also came to be conceptualised not as a denial of justice, but rather as complementary to prosecution as a means of pursuing justice in transition.[22] As Leebaw highlights, 'Where truth commissions and trials were once viewed as advancing distinctive and conflicting agendas, they were now seen as promoting complementary and mutually-reinforcing goals.'[23]

With each new step, the field of transitional justice expanded to incorporate a broader range of objectives, held together by the goal of achieving reconciliation. The interplay of these seemingly oppositional concepts exposed the way in which the boundaries of transitional justice were subject to ongoing and contested interpretation. As seemingly peripheral concepts, such as truth and reconciliation, jostled for position and were represented as integral to justice rather than opposed to it, the parameters for inclusion within the definition of transitional justice expanded. Transitional justice also began to encompass many of the political elements it had previously worked alongside.[24] They became subsumed into a much broader narrative of transition, increasingly regulated by law. This (international) mandate was confirmed in the 2004 Report of the UN Secretary General on Transitional Justice and the Rule of Law in Conflict and Post Conflict Societies, in which the goals of transitional justice were explicitly linked with those of peace and democracy and, in particular, with the consolidation of the rule of law. Adopting a broadly defined purpose and *modus operandi* was central to the evolution of the model of transitional justice.

19 Orentlicher (n. 16).

20 See Bronwyn Leebaw, 'The Irreconcilable Goals of Transitional Justice' (2008) 30 *Human Rights Quarterly* 95.

21 Payam Akhavan, 'Justice in The Hague, Peace in the former Yugoslavia? A Commentary on the United Nations War Crimes Tribunal' (1998) 20 *Human Rights Quarterly* 737.

22 Leebaw (n. 20) 102. On the significance of truth and the South African experience, see Alex Boraine, *A Country Unmasked: Inside South Africa's Truth and Reconciliation Commission* (Oxford University Press 2000).

23 Leebaw (n. 20) 105.

24 Bell (n. 1). For a different interpretation see Harvey Weinstein *et al.*, 'Editorial Note' (2007) 1(1) *International Journal of Transitional Justice* 1.

2.1.2 Transitional justice and the rule of law

In 2000 Ruti Teitel published her seminal text *Transitional Justice*, in which she outlined what she saw as an emerging conception of the field and its core underlying assumptions.[25] In this work Teitel brought together discussion of previously disparate mechanisms for dealing with the past – including trials, truth commissions, lustration and constitutional reform, each of which had their own distinct aims and objectives – and discussed them within the new conceptual framework of transitional justice. A significant focus of this inquiry was the role that law could play in facilitating political transition. From the year 2000 transitional justice, it has been argued, has existed as a 'self conscious field of practice and study',[26] the label used to denote a general conception of justice in political transition characterised by legal responses to past injustice.[27] In particular, the shift that occurred at this time was one from viewing justice as operating alongside other political mechanisms in transition, to transitional justice as necessary to deliver successful transitions – peace through justice. In particular, Teitel's conceptualisation of the field highlights the shift in understandings of the role of law in post-conflict situations, moving away from existing and clearly defined regimes of legality to one which is more contingent and shaped by the circumstances in which it operates. The reconception of law as fluid and capable of providing a framework for transformation laid the foundations for the domination of the field by law. Once the traditional rigidity of law and legal process had been stripped away, almost any reform or transformative initiative could be justified using the mantle of law.

As outlined, the unifying feature of transitional justice has become the idea that law can be a means to achieve justice. The promotion of the rule of law through international human rights norms underpins the entire discourse of transitional justice.[28] It is therefore worth explaining in more detail how the role of law is characterised in transitional justice and how law is viewed as responding to the particular circumstances of post-conflict societies.

Transitional justice rests on the paradox that it seeks to address past failings of the law by replacing it with law. While transitional justice may operate in contexts where law and order has irreparably broken down, in many conflicted societies what is at issue is not the existence of the law but rather its legitimacy in the eyes of the population. Legitimacy may be contested, with ongoing struggle for 'ownership' of the law, leaving debates polarised between those who seek to maintain the continuity of law and those who reject the legality of the existing law and

25 Ruti Teitel, *Transitional Justice* (Oxford University Press 2000). This text is chosen as the most cited authority on the meaning and scope of transitional justice.

26 Bell (n. 1) 8.

27 Teitel (n. 25).

28 United Nations, 'Report of the Secretary General on the Rule of Law and Transitional Justice in Conflict and Post Conflict Societies' (UN Doc. S/2004/616, United Nations 2004).

demand reform or overthrow of the system.[29] To try and mediate this dispute, the role of law (and indeed the rule of law) in transition has been vested with particular meaning whereby the stability and continuity of the 'rule of law' is maintained but the substance of the law is re-envisaged as a substantive model that encompasses clearly defined principles of justice. As Teitel states, the role of law in transitional contexts is to 'mediate the normative shift in values that characterises these extraordinary periods'.[30] Law in transition is constructed in relation to the nature of the injustice of the previous regime, which is deemed to be illegitimate and discredited. This, according to Teitel, provides legitimacy for legal change. What is being advanced, therefore, is not only a shift in understanding of the politics of law in the transitional phase but also a fundamental shift in understandings of the role and function of law itself. One of the core and accepted premises of transitional justice is that the role of law in transition is fundamentally different from that in ordinary or settled regimes. The operation of law in transition speaks directly to the idea that there is a need to move from one form of society to another, thus responding to the history and narrative of conflict, and therefore law. Teitel highlighted three key features of law in transition. These were that law was socially constructed; that international law could transcend domestic legal understandings; and finally that the rule of law could transcend politics.

2.1.2.1 Law as socially constructed

Central to transitional justice is the idea of a shift from one illegitimate form of government to a more democratic order. Fundamentally, it is assumed that there is a gap between the 'law as written' and 'law as perceived'. The idea of law as socially constructed rests on the assumption that the legitimacy of the law depends on popular understandings of legality. Where there is civic or armed resistance to the posited law of the state, this is read as sufficient to undermine the quality of that law as legal. This gap feeds conflict, which will continue until the gap is closed and legality and popular perceptions of legitimacy are aligned.

The gap between law and popular perceptions in conflict situations gives rise to some of the key antinomies of transitional justice, those between the 'is' and the 'ought' of law, as well as between procedural and substantive versions of democracy.[31] These are held out as the key points of tension in repressive or conflicted societies, the points around which conflict over the legitimacy of law is most likely to arise.[32] These distinctions are also integral to the *raison d'être* of transitional justice, in that it is precisely these gaps that transitional justice aims to

29 Genealogy (n. 2). For discussion of this in context, see Catherine Turner, 'Political Representations of Law in Northern Ireland' [2010] *Public Law* 451.

30 Teitel (n. 25) 11.

31 Colm Campbell and Fionnuala Ní Aoláin, 'The Paradox of Transitions in Liberal Democracies' (2005) 27 *Human Rights Quarterly* 172.

32 Ibid.

close, using legal form itself to move from one form of legality to another. This is not an altogether uncontroversial claim from a legal point of view. All instances of transitional justice will give rise to conflict over the desirability of maintaining legal certainty as opposed to justifying a new and distinctive conception of law forged in response to an existing set of circumstances – one clearly rooted in history and narrativity.[33] To try and obviate some of this criticism, transitional justice theorists have sought to shift the locus of legal legitimacy from the domestic order to the international, looking particularly to international human rights law as a standard external to the parties that can provide guidance on the necessary course of action.[34]

2.1.2.2 International law can transcend domestic concepts of legality

International human rights law is regarded as a means of bridging the gap in understandings of the role and function of law in transition. Whereas the antinomies of positive and natural law and procedural and substantive law present dilemmas for the domestic law theorist, Teitel suggests that international law can successfully mediate this tension. She states, 'grounded in positive law but incorporating values of justice associated with natural law, international law mediates the rule of law dilemma.'[35] This emphasis on the incorporation of the values of justice into the substance of law highlights both the link being made in transitional justice between law and justice and also the fundamental shift from established notions of legality. Where the legality, rather than the existence, of the law is called into question, the new regime speaks directly to the experience of injustice or repression, implicitly acknowledging the failure of law in the past.[36] The role of international law is simply to ease the passage of this new vision of legality, providing independent standards against which the action can be judged.[37] The importance of incorporating international law, and with it values of justice, in a transitional context is also reflected in Teitel's third understanding of the role of law in transition – that it is capable of transcending the passing politics of the time.

2.1.2.3 International law can transcend politics

This understanding goes to the heart of transitional justice, and in particular the use of law, to achieve transitional outcomes. 'Rule of law' is viewed as a means of simultaneously preserving the continuity of legal form, while marking a break from the old regime and enabling normative change. Although critical of the turn

33 Genealogy (n. 2).

34 Christine Bell, Colm Campbell and Fionnuala Ní Aoláin, 'Justice Discourses in Transition' (2004) 13 *Social and Legal Studies* 305, 306.

35 Teitel (n. 25) 21.

36 This also distinguishes transitions in contexts of social conflict from those in which war has caused a complete collapse of legal systems, which are comparatively rare.

37 Bell *et al.* (n. 34) 308.

to legalism, McEvoy succinctly outlines what he terms the 'seductive qualities of legalistic analysis'. He states, 'Claims that the rule of law speaks to values and working practices such as justice, objectivity, uniformity, rationality etc are particularly prized in times of profound social and political transition.'[38]

Although Teitel and others acknowledge the politically contingent nature of law in transition, most agree that law fulfils an important symbolic function in such contexts. Campbell and Ní Aoláin see law in transition as providing the means to confront human rights abuses through the application of legal procedure to narrative forums, and providing a 'safe and stable' means to assist the journey.[39] The conception of law in the transitional justice literature is also regarded as a key source of democratic legitimacy. Rather than being held hostage to politics, the application of legal form is seen as a means of transcending existing political conflict and allowing a society to move towards a new form of governance, shielded by the formality of law and legal procedure.[40] The rule of law is represented as providing a new site of contestation, bounded by legality. In this way the interpretation of the role of law in transition ensures the ongoing constitution of the field.

This understanding of the rule of law in transition demonstrates the way in which law is regarded both as a means to deliver justice for past human rights abuses and to deliver sustainable political reform in conflicted societies. Law under this conception has a role to play in telling the story of the conflict, in forging narratives of right and wrong and in responding to those charges. The application of legal form is, in and of itself, regarded as assisting with the establishment of democratic legitimacy and providing a mediated framework for political conflict. What Teitel's conceptualisation of the role of law in transition demonstrates is that law is intended to have a reflexive function, in that it can be flexible enough to respond to a past history of injustice while at the same time maintaining the stability of legal form. As the idea of transitional justice gained traction and became more widely applied in policy circles, however, this reflexive aspect of law became subordinated to the desire of policymakers and funders for determinate goals that could be measured.[41] This has led to a more rigid use of law in transition than that originally proposed by Teitel.

2.2 Transitional justice: the margin and the mainstream

The emergence of a theorised concept of transitional justice represented the constitution of a new field, a new way of constructing meaning in relation to justice. Once a normative element was established in transitional justice literature, all efforts at peace-making became subject to evaluation according to the

38 McEvoy (n. 6) 417.

39 Campbell and Ní Aoláin (n. 31) 188.

40 Teitel (n. 25) 6. See also Leebaw (n. 20) 103, suggesting that, as the role of international law and institutions in transitional justice expanded, the model itself became ostensibly less political.

41 Subotić (n. 7).

requirements of that framework. This was clearly evident in respect of the belief in the rule of law inherent in transitional justice thinking. This new international order facilitated the emergence of new normative frameworks for action and evaluation.[42] Despite the existence of a complex web of interrelated claims to the genesis and aims of transitional justice, an overarching and dominant narrative emerged. This narrative is evidenced in a convergence of opinion that certain unifying principles of justice in transition exist and that these normative principles are embodied in mechanisms such as trials, truth commissions and reparations.[43] Transitional justice initiatives could be evaluated on the extent to which they delivered 'justice' as defined in international law, and action in transitional contexts came to be legitimated by the label of transitional justice.

2.2.1 The emergence of the transitional justice norm

From a practical perspective, the emergence of a bounded conceptual space of transitional justice is evident in the increasing volume of international law and policy that regulates transitional processes. The United Nations has published an extensive range of rule of law toolkits in relation to transitional justice, covering all aspects of transitional justice policy.[44] Specific guidance exists in the form of 'Rule of Law Tools' in respect of amnesties,[45] prosecution initiatives,[46] truth commissions,[47] reparations programmes[48] and vetting,[49] to name but a few. Each of these toolkits is intended to fit into a 'coherent operational perspective' that outlines the basic principles involved in transitional justice.[50] These are complemented by a range of documents, such as guidance notes, that shape the institutional response to transitional justice at an international level.[51]

From toolkits to expert reports, this approach seeks to draw general conclusions from the experience in practice of transitional states, thereby committing

42 Bell (n. 1).
43 Subotić (n. 7) 120.
44 These are all available on the UN Rule of Law website www.unrol.org.
45 United Nations, 'Rule of Law Tools for Post Conflict States: Amnesties' (UN Doc. HR/PUB/09/1, United Nations 2009).
46 United Nations, 'Rule of Law Tools for Post Conflict States: Prosecution Initiatives' (UN Doc. HR/PUB/06/4, United Nations 2006) (hereinafter 'Prosecution Initiatives').
47 United Nations, 'Rule of Law Tools for Post Conflict States: Truth Commissions' (UN Doc. HR/PUB/06/1, United Nations 2006).
48 United Nations, 'Rule of Law Tools for Post Conflict States: Reparations Programmes' (UN Doc. HR/PUB/08/1, United Nations 2008).
49 United Nations, 'Rule of Law Tools for Post Conflict States: Vetting: An Operational Framework' (UN Doc HR/PUB/06/5, United Nations 2006).
50 Prosecution Initiatives (n. 46).
51 See, for example, United Nations, 'Guidance Note of the Secretary General: United Nations Approach to Transitional Justice' (United Nations 2010); United Nations, 'Guidance Note on Gender and Transitional Justice' (United Nations 2010); United Nations, 'Human Rights and Transitional Justice: Report of the United Nations High Commissioner for Human Rights' (UN Doc. A/HRC/4/87, United Nations 2006).

to text the principles of the conceptual model. Transitional goals are articulated as legal imperatives, embedded in the normative framework of international law. What it attempts to frame is not so much a blueprint for action, but rather an objective set of standards, rooted in best practice, which can be said to define the requirements of justice in transition. Once clear normative guidance is in place, deadlines can be set for the implementation of frameworks for action, allowing for targets against which the achievement of transition can be measured.[52] The boundaries of transitional justice are therefore determined by a system of positive laws and conventions that define its character.[53] It is clear from these guidelines what is included within the scope of transitional justice and, by implication, what is excluded. There is, inevitably, some degree of a 'right' and a 'wrong' response to conflict. Transition is constructed as a linear progression in which the problem is defined, transitional justice mechanisms are implemented and the desired outcome is achieved. The legal character of this model serves to portray this progression, and the means by which it is achieved, as 'universally objective and uncontroversial'.[54] Subotić notes how a state's choice is now 'one of which model of justice to adopt, not whether any should be adopted at all'.[55]

Transitional justice has therefore become established as the only legitimate response to conflict. It is suggested that the effects of this dynamic are experienced at both the macro- and micro-levels. At the macro-level, the emergence of an institutionalised transitional justice norm has led to the creation of a mainstream of scholarship and advocacy that is easily translated into policy and practice, and a margin that retains its critical distance but as a result remains less 'visible' in international advocacy and policy. At the micro-level, the use of the language of transition can marginalise those who do not chose to engage, for whatever reason, in 'transitional' mechanisms in local contexts.[56]

2.2.2 *Transitional justice and opposition*

This emergence of a clearly defined model of transitional justice means that it is possible to interrogate the core assumptions upon which it has been constructed. The existence of a clear inside and outside of transitional justice reflects a broader trend in the field whereby it is characterised by opposition. In addition to the apparent existence of a 'right' and a 'wrong' way to approach justice in

52 See in particular the setting of deadlines on transitional constitutional processes that are deemed to mark the end of the transition. See Catherine Turner and Ruth Houghton, 'Constitution Making and Post-Conflict Reconstruction' in Matthew Saul and James Sweeney (eds), *International Law and Post-Conflict Reconstruction* (Routledge 2015) 119.

53 Subotić (n. 7). This maps on to Derrida's understanding of the nature of law, discussed in Chapter 3.

54 Ibid. 118.

55 Ibid.

56 See Siphiwe Ignatius Dube, 'Transitional Justice Beyond the Normative: Towards a Literary Theory of Political Transitions' (2011) 5 *International Journal of Transitional Justice* 177.

transition, the 'inside' of the field itself is constructed on a series of oppositions.[57] These are the core assumptions upon which the model rests. The most fundamental opposition is that between war and peace (war/peace). The underlying aim of transitional justice is to move from a situation where direct physical violence is replaced with the more civilised instruments of law (violence/law). The distinction between victim and perpetrator that shapes the boundaries of political inclusion and exclusion in the transitional context operates in a similar way.[58] The way in which conflict is narrated in transitional justice requires a distinction to be visible between right and wrong (legitimate/illegitimate). This underpins the drive for accountability that underpins transitional justice (acknowledgement/denial), which in turn contributes to the transformation of repressive societies into liberal ones. The method by which this is achieved is by replacing volatile political contestation with legal regulation (politics/law) and embedding a thicker or more substantive version of democracy, which incorporates key principles of human rights and good governance, in place of a purely procedural version in which the legitimacy of law as posited is challenged (procedure/substance). Finally, the outcome of transition is to replace repression and injustice with justice. The divided community is reconciled; division is replaced with unity (division/reconciliation).[59]

What has been created is a system of opposites, where transitional justice mechanisms are used to move societies from one state of being towards another. Rather than problematising or interrogating these binaries, transitional justice scholars and practitioners to date have tended to speak of law as a means of moving from one to the other.[60] Opposition therefore goes to the very heart of transitional justice and is the foundation upon which theorising has occurred. It is suggested that this opposition is an inherent feature of the use of law to conceptualise and implement transitional justice. However, the oppositional nature of the discourse has implications for the impartiality from which the legitimacy of the model derives, as well as for its capacity to either transcend or mediate political conflict. This is particularly apparent with the application of transitional justice to 'non-paradigmatic' transitions, where there is a higher degree of division over the causes of the conflict and how it should be resolved.[61] This applies particularly where armed violence has been brought to an end by negotiated settlement, but

57 Campbell and Ní Aoláin (n. 31) highlight these binaries as arising from the paradigmatic transitions upon which the field of transitional justice is constructed.

58 Claire Moon, 'Narrating Political Reconciliation: Truth and Reconciliation in South Africa' (2006) 15 *Social and Legal Studies* 257.

59 See Harvey Weinstein, 'Editorial Note: The Myth of Closure, the Illusion of Reconciliation: Final Thoughts on Five Years as Co-Editor-in-Chief' (2011) 6 *International Journal of Transitional Justice* 1 on the role of the concept of reconciliation in driving transitional justice. See also Emilios Christodoulidis, 'Truth and Reconciliation and Risks' (2000) 9 *Social and Legal Studies* 179.

60 See e.g. Campbell and Ní Aoláin (n. 31). There is also an implicit assumption that the move from one to the other is positive. See Dube (n. 56) 181.

61 In this regard, Northern Ireland, discussed in Chapters 4 to 6, is a clear example.

'conflict' remains over the causes of the conflict and the nature of the state.[62] Just as struggle over ownership of the law can lead to conflict, and ultimately transition, the power of the label of transitional justice can lead to struggle over ownership of the transition and conflict over the scope, definition and priority to be afforded to transitional mechanisms.[63] The model of transitional justice assumes a rupture with a prior regime that is discredited on account of a breach with public support and perceptions of legality. It also assumes that this moment of rupture, most often the physical manifestation of conflict, can be isolated from political and social dynamics that have preceded it and be addressed as an exceptional event rather than part of ongoing contestation of norms. Where there are contested narratives of the conflict at play, demands for transitional justice are not necessarily value free.[64] Applying the label of transitional justice allows one side to take control of the direction of reform in a way that simply replicates the politics and the violence of open conflict.[65]

The interpretation of the concept of transitional justice in a way that seeks to apply ostensibly neutral legal principles to mediate reform serves to replicate patterns of inclusion and exclusion on a micro-level.[66] Adopting one narrative of conflict over another and favouring it through the application of the rhetoric of transition simply reflects the bounded nature of the transitional space and creates new sites of silence and invisibility. However, this aspect of transitional justice is one in which there is now a rich vein of critique that has sought to subject these foundational assumptions to greater scrutiny. Some of these critiques have had considerable success in exposing the limits of the model of transitional justice and, by working within the model, are themselves now considered to be becoming mainstream. Others, however, seek to question the foundations of the model and, as such, the existence of the boundaries rather than where they are drawn. These critiques are less easily translated into law and policy and thus remain at the margins of the field,[67] certainly in terms of policy and practice at least. The remainder of this chapter seeks to map the existence of critique in transitional justice literature and to explore what it has contributed to our understanding of transitional justice.

62 This is now the dominant means by which wars are ended. See Christine Bell, *Peace Agreements and Human Rights* (Oxford University Press 2000).

63 See McEvoy (n. 6) 420, who suggests that this tension is not in itself surprising. Rather, what is more significant is the tendency to represent law as somehow existing above this political fray.

64 The existence of contested narratives refers not only to competing 'sides' of the conflict, but also more broadly to a range of voices that may be silenced by a dominant transitional justice narrative. See Dube (n. 56). This is discussed in detail in Chapter 6.

65 This trend has been noted in the Northern Ireland context by Christine Bell and Johanna Keenan, 'Lost on the Way Home? The Right to Life in Northern Ireland' (2005) 32(1) *Journal of Law and Society* 68; Campbell and Ní Aoláin (n. 31).

66 Kirk Simpson, 'Voices Silenced, Voices Re-discovered: Victims of Violence and the Reclamation of Language in Transitional Societies' (2007) 3 *International Journal of Law in Context* 89.

67 Dube (n. 56).

2.3 Transitional justice and critique

Before beginning this mapping, a note on the understanding of critique that informs the exercise is useful. The categorisation employed here is centred around the distinction between 'internal' and 'external' critique.[68] Just as it has been argued that a mainstream of transitional justice has emerged, it is also suggested that there is a dividing line between two types of critique visible in transitional justice literature. One seeks to challenge the mainstream by demanding inclusion therein. Termed 'internal critique', this type of critique is understood as working within the model or the language of transitional justice with the aim of expanding the boundaries of the model. Therefore, while the model, and in particular the outcomes that it can reasonably deliver, are subjected to robust questioning, the model itself is not subject to challenge. The reason for this may be a belief in the validity of the model, but may also be strategic, in that although imperfect, the model of transitional justice is seen as the best opportunity to deliver the change or outcomes desired, particularly for groups whose needs or demands have been stubbornly ignored in traditional politics.[69]

External critiques, on the other hand, are those concerned with revealing the deeper assumptions on which the model of transitional justice rests and, as such, subjecting the model itself to scrutiny. With this type of critique the validity of the model is not taken as a given, but rather the model itself, and not simply the effectiveness of its operation, is questioned. These critiques have challenged key goals of transitional justice, such as the possibility of truth, forgiveness and reconciliation, as well as some of the ideological bases upon which it is founded. While this distinction is for the most part discernible throughout the literature, there are areas in which it becomes blurred, for example where internal critique begins to touch on deeper questions of how we conceptualise transition. Nevertheless, the distinction remains useful in thinking through how and why scholars engage in critique of transitional justice.

Beginning with internal critiques, this section poses two core questions: where do we find these critiques? And what do they add to our understanding of transitional justice?

2.3.1 Internal critique and the boundaries of 'transition'

It is suggested that the primary contribution of internal critiques has been to expose the blind spots in protection offered by transitional justice, and as a result to expand the parameters and goals of what is or should be included within the

68 In using this distinction, I take inspiration from the work of Karen Engle, who uses these categories to explore the relationship between international human rights and feminism. Karen Engle, 'International Human Rights and Feminism: Where Discourses Meet' (1992) 13 *Michigan Journal of International Law* 517.

69 For a good discussion of this dynamic, see Christine Bell and Catherine O'Rourke, 'Does Feminism Need a Theory of Transitional Justice?' (2007) 1 *International Journal of Transitional Justice* 23.

transitional justice model. These critiques are now firmly established in transitional justice literature and have achieved remarkable progress in ensuring that a light has been shone on the needs of traditionally vulnerable populations, by consistently asking how transitional justice can be used to benefit these groups.[70] These works have advocated transitional justice as a site of critical engagement – as a useful space for opening up opportunity. The unique nature of law in transition is seen as providing sites of activism that would not otherwise be available. There are two particularly good examples of this type of critique, which exemplify the way in which critique has been employed to call for greater inclusivity in transitional justice processes. The first is the literature on the relationship between transitional justice and gender.[71] The second is that on the relationship between transitional justice and social justice.

2.3.1.1 Transitional justice and gender justice

The feminist critique of transitional justice remains an emergent stream of critique.[72] Drawing on a deeper vein of critique of international law that emerged in the early 1990s, it is an area that has gained significant policy traction in recent years.[73] As such, it is a good example of the way in which critique can not only expand scholarly understanding of transitional justice but also have an impact in practice. The successes of feminist scholarship include making women visible to law in transition; redefining what we understand 'harm' to mean in the transitional context; and exposing the limits of key organising binaries of transitional justice, such as public/private and war/peace. However there are also limitations of the feminist critique to date, and feminist scholars continue to call for a more radical or transformative approach to transitional justice that would take feminist critique beyond the existing boundaries of the field.

As noted in section 2.1, transitional justice is rooted largely in international legal scholarship. It is therefore inevitable that internal critiques of the field will engage with the question of law and how it is constructed. Feminist engagement in the field of transitional justice emerged from broader engagement with international

70 The gender critique has been so successful that it is now incorporated into UN policy and practice in transitional justice. See UN Women, *A Window of Opportunity: Making Transitional Justice Work for Women*, 2nd edn (United Nations 2010).

71 This relationship has been explored in detail in Catherine O'Rourke, 'Feminist Scholarship in Transitional Justice: A De-Politicising Impulse?' (2014) 51 *Women's Studies International Forum* 118. My aim here is not to replicate this analysis, but simply to provide an overview of the contribution of critical feminist scholarship to the field of transitional justice.

72 Sari Kuovo, 'Review Essay: Feminism, Gender and International (Criminal) Law: From Asking the "Woman Question" in Law to Moving Beyond Law' (2014) 16 *International Feminist Journal of Politics* 669. There are nevertheless a number of 'overview' pieces that are useful in mapping feminist engagement in transitional justice. See, for example, Bell and O'Rourke (n. 69); Fionnuala Ní Aoláin, 'Advancing Feminist Positioning in the Field of Transitional Justice' (2012) 6 *International Journal of Transitional Justice* 205; O'Rourke (n. 71).

73 UN Women (n. 70).

law.[74] Drawing on an emergent strand of critique that highlighted the gendered nature of international law, the origins of the gender critique in transitional justice lie with the international legal regulation of conflict.[75] Kuovo describes how in the 1990s '[f]eminist scholars and activists turned to international law ... because of the potential it *might* have for women'.[76] Feminist interventions highlighted the absence of gendered approaches to international law and policy and called for both the participation of women in international decision-making, as well as the mainstreaming of gender in international policy.[77] Where this approach intersects with transitional justice is in the increasing demands for harms committed against women during conflict to be recognised in transitional justice mechanisms. The evolution of the feminist critique of transitional justice is therefore integrally bound up with that of international criminal law.[78] Early feminist successes in having women included within transitional mechanisms lay in the recognition of sexual violence as a war crime for which accountability could be sought in the aftermath of conflict.[79]

And yet it became clear that this was not enough. As Kuovo suggests, the result of this approach, sometimes referred to as the 'add women' approach,[80] was that women's lived experiences were 'moulded to the realities of international law, politics and institutions, adapting to what is possible rather than what is necessary'.[81] While prosecuting sexual violence against women at least made women visible in transitional justice, an exclusive focus on sexual violence simply applied existing male-centric conceptions of 'harm' to women and in so doing perpetuated the exclusion of the majority of women from these forums.[82] If the 'harm' experienced did not map onto existing understandings of 'violations of human rights', most

74 While international law has been the main locus of this engagement, interesting intersections with domestic law and politics are also a key feature of this scholarship. See Catherine O'Rourke, *Gender Politics in Transitional Justice* (Routledge 2013).

75 At this time, feminist scholarship was interrogating both the gendered nature of international law (see Hilary Charlesworth and Christine Chinkin, *The Boundaries of International Law: A Feminist Analysis* (Manchester University Press 2000)) and the relationship between human rights and women's rights (see Niamh Reilly, *Women's Human Rights: Seeking Gender Justice in a Globalising Age* (Polity 2009).

76 Kuovo (n. 72) 666. Emphasis in original.

77 Beijing Declaration and Platform for Action (1995) www.un.org/womenwatch/daw/beijing/, accessed 16 March 2016.

78 For an overview of this, see Catherine O'Rourke, 'International Law and Domestic Gender Justice, or Why Case Studies Matter' in Martha Fineman and Estelle Zinsstag (eds), *Feminist Perspectives on Transitional Justice: From International and Criminal to Alternative Forms of Justice* (Intersentia 2013) 11.

79 Christine Chinkin, 'Rape and Sexual Abuse of Women in International Law' (1994) 5 *European Journal of International Law* 326; O'Rourke (n. 78).

80 Kuovo (n. 72).

81 Ibid. 666.

82 See, for example, Fiona Ross's searing analysis of the role of the testimony of women before the South African Truth and Reconciliation Commission. Fiona Ross, *Bearing Witness: Women in the Truth and Reconciliation Commission in South Africa* (Pluto 2003). See also Vasuki Nesiah, 'Missionary Zeal for a Secular Mission: Bringing Gender to Transitional Justice and Redemption to Feminism' in Sari Kuovo and Zoe Pearson (eds), *Feminist Perspectives on Contemporary International Law: Between Resistance and Compliance* (Hart 2011) 137. Nesiah is critical of the limitations of sexual violence as the 'privileged frame narratives for women's subjectivity'.

notably violations of bodily integrity resulting in death, then it remained invisible to the law.[83] International criminal law was not concerned with the experience of harm *per se*, but simply how it could be used to prove a case against an accused.[84] Feminist scholarship highlighted this blind spot. In this way, however, feminists, by demanding the inclusion of women, were not expanding the parameters of transitional justice, nor remedying the exclusion of women. They were simply demanding that women be accommodated within the existing limited parameters. While the trend emerged with trials, the ostensibly more flexible mechanism of the truth commission also suffered from the same limitation. Feminist scholarship highlighted how, despite the claims for flexibility in the terms of reference of truth commissions, they were often constrained by the same legal formality that constrained trials.[85] Central to feminist strategy, therefore, was revealing how law constrains what is or is not considered to be worthy of consideration in the transitional phase.

Having succeeded in expanding the definition of the crimes of concern in transitional justice to include those committed against women, feminist critique moved on to expand the definition of harm that underpinned calls for accountability, and in so doing expanded the definition of 'justice' in transition.[86] Feminist scholarship highlighted the gendered ways in which women experience conflict and, in particular, the disproportionate effect of violations of social and economic rights, which remained invisible to the law that framed intervention in the transitional phase.[87] By doing this, it has attempted to articulate a specifically gendered account of harm, rooted in women's lived experience, that extends well beyond the traditional legal definitions. This incorporates what O'Rourke describes as the 'web of harms' that encapsulates a number of different ways in which women experience violence.[88] By using this concept of harm, feminist scholarship has highlighted the ways in which transitional justice has prioritised public violations of civil and political rights over those committed in the private sphere. It has also exposed the prioritisation of accountability for violations of discrete and individual violations at the expense of questioning the deeper patterns of structural violence that underpin conflict and that often affect women disproportionately. This prioritisation of public harms, it has been suggested, serves to 'neatly separate the harms in women's lives from the concerns (and obligations) of the state,

83 For discussion of this in the Chilean context, see Fionnuala Ní Aoláin and Catherine Turner, 'Gender, Truth and Transition' (2007) 16 *UCLA Women's Law Journal* 229.

84 There is also a very compelling critique of the impact that the need to fit the story of violation into an existing narrative of conflict and transition had on women's testimony before transitional justice bodies. See in particular Ross (n. 82); For a more recent analysis of this trend that extends beyond the feminist critique, see Jill Stauffer, *Ethical Loneliness: The Injustice of Not Being Heard* (Columbia University Press 2015).

85 Ní Aoláin and Turner (n. 83).

86 Ibid.

87 On the failure of law to capture these experiences of conflict, see Colm Campbell and Catherine Turner, 'Utopia and the Doubters: Truth, Transition and the Law' (2008) 23 *Legal Studies* 374.

88 Catherine O'Rourke, *Gender Politics in Transitional Justice* (Routledge 2013).

and to consign women to an apolitical space'.[89] The effect of this is not only to deny accountability for the effects of structural violence, but also to deny women agency in conflict. It also exposes the myth that there can be one unitary account of conflict. Exposing the ways in which women experience conflict exposes the multi-layered nature of conflict and the many divergent accounts that compete for priority in the quest for 'truth' in the transitional phase.[90] The way in which conflict is narrated often obscures many different sites of intersection of identity and experience, and feminist scholarship has sought to highlight this.

A further aspect of this problematic public/private divide highlighted by feminist scholarship is the artificial division between conflict (or violence) and peace as experienced by women. Whereas transitional justice assumes a move away from violent conflict towards legally regulated peace, this does not correspond with the lived reality for many women. Feminist scholarship has used the concept of the continuum of violence to highlight how violence against women that occurs during times of conflict cannot be neatly separated from violence that occurs during 'peace' time.[91] In particular, it has drawn attention to the ways in which violence against women alters in form rather than prevalence post-transition, but that this violence, occurring in the private rather than the public sphere, remains invisible to transitional justice.[92] Therefore, the linear model of transitional justice, from war to peace, as well as the definition of peace itself, is called into question.

Feminist scholarship has therefore contributed significantly to expanding the parameters of transitional justice scholarship and policy. However, scholars themselves acknowledge that there are limitations to the approach that has been adopted to date. Kuovo characterises the feminist approach to international law that also underpins feminist scholarship on transitional justice as between resistance and compliance.[93] It is a project of resistance in that it calls into question established models of theory and practice and demands the inclusion of gender in those models. And yet it does not seek to destroy the model altogether. It has to date worked within the existing parameters of the field to affect change. In this way it is compliant. According to Kuovo, this is a necessary strategy. To seek to deconstruct the model altogether would remove its potential to affect change, or in Kuovo's words, undo its 'potential as a feminist tool'.[94] Therefore, feminist scholars have self-consciously engaged with transitional justice strategically, aware of the compromises that were being made. O'Rourke highlights some of

89 O'Rourke (n. 71).

90 See Eilish Rooney, 'Intersectionality: A Feminist Theory for Transitional Justice' in Martha Fineman and Estelle Zinsstag (eds), *Feminist Perspectives on Transitional Justice: From International and Criminal to Alternative Forms of Justice* (Intersentia 2013) 89.

91 For a more detailed overview of this scholarship, see O'Rourke (n. 88).

92 Rama Mani, 'Dilemmas of Expanding Transitional Justice, or Forging the Nexus between Transitional Justice and Development' (2008) 2 *International Journal of Transitional Justice* 253.

93 Sari Kuovo and Zoe Pearson 'Introduction' in Sari Kuovo and Zoe Pearson (eds), *Feminist Perspectives on Contemporary International Law: Between Resistance and Compliance* (Hart 2011).

94 Kuovo (n. 72) 667.

the difficulties that have arisen as a result of this strategic engagement. By working within the existing model, the emphasis of feminist intervention has remained on technical rather than transformative change.[95] This has meant that bigger questions have not been asked in terms of the capacity of transitional justice to accommodate conceptual challenges, such as those posed by feminist constructs of the web of harms or the continuum of violence, for example. These are questions that remain for feminist scholars to address.

Despite the progress made by feminist scholarship in expanding the boundaries of transitional justice, it is acknowledged that 'feminist presence in transitional justice is complex, multi-layered, and still in the process of engagement'.[96] Indeed, there are risks inherent in trying to impose order onto this critique. This is highlighted by Ní Aoláin, who cautions us to reflect on the potential drawbacks of focusing exclusively on Western liberal feminist discourse, which risks excluding other feminisms.[97] Nesiah goes further, suggesting that '[r]ather than challenge the mainstream of the transitional justice field, feminism has become mainstreamed within transitional justice'.[98] In particular, she advocates a feminist approach to transitional justice that goes beyond simply 'expanding the scope of the dominant subject to be more inclusive'.[99] This dynamic is also reflected in O'Rourke's concern that, to date, feminism has focused on technical reform at the expense of a genuinely transformative approach to transitional justice born of a persistent 'reluctance to engage with the political dynamics that drive transitional justice in particular contexts'.[100] Nevertheless, as a site of critical engagement with transitional justice, feminist critique has added significantly to our understanding of the gendered nature of transitional justice and in particular the ways in which law shapes our understanding of harm.

2.3.1.2 Transitional justice and social justice

The second area of critique relates to the relationship between transitional justice and social and economic rights. This is an area of critique that is less established than that based on gender, notwithstanding the significant degree of overlap between the two.[101] It is, however, an area in which there is currently a strong emergent literature, some evidence of policy traction, and one that is likely to

95 O'Rourke (n. 71).
96 Ní Aoláin (n. 72).
97 Ibid. 206. For a more detailed analysis of these intersections, see Nikita Dhawan, 'Transitions to Justice' in Susanne Buckley-Zistel and Ruth Stanley (eds), *Gender in Transitional Justice* (Palgrave MacMillan 2011).
98 Nesiah (n 82) 137, 138.
99 Ibid. 157.
100 O'Rourke (n. 71).
101 See e.g. Diana Sankey, 'Towards the Recognition of Subsistence Harms: Reassessing Current Approaches to Socio-Economic Forms of Violence in Transitional Justice' (2013) 8 *International Journal of Transitional Justice* 121.

represent a new focal point for critique. As with the literature on gender, this critique operates on a number of different levels. From the basic suggestion that the mandates of existing transitional justice mechanisms, such as trials and truth commissions, should address violations of social and economic rights, to the more conceptually demanding idea that transitional justice as a model cannot adequately incorporate broader questions of social justice that underlie conflict, the persistent exclusion of social and economic issues from the purview of transitional justice has now led to an increased interest in how the model can be adapted to remedy this particular blind spot.

As with the gender critique, scholars concerned with social and economic rights have sought to highlight the persistent silence of the field, both in theory and practice, on the question of social and economic justice.[102] They have also called into question the nature of the 'harms' that are to be accounted for in transition.[103] There are three discernible schools of thought evident in the literature on the relationship between transitional justice and social and economic justice. The first is a straightforward analysis that suggests that there are some economic and social rights that can fit, and indeed have fitted, within the existing legal framework of transitional justice.[104] Rather than viewing violations of economic and social rights as qualitatively different from those of civil and political rights, scholars have identified rights, such as forced eviction, for which accountability could be established within existing transitional justice frameworks.[105] This approach does not require a fundamental critique of the legalistic nature of transitional justice, nor of the role in prioritising harms, but rather asserts that violations of an economic or social nature should be treated as direct violations for which accountability should be sought where possible.[106] This approach equates with that of the 'add women' approach discussed above, in that it does not seek to fundamentally challenge the model or goals of transitional justice, but simply seeks to expand its parameters to include new categories of legal rights. The need for such expansion relates to the second school of thought – that which identifies the tendency of legal transitional justice mechanisms to prioritise civil and political rights at the expense of economic and social rights. These rights, it is argued, are seen as less justiciable and less achievable, and are therefore marginalised in transitional justice.[107] Miller refers to the tendency of transitional justice mechanisms to 'background' economic and social violations, treating them simply as the historical or social context in which

102 Louise Arbour, 'Economic and Social Justice for Societies in Transition' (2007) 40(1) *International Law and Politics* 1.

103 Sankey (n. 101).

104 See Office of the High Commissioner for Human Rights, *Transitional Justice and Economic, Social and Cultural Rights* (UN Doc. HR/PUB13/5, United Nations 2014) on where transitional justice mechanisms have addressed violations of economic and social rights.

105 Arbour (n. 102).

106 Ibid. 16. This may also include using legal forums beyond criminal tribunals, such as human rights or constitutional courts, to give effect to these rights.

107 Arthur (n. 2).

the 'more serious' violations of civil and political rights occur.[108] In these cases, the violation of economic and social rights are narrated, often in truth commission reports, as the incidental effects of the violation of rights – such as the right to life and the prohibition of torture.[109] Rather than being viewed as direct violations themselves, for which accountability could be sought, they are mentioned, then dismissed. As Miller powerfully highlights, this approach 'temporarily mak[es] visible what was hidden, without substantively addressing it. The utterance might appear as a remedy, when, in fact, it further backgrounds the problem.'[110]

What these two schools of thought demonstrate is the problematic absence of accountability for economic and social rights in transitional justice. Where the critique becomes really interesting, however, is in the competing approaches to how this absence should be addressed. While some advocate expanding the legal parameters of transitional justice to include these violations, there is a much stronger push in the literature to use the absence of economic and social rights within transitional justice discourse and practice as an opportunity to challenge the concept of justice that underpins the field. The third school of thought is therefore a much bigger and more ambitious project, concerned with expanding the conceptual boundaries of 'justice' to include social justice and address structural inequality. While this school of thought has been criticised for a lack of conceptual clarity,[111] the use of the language of economic and social rights has nevertheless allowed scholars to highlight the invisibility of broader questions of economic inequality and social injustice within transitional justice. As such it raises interesting questions of where the dividing line between (legal) economic and social rights and social justice lies.

Central to this school of thought is an understanding of economic and social injustice as root causes of conflict. Mani identifies practices such as systematic discrimination, exclusion and marginalisation of groups as underlying conflict. Yet the extent of victimisation caused by such practices poses very real difficulties for any attempt to incorporate these types of harm into existing transitional justice models.[112] Existing mechanisms, including truth commissions and reparations, that are premised on the identification of a specific harm, caused to a named victim by a named perpetrator, will simply be unable to expand their mandates to encompass this range of harms. And yet it is increasingly asserted that failure to adequately address structural inequalities and systemic violence will undermine the chances of a successful transition.[113] Therefore, addressing this injustice is a

108 Zinaida Miller, 'Effects of Invisibility: In Search of the "Economic" in Transitional Justice' (2008) 2 *International Journal of Transitional Justice* 266.

109 Ní Aoláin and Turner (n. 83).

110 Miller (n. 108).

111 Evelyne Schmid and Aoife Nolan, 'Do No Harm? Exploring the Scope of Economic and Social Rights in Transitional Justice' (2014) 8 *International Journal of Transitional Justice* 362.

112 Mani (n. 92).

113 Ismael Muvingi, 'Sitting on Powder Kegs: Socioeconomic Rights in Transitional Societies' (2009) 3 *International Journal of Transitional Justice* 163.

necessary element of delivering sustainable peace and reconciliation. However, in order to do this, a re-evaluation of the priorities of transitional justice is called for. Scholars highlight the preference for market-friendly liberal democracy that underpins transitional justice at the expense of redistributive justice and equality.[114] They highlight the invisibility of economic questions and the ways in which a narrative of transitional justice constructed on stories of civil and political violations renders invisible a background of structural violence and its contribution to conflict.[115] The invisibility of this violence then absolves transitional justice of the responsibility for addressing it.

To address this gap, a more holistic approach to transitional justice is called for – one that recognises the underlying importance of structural violence to any project of transition. As with feminist scholarship, adopting a more holistic approach that addresses economic and social injustice would also 'situate violence on a continuum that spans interpersonal and structural violence rather than simply focusing on acts of political violence'.[116] Fundamentally, however, this school of thought argues not that social justice as a construct should somehow replace transitional justice, but that how we conceptualise 'justice' in transition needs to expand to incorporate social justice.[117] In this way it is also a strategic engagement with transitional justice. It draws on the potential of the unique role of law in transition to advocate a more holistic approach that will address a much broader range of harms. Rather than abandoning the concept altogether, scholarship in this field calls for a radical engagement with transitional justice to ensure that questions of inequality and structural violence are brought to the forefront.

It can be seen both from the feminist critique, and from work seeking to expand the definition of justice in transition to include social justice, that the field of transitional justice has been seen as a site of critical engagement. These critiques draw on key themes of silence and invisibility to expose the blind spots and the limitations of the field as constructed, and to call for a more inclusive approach to justice in transition.

2.3.2 External critiques and the meaning of 'transition': truth and reconciliation

The critiques discussed so far have focused on exploring the silences of transitional justice and, in so doing, revealing its blind spots. However, this has been done in a strategic manner, with the aim of expanding the definition of 'justice' in transition and thereby the range of people, groups and harms included within its operation.

114 Ibid; Lisa Laplante, 'Transitional Justice and Peacebuilding: Diagnosing and Addressing the Socioeconomic Roots of Violence through a Human Rights Framework' (2008) 2 *International Journal of Transitional Justice* 331.

115 Miller (n. 108).

116 Paul Gready and Simon Robbins, 'From Transitional to Transformative Justice: A New Agenda for Practice' (2014) 8 *International Journal of Transitional Justice* 344.

117 See Laplante (n. 114).

In revealing the exclusion of certain groups from the reach of transitional justice, this scholarship has made demands for inclusion. In this way, it does not question the inevitability of transitional justice in a sustained manner, but rather concentrates on providing a multi-layered engagement with the aim of achieving transformative change. The next set of critiques considered are also concerned with the themes of silence and invisibility. However, these critiques express much greater scepticism about the stated goals of transitional justice. In particular, the possibility of truth, and that of reconciliation, are questioned. These critiques present a much greater conceptual challenge to transitional justice, in that they seek to reveal fundamental limitations of the model and the assumptions upon which it is premised. What these critiques ultimately call into question is the temporality of transitional justice – the extent to which we can ever speak of a before and an after of transition and the ways in which past, present and future intersect in the transitional context.

Remaining with the theme of silence, the next site of critical engagement is that relating to the possibility of truth in transitional justice. As research and practice in transitional justice began to expand beyond its origins as a criminal justice response to past human rights abuses, the idea of truth began to emerge as a site of engagement. In 1994 the South African Truth and Reconciliation Commission (TRC) captured the imagination of the world. Rooted in theological concepts such as forgiveness and reconciliation, the Commission appeared as a direct challenge to the imperatives of transitional justice, not least because of its model of exchanging amnesty for truth. However, what was most significant about the TRC, and what it contributed to the conceptualisation of transitional 'justice', was that it introduced the idea that truth-telling (even in exchange for amnesty) could be a means of achieving justice rather than sacrificing it.[118] Notions such as reconciliation began to creep into the discourse of transitional justice, and the parameters of the debate shifted from the dichotomy between peace and justice to that between retributive and restorative justice.[119] It also introduced the idea that justice can be achieved by pursuing the 'truth' of a conflict, and indeed that it might be possible for such inquiry to achieve an agreed form of truth capable of transcending established narratives of blame. Such inquiry was represented as a necessary condition of lasting peace and the influence of this school of thought remains evident in transitional justice discourses today. Claims for transitional measures to establish the truth are often framed in the language of

118 Kader Asmal, 'Truth, Reconciliation and Justice: The South African Experience in Perspective' (2000) 63 *Modern Law Review* 1.

119 Ibid.; John Dugard, 'Retrospective Justice: International Law and the South African Model' in A James McAdams (ed.), *Transitional Justice and the Rule of Law in New Democracies* (University of Notre Dame Press 1997); Mahmood Mamdani, 'From Justice to Reconciliation: Making Sense of the African Experience' in Colin Leys and Mahmood Mamdani (eds), *Crisis and Reconstruction: African Perspectives* (Nordisk Afrikainstitut 1997); Jeremy Sarkin, 'The Tension Between Justice and Reconciliation in Rwanda: Politics, Human Rights, Due Process and the Role of Gacaca Courts in Dealing with the Genocide' (2001) 45 *Journal of African Law* 143.

necessity – represented as a precondition to progress.[120] Since truth first emerged as a foundational concept of transitional justice, it has been linked with the idea of reconciliation. Truth, it is argued, will purge the past. It will lead to catharsis, and produce an agreed history of the conflict that will allow society to put the past behind it and look to the future.[121]

One point to note here is that although 'truth' has become the 'darling of transitional justice',[122] it cannot be said that there is any clear agreement on the relationship between truth and reconciliation or between truth and justice. While the claim is often made that truth can lead to reconciliation, the opposite can equally be true.[123] Similarly with justice, there is no clear basis on which to argue that truth leads to justice or otherwise. These claims remain largely rhetorical and unfounded by empirical evidence. Nevertheless, they remain influential in transitional justice scholarship and practice. Critical scholarship has not only questioned the possibility of establishing the 'truth' of a conflict, but has also interrogated the broader claim that truth can contribute to reconciliation.

2.3.2.1 Truth

The first aspect is relatively straightforward. Scholars have sought to highlight the limits of 'truth' as a goal of transitional justice and, in particular, the difficulty in establishing truth.[124] This critique can be as simple as highlighting the institutional constraints faced by truth commissions, such as distilling a conflict down into achievable terms of reference.[125] It can also relate to some of the dilemmas inherent in seeking truth, such as the truth versus amnesty debate that characterised the South African case, or the political difficulties associated with establishing authority, helping victims and making recommendations for reform.[126] Truth commissions bear a heavy weight of expectation and the first step in a critique of the value of truth will necessarily be to highlight the practical limitations of the model. These critiques assume that there is intrinsic value to truth-seeking in transition and that the model should address these limitations. However, there is another strand of critique that goes beyond these limitations to question the concept of truth itself, and its application in the transitional context.

120 See e.g. Louis Bickford *et al.*, *Documenting Truth* (International Centre for Transitional Justice 2009); Consultative Group on the Past, 'Report of the Consultative Group on the Past' http://cain.ulst.ac.uk/victims/docs/consultative_group/cgp_230109_report.pdf, accessed 17 November 2015.

121 See Priscilla Hayner, *Unspeakable Truths: Transitional Justice and the Challenge of Truth Commissions* (Routledge 2010).

122 Jeremy Sarkin and Erin Daly, 'Too Many Questions, Too Few Answers: Reconciliation in Transitional Societies' (2004) 35(3) *Columbia Human Rights Law Review* 101.

123 See Campbell and Turner (n. 87). See also Weinstein (n. 59).

124 For a more detailed discussion of these critiques, see Ní Aoláin and Turner (n. 83).

125 Campbell and Turner (n. 87).

126 Erin Daly, 'Truth Skepticism: An Inquiry into the Value of Truth in Times of Transition' (2008) 2 *International Journal of Transitional Justice* 23.

Central to the claims for truth in transitional justice is the idea that it will encourage acknowledgement of past abuses and break down barriers caused by denial. The assumption upon which this claim is based is that there is an objective truth that exists and must be discovered. For critical scholars, the difficulty lies in the element of acknowledgement and denial and the oppositional logic that it creates. Where the history of the conflict remains contested, framing truth as something to be acknowledged, rather than a multi-layered and complex discursive process, becomes problematic. Truth-seeking in an institutionalised format, undertaken by a body charged with producing a final report and recommendations for reform, encourages the imposition of rigid binaries of right and wrong that will allow for the apportionment of blame and the allocation of reparations. This approach, however, ignores the grey zones that inevitably arise in deep-rooted social conflict.[127] In the aftermath of conflict, as Daly highlights, most people will be able to agree on the facts of what has happened during that conflict. It is their interpretation of the moral significance of events that will vary.[128] Truth-seeking therefore becomes a new site of conflict. It requires the designation of the distinct categories of victim and perpetrator, those 'authorised to speak the truth about the past'.[129] Both sides jostle to establish a monopoly of victimhood, using truth-seeking as a mechanism to legitimate their superior claim to suffering. The concept of truth itself becomes politicised, becomes contested. Silence assumes meaning. For example, the unwillingness of some groups to take part in truth-seeking initiatives is read as a form of denial, as an unwillingness to acknowledge responsibility for conflict.[130]

This reading of silence has the dual effect not only of politicising truth but also of excluding those who are unwilling to engage in a process where they feel that the rules have been set in such a way that their own story will not be heard.[131] Stauffer sums this up well when she speaks of ethical loneliness.[132] By this, she refers to the element of truth-seeking whereby, on a metaphysical level, whether testimony is heard or not depends on whether or not it supports the narrative being sought. This applies in the context of trials when victim testimony is selected or not on the basis of its contribution to the case against an accused, but also operates much more subtly in the context of truth commissions where

127 Bronwyn Leebaw, *Judging State Sponsored Violence, Imagining Political Change* (Cambridge University Press 2011).

128 Daly (n. 126).

129 Moon (n. 58) 261.

130 Cheryl Lawther, *Truth, Denial and Transition: Northern Ireland and the Contested Past* (Routledge 2014); Jelena Obradović-Wochnik, 'The "Silent Dilemma" of Transitional Justice: Silencing and Coming to Terms with the Past in Serbia' (2013) 7 *International Journal of Transitional Justice* 328.

131 For a good example of this, see Simpson on the attitude of the Unionist community towards dealing with the past in Northern Ireland. Kirk Simpson, *Unionist Voices and the Politics of Remembering the Past in Northern Ireland* (Palgrave 2009). See also Tshepo Madlingozi, 'Good Victim, Bad Victim: Apartheid's Beneficiaries, Victims and the Struggle for Social Justice' in Wessel Le Roux and Karin Van Marle (eds), *Law, Memory and the Legacy of Apartheid: Ten Years after AZAPO v President of South Africa* (Pretoria University Law Press 2007) 107 on the South African context.

132 Stauffer (n. 84).

the interpretation of testimony will depend on the narrative that underpins the work of the commission. Put neatly, Stauffer claims that 'Some truths get heard more loudly than others'.[133] This is due to factors such as power, institutional bias and receptiveness of the audience.[134] It occurs where the pursuit of truth involves locating particular occurrences of violence within a much longer history of domination or conflict,[135] for example, or where harms are prioritised to fit institutional terms of reference,[136] as discussed above. Far from achieving catharsis or reconciliation, the effect of not having one's story heard, or of having one's story interpreted in a manner other than how it was intended, claims Stauffer, is to compound the feeling of isolation and violation.[137]

Therefore, it is truth that is the contested concept. These critiques reject the idea of one objective version of truth and highlight the potentially divisive nature of truth-seeking in transition.[138] Where the quest for truth is a quest for a unified narrative of the causes of conflict, it will inevitably perpetuate division, setting new boundaries of inclusion and exclusion,[139] denying victimhood to those whose story does not 'fit'[140] and eliding alternative histories.[141] Truth-seeking, when seen through a critical lens, risks perpetuating hierarchies of victimhood by using the designations of victim and perpetrator, making an institutional statement of who has the right to call themselves a victim. By doing this, it determines who can legitimately claim to have been wronged and thereby seek justice. The performative element of truth-seeking in transition, whereby truth is 'produced' by a commission, conceals a complex web of reasons people may have for supporting or rejecting the narrative of a truth commission.[142] This applies not only across the macro-axis of conflict, such as state versus non-state actors, for example, but also engages the critique of the rigidity of law in framing violations, and denying the victimhood of those who suffer violations outside the traditional purview of civil and political rights, as discussed above. Wilson's ethnographic approach to the exploration of truth in the South African context, for example, revealed a number of different axes around which attitudes to the TRC could be organised, an approach that stands in contrast to the unified version of history put forward by the Commission.[143]

133 Jill Stauffer, 'Speaking Truth to Reconciliation: Political Transition, Recovery and the Work of Time' (2013) 4 *Humanity* 27, 36.
134 Ibid.
135 See Moon (n. 58).
136 Ross (n.82).
137 Stauffer (n. 84).
138 See Panu Minkinnen, 'Ressentiment as Suffering: On Transitional Justice and the Impossibility of Forgiveness' (2007) 19 *Law and Literature* 513, 529.
139 Moon (n. 58); Madlingozi (n. 131).
140 Campbell and Turner (n. 87) 377.
141 Moon (n. 58) 260.
142 Richard Wilson, *The Politics of Truth and Reconciliation in South Africa: Legitimising the Post-Apartheid State* (Cambridge University Press 2001).
143 Ibid.

However, it has been suggested that the element of righting wrong that underpins the quest for truth as transitional justice can also be read as an alternative to retributive justice because of the way in which it encourages forgiveness. Atria suggests that balance can be restored between victim and perpetrator either through the punishment of a perpetrator or through the forgiveness by the victim of the perpetrator.[144] The problem of truth is therefore linked to a bigger issue – that of forgiveness.

2.3.2.2 Forgiveness

Because of the theological influence that guided the South African TRC, forgiveness has become a constituent element of transitional scholarship.[145] The idea of forgiveness is linked to that of acknowledgement – a linear progression in which the perpetrator of a human rights abuse admits their crime, acknowledges the hurt it caused and seeks the forgiveness of the victim.[146] The victim, having heard the acknowledgement and apology, is expected to forgive, so that reconciliation can be achieved. Moon characterises this bargain as contractual, whereby victims are expected to forgive, and thereby to 'give up the right to perpetuate old grievances' in exchange for the perpetrator being 'bound not to repeat violations and constructively to make amends'.[147]

However, critical scholarship has sought to destabilise this neat progression by demonstrating the limits of forgiveness in transitional contexts. Foremost of these critiques is that provided by Jacques Derrida in his work, *On Cosmopolitanism and Forgiveness.*[148] Addressing the contractual nature of the forgiveness transaction that takes place in a truth commission, Derrida explores the tension between conditional and unconditional forgiveness. The exchange of forgiveness for apology that characterised the approach of the South African TRC speaks directly to the acknowledgement and denial binary that has been identified as problematic in respect of truth-seeking. For Derrida, forgiveness in its true form is unconditional, in that it is given even in the absence of apology. However, under the TRC model forgiveness is conditional, in that it is 'proportionate to the recognition of the fault', meaning that repentance of the sinner, the perpetrator, is a condition of forgiveness. Forgiveness in this context makes sense not as an unconditional and gracious act, but only when seen as an element of, or move towards, the broader goal of reconciliation or atonement.[149] For Derrida this means that

144 Fernando Atria, 'Reconciliation and Reconstruction' in Scott Veitch (ed.), *Law and the Politics of Reconciliation* (Ashgate 2007) 42.

145 Claire Moon, 'Prelapsarian State: Forgiveness and Reconciliation in Transitional Justice' (2004) 17 *International Journal for the Semiotics of Law* 185, 186–187. See also Atria (n. 144) on the transposition of the theological concept into politics.

146 Moon (n. 145).

147 Ibid. 190.

148 Jacques Derrida, *On Cosmopolitanism and Forgiveness*, Mark Dooley and Michael Hughes tr. (Routledge 2001).

149 Ibid. 36.

forgiveness is reduced to a calculated transaction, a strategic calculation, that, in the worst cases, is deprived of all meaning.[150] The tendency of the truth commission is to replace unconditional forgiveness with juridical concepts such as amnesty, which can be administered according to technical criteria,[151] allowing a story of forgiveness and reconciliation to be told. If the goal of forgiveness is to promote national reconciliation, however, then the strategic or instrumental use of the concept is meaningless where there is no shared understanding of its significance, particularly on the part of victims. Thus forgiveness risks being reduced to no more than a rhetorical device behind which governments can hide the absence of meaningful change.[152]

However, while an instrumentalised use of forgiveness presents both a challenge and an opportunity to the perpetrator, it also presents challenges to victims. Critical literature recognises that there are some victims who are simply not willing to forgive, and that that is their right.[153] Indeed, it has been suggested that the focus on forgiveness could be profoundly damaging for victims, particularly where they feel under pressure to forgive as the price of peace.[154] The effect of the truth commission, in reconstructing the narrative of the past, is to perpetuate the exclusion of the victim who finds themselves unwilling to forgive, and therefore to take part in the version of the present propagated by the truth commission.[155] As Minkinnen claims, 'there is no objective truth to claim, no common history to recognize, but only the subjective moral truth of a victim who will persistently refuse to forgive.'[156] Therefore, any transitional justice mechanism that refuses to recognise this right of the victim not to forgive will be limited in its potential, because 'in the theory of transitional justice, the possibility of forgiveness becomes dependent on how theory confronts the suffering of the victim'.[157] If transitional justice mechanisms do not have the capacity to recognise the unreconciled victim, effectively compounding their feeling of violation,[158] then their value is open to question.

What critical scholarship reveals is that the use of the concepts of both truth and forgiveness in transitional justice discourse are potentially problematic on one level because of the way in which they can become instrumentalised as a way of achieving set political goals. But these critiques go further than simply providing a critique of how these concepts are applied, to question their utility in transitional justice – in particular their use as determined goals of transition.

150 Ibid. 39.
151 Minkinnen (n. 138) 528.
152 See also Sarkin and Daly (n. 122).
153 Minkinnen (n. 138) 519. See also Stauffer (n. 133).
154 Rebecca Saunders, 'Questionable Associations: The Role of Forgiveness in Transitional Justice' (2011) 5 *International Journal of Transitional Justice* 119.
155 Minkinnen (n. 138) 523.
156 Ibid. 526.
157 Ibid. 527.
158 See Stauffer (n. 84).

The final goal that has been critiqued is that of reconciliation. A concept transposed from the religious to the political sphere, this is an area where critical inquiry poses a direct challenge to transitional justice scholarship in particular.

2.3.2.3 Reconciliation

Resistance to the idea of truth can also be read as an inevitable consequence of the linking of truth and reconciliation in transitional justice discourse. While truth, and to a lesser extent forgiveness, have become central elements of transitional justice scholarship and practice, they are not often seen as end goals in themselves. Rather they are seen as constituent elements in the much broader process of achieving reconciliation.[159] Critical scholars have explored how reconciliation, a concept rooted in theology, has been framed as both a political and a juridical concept in transitional justice discourse.[160] While the concept of reconciliation holds much promise, particularly as an alternative to potentially divisive retributive justice strategies, critical scholarship has identified the way in which law, and particularly the legal institutional form adopted by truth commissions, has shaped our understanding of reconciliation in transitional contexts.[161]

The etymology of 're-conciliation' suggests the recreation of an existing bond, the restoration of unity in a community that has become fractured.[162] The role of law in transition is therefore foundational, facilitating the reconstitution of society through transitional justice processes.[163] In so doing, it attempts to construct an authoritative narrative of the conflict that reconciles different accounts of conflict into an agreed narrative that creates the unity necessary for a new society, thereby transcending former political enmity.[164] What law does in transition, therefore, is to set parameters within which conflict must be resolved. In this way it plays a useful function in that it requires the settlement of dispute through legal means rather than through violence. It seeks to restore a fractured community by creating a shared narrative on the past that will frame shared norms in the present and future. However, the other, and to some inevitable, side of this function is that in setting parameters, law forecloses further debate on political issues. The limits of what can and cannot be challenged are set by law, leaving no

159 See Joanna Quinn (ed.), *Reconciliation(s): Transitional Justice in Postconflict Societies* (McGill-Queen's University Press 2009).

160 See Andrew Schapp, 'The Time of Reconciliation and the Space of Politics' in Scott Veitch (ed.), *Law and the Politics of Reconciliation* (Ashgate 2007) 10; Christodoulidis (n. 59).

161 In particular, the question of the extent to which ideas of reconciliation between individuals can usefully be applied in a communal context is explored. See Atria (n. 144). For a discussion of this dynamic in context, see Catherine Turner, 'The Art(s) of Dealing with the Past' (RightsNI, 1 April 2015) http://rightsni.org/2015/04/the-arts-of-dealing-with-the-past/, accessed 19 October 2015.

162 For more detailed discussion, see Campbell and Turner (n. 87).

163 Christodoulidis (n. 59).

164 For a detailed critique of this dynamic, see Schapp (n. 160).

further space for dissensus.[165] The goal of reconciliation is to recreate reconciled subjects of liberal democratic nations, thus linking it to a much broader project of nation-building.[166] There remains no legitimate space for challenging the narrative of transition or of reconciliation. In short, seen through this lens, law shuts down the possibility of politics.

The difficulties associated with defining, let alone achieving, truth and forgiveness, either on practical or metaphysical levels, have led critical scholars to question whether reconciliation is an appropriate concept to apply to transitional contexts.[167] If reconciliation requires a shared understanding of the causes of conflict, as well as a clearly defined 'victim' who is willing to forgive a 'perpetrator', then the critiques outlined demonstrate the difficulty with expecting reconciliation to be possible in deeply divided societies.[168] Christodoulidis explains this impulse towards a unified narrative in terms of the law's desire for certainty – certainty that can be contrasted with the openness, and therefore risk, inherent in reconciliation.[169] Law requires determination – the certainty of one agreed narrative rather than the uncertainty of a number of competing accounts of the conflict. It also, through the setting of time limits within which the work of transitional justice must be complete and naming a criteria by which the achievement of 'reconciliation' can be judged, sets a horizon on the achievement of reconciliation. 'Closure' is achieved when society is reconstituted, 'based upon democratic principles, rule of law and observance of human rights norms'.[170] Reconciliation becomes a determinate outcome rather than an ongoing process for managing enmity.[171] Critical perspectives on reconciliation in transitional justice suggest that it is simply not possible to whitewash the past. It is not possible to ignore the existence of radically divergent versions of the conflict and the identities that they produce.[172] If the outcome of transition is to be sustainable, then it is necessary to leave a space for politics, where reconciliation is based on recognition of the 'other', not denial of the existence of difference.

What we see with these critiques of truth, forgiveness and reconciliation is the linear impulse of transitional justice. Truth-seeking looks to the past to establish the truth of events. The past is viewed from the vantage point of the present, but with a view to establishing a different future. This impulse is summed up

165 See ibid.

166 Wilson (n. 142). See also Anne Orford, 'Commissioning the Truth' (2006) 15 *Columbia Journal of Gender and Law* 851.

167 Weinstein (n. 59).

168 See Christodoulidis (n. 59) for a particularly good discussion of the 'politics of naming', in which he addresses the labelling of right and wrong.

169 Ibid. See also Zenon Bankowski, 'The Risk of Reconciliation' in Scott Veitch (ed.), *Law and the Politics of Reconciliation* (Ashgate 2007).

170 Weinstein (n. 59).

171 This is in distinct contrast to the view of reconciliation as a process advocated in the leading policy handbook on the issue. See International Institute for Democracy and Electoral Assistance, *Reconciliation After Violent Conflict: A Handbook* (Stockholm, 2003).

172 Christodoulidis (n. 59).

in Teitel's well-known assertion that transitional justice is both backward- and forward-looking.[173] From the standpoint of the present, the past is reinterpreted with the future in mind. The meaning of events is read in the context of an overall beginning, middle and end,[174] in which injustice and violence is replaced with law and ultimately peace and justice. The desired endpoint of the transition – reconciliation – colours the interpretation of the past and the way the story of the conflict will be told. As Moon states, 'Reconciliation as the prefigured closure of transition thus shapes the new official history *from its very beginning*.'[175] Each of these critiques has sought to destabilise this neat progression, and to challenge the idea that a teleological reading of the past can accurately reflect the political dynamics of conflict. Ultimately critical scholarship has highlighted the impossibility of reaching one unified account of conflict and transition, and has advocated the protection of a political space in which difference can exist.

The final critique to be considered, the 'ideology critique', moves beyond deconstruction of individual elements of transitional justice discourse and focuses more broadly on the dominant understanding of transition. In particular it reveals and interrogates the embeddedness of the discourse of transition within the liberal democratic paradigm.

2.3.3 Transitional justice and the ideology critique

While transitional justice as a field has expanded well beyond its origins, it can be argued that it remains stubbornly rooted in a particular ideological tradition. Mutua characterises transitional justice as an enterprise whose 'normative seeds are in the garden of liberal theory'.[176] Transitional justice, from its inception, has been deeply rooted in liberalism. Both in terms of its goals and its methods, it is very much a product of the resurgence of ideas of a liberal peace that accompanied the end of the Cold War.[177] This embeddedness in Western liberal theory has given rise in critical literature to a number of challenges in respect of *inter alia* the claims to universality of transitional justice, the dominance of civil and political rights as the frame of reference for justice in transition, and the individual versus collective rights dichotomy.[178] However, while all of these critiques ask important questions of transitional justice, there is also a body of literature that seeks to highlight further the ideological embeddedness that underpins theory and practice in transitional justice.[179]

173 Teitel (n. 25).
174 See Moon (n. 145) 268.
175 Ibid. 271. Emphasis in original.
176 Makau Matua, 'What Is the Future of Transitional Justice?' (2015) 9 *International Journal of Transitional Justice* 1.
177 For detailed discussion of this, see Catherine Turner, 'Delivering Lasting Peace, Democracy and Human Rights in Transition: The Role of International Law' (2008) 2 *International Journal of Transitional Justice* 126.
178 Matua (n. 176).
179 See, in particular, the work of Wilson (n. 142) on truth as a project of nation-building.

The value of separating critique of the operation within a particular ideology, and interrogating the role of ideology in constructing the field, lies in the potential of the critical scholar to expose on a macro-level the political dynamics that shape our understanding of the meaning and goals of transition *per se*, and how these impact the effectiveness or otherwise of transitional justice.[180] Or, put more simply, what we need to consider is not just how existing transitional justice mechanisms might be adapted to fix divergent contexts, but how divergent contexts can shape our understanding of transitional justice. From this perspective, Third World and post-colonial critiques offer new insights into the operation of a field whose evolution has been driven by European and North American scholars and policymakers. For example, post-colonial critiques of transitional justice identify the way in which it operates within the framework of law and society created by colonialism, without taking into account differing political priorities and models of social organisation that might make these frameworks inappropriate.[181] As Dawan highlights, 'colonial relations still inform how problems are perceived and what solutions are offered.'[182] This is evident in the teleological approach to transition outlined above, in which endpoints of the reconstituted society are represented by human rights and democratic governance, for example, or the association of justice in transition with Western notions of accountability and legal institutional reform.[183] Similarly, Nesiah characterises transitional justice as 'incorporated into a North–South trajectory' in which the global North 'tilt[s] the field'.[184] She therefore challenges feminist scholars to resist becoming mainstream within the field and rather to counter the hegemonic project.

Ideology critiques challenge us to ask important questions – such as for whose benefit does transitional justice exist?[185] They also ask explicitly that which is only hinted at by other critiques, namely what are we transitioning from, and what are we transitioning to? How do we strike the balance between liberty and equality?[186] These are fundamental questions that relate to the organisation of society, the answers to which are simply taken for granted in transitional justice discourse, but which may nevertheless be the subject of considerable political division within affected states.[187] The liberal framework assumes the impartiality of law as between competing conceptions of law and state, presenting itself as a

180 See Abdullahi An Na'im, 'Editorial Note: From the Neo-colonial "Transitional" to Indigenous Formations of Justice' (2013) 7 *International Journal of Transitional Justice* 197.
181 See, for example, Khanyisela Moyo, 'Mimicry, Transitional Justice and the Land Question in Racially Divided Former Settler Colonies' (2015) 9 *International Journal of Transitional Justice* 70.
182 Dhawan (n. 97) 264.
183 Dustin Sharp, 'Emancipating Transitional Justice from the Bonds of the Paradigmatic Transition' (2014) 9 *International Journal of Transitional Justice* 150.
184 Nesiah (n. 82) 156.
185 See Rosemary Nagy's critique, 'Transitional Justice as Global Project: Critical Reflections' (2008) 29 *Third World Quarterly* 275.
186 Ibid.
187 See e.g. Catherine Turner, 'Transitional Constitutionalism and the Case of the Arab Spring' (2015) 64 *International and Comparative Law Quarterly* 267.

depoliticised framework that transcends political division, and yet in transitional contexts it may be unable to play the neutral role it assumes.[188] So it is perhaps from an ideological perspective that critique is most required. Robbins highlights how 'transitional justice appears to have become ossified in an incantation that is directly linked to the transitions of the post-Cold War era and the hubris of the end of history'.[189] As such it has been unable or unwilling to adapt to the changed contexts in which it is now applied.[190]

2.4 Conclusion

The purpose of this chapter was to explore the way in which transitional justice has evolved to become the dominant language in which the move from war to peace is discussed.[191] By tracing the progression from the articulation of a 'concept' of transitional justice and its institution in law and policy, the chapter has demonstrated how law and legal form have come to dominate how transitional justice is understood.[192] The review suggests that the effect of the institution of transitional justice into law and policy has been to create a 'theatrical space' within which efforts at peace-making must play out.[193] The effect of the creation of this 'theatrical space' has been to create a mainstream and a margin in transitional justice research. The critical approaches outlined have all sought to expose the existence of this dynamic. All of the critiques discussed have shared the concern that transitional justice attempts to neatly package complex dynamics into a progressive narrative of war and peace. In this narrative, conflict is categorised as rupture, as an aberration that interrupts normal life, but that can be addressed by properly designed (legal) institutions. The proper design and implementation of these largely legal solutions has the effect of fitting the conflict into a neat linear account of historical factors that caused the conflict, and that can then be isolated as a means of addressing that conflict and preventing its recurrence. This requires the acceptance of the possibility of a unified and progressive narrative in which the past can be separated from the present, and indeed from the future. Each of the critiques discussed has demonstrated how the separation of past, present and future, and the presentation of a progressive temporality, obscures the deeper dynamics of transition. Although the model of transitional justice, both in theory and practice, has been subjected to increasingly rigorous critique that has begun to question the very existence of the field, there is little sense from this

188 Ibid.

189 Simon Robbins, 'Mapping a Future for Transitional Justice by Learning from its Past' (2015) 9 *International Journal of Transitional Justice* 181.

190 See for example Reem Abou-El-Fadl, 'Beyond Conventional Transitional Justice: Egypt's 2011 Revolution and the Absence of Political Will' (2012) 6 *International Journal of Transitional Justice* 318; Turner (n. 187).

191 Bell (n. 1).

192 McEvoy (n. 6).

193 *On Cosmopolitanism and Forgiveness* (n. 148) 29.

literature that there is no role for 'transitional justice'.[194] This is a remarkable testimony to the resilience of the *idea* of transitional justice – to the idea that there should be an exceptional space carved out of everyday politics in which questions of truth, justice and reconciliation are addressed. Rather than a dismissal of the idea of transitional justice altogether, what emerges both from the internal and the external critiques is the idea that transitional justice has both determinate and reflexive aspects. As the model currently operates, it has tended to focus on a set of narrowly defined priorities, which has effectively precluded the transformative potential of the model itself. The vast majority of these critiques are an appeal to rethink the way in which transitional justice is conceptualised to leave open the transformative potential of transition, so that it can achieve its potential.

This book argues that if transitional justice is to act as a transformative force, a broader view needs to be taken of its aims and its operation. The aim is not to replicate the critical analysis outlined, nor to critique any particular mechanism of transitional justice. Rather the aim is to ascertain how critical engagement can contribute to our understanding of transitional justice. To this end it explores in greater detail the operation of the *model* of transitional justice, and the effect that the emergence of a 'theatrical space' of transition has had on the way we think about conflict resolution. By taking a step back and working at a slightly higher level of abstraction, it aims to join the dots between each of the separate critiques presented. Rather than exploring discrete sites of silence and invisibility, it seeks to ask the bigger question of *why* some voices and some experiences are excluded from transitional justice discourse. In so doing, it proposes a coherent theoretical framework within which these disparate critiques can be understood. This is achieved by highlighting the relationship between violence, law and justice in constructing understandings of conflict and transition. The following chapter explores how deconstructive analysis can provide useful insights into the way in which the meaning of justice is constructed. It therefore casts new light on the reasons that some groups resist participating in transitional justice, highlighting points of convergence between apparently distinct sites of resistance and considering the macro-structure of contestation over the meaning and purpose of transition. By reflecting on the overarching concept rather than the individual mechanisms of justice, the book asks whether silence and exclusion are immanent to transitional justice as we currently understand it.

194 On a note of caution, however, these are the critiques that engage with and are themselves visible to transitional justice. This claim does not take account of those silences born of an unwillingness to participate in the discourse and thereby legitimate its application.

Chapter 3

Introducing uncertainty

Deconstruction and transitional justice

Transitional justice as a field of inquiry has, until recently, been relatively under-theorised. This can be seen as a logical consequence of its recent emergence, and the fact that a field must become established before it can be robustly critiqued.[1] However, as the previous chapter has demonstrated, transitional justice is now subject to increasingly critical interrogation, from disciplines ranging from anthropology to theology. These critical perspectives that have been brought to bear on transitional justice have highlighted its blind spots, and the ways in which the model of transitional justice itself has set the boundaries of inclusion and exclusion in the transitional space. Building on the critiques of transitional justice outlined in the previous chapter, this chapter now seeks to expound at a theoretical level the points of convergence between these critiques. In so doing, it explores how critical engagement can contribute to our understanding of transitional justice. The purpose of this exercise is to move the critique beyond simply asking 'who' or 'what' is excluded from transitional justice, to also asking 'how' and 'why' this exclusion occurs. Drawing on the work of Jacques Derrida, and in particular on the approach of deconstruction, this chapter builds on the analysis presented in Chapter 2 by examining in more depth the way in which our understanding of transitional justice is premised on a series of oppositions. The aim of this approach is to ascertain the significance of an oppositional structure for the possibility of resolving conflict. At this point it should be noted that this book is first and foremost a book about transitional justice. There are critical scholars who focus more closely on the specific texts of Derrida drawn upon here.[2] Where this work differs is in the application of the deconstructive premise of Derrida's reading of law, politics, ethics and justice to the relatively newly constituted field of transitional justice. It therefore proposes a new reading of transitional justice

1 Christine Bell, 'Transitional Justice, Interdisciplinarity and the State of the "Field" or "Non-Field"' (2009) 3 *International Journal of Transitional Justice* 5 on the establishment of the field and how critique is beginning to emerge.

2 See, for example, Richard Beardsworth, *Derrida and the Political* (Routledge 1996); Peter Goodrich *et al.*, 'Introduction: A Philosophy of Legal Enigmas' in P Goodrich *et al.* (eds), *Derrida and Legal Philosophy* (Palgrave Macmillan 2008); Jacques De Ville, 'Sovereignty without Sovereignty: Derrida's Declarations of Independence' (2008) 19 *Law and Critique* 87.

that uses deconstruction as a means of exploring both the promise and the pitfalls of the field.

This chapter explores the origin and development of the term 'deconstruction' in the context of linguistics and the power of language to shape meaning. It begins by discussing deconstruction in the context of institutions and systems of thought, and analyses the emergence of the concept of '*différance*' that is central to deconstruction. It then moves on to outline the understanding of deconstruction that informs the analysis presented in the rest of the book. In particular it distinguishes between deconstruction and other methodological approaches to transitional justice. Finally, the chapter builds on this analysis by considering the application of the idea of deconstruction to the law. It explores Derrida's work on the nature of law, and on the relationship between law and justice that makes law essentially deconstructible. In this way the chapter progresses with Derrida's own work, beginning with the philosophical origins of his deconstructive approach, and culminating in its logical engagement with the question of violence and transition. It is suggested that, by its very nature, deconstruction provides a valuable tool for interrogating the underlying assumptions not only of the subject with which it is immediately concerned, but also of broader structures of philosophical thought and method that underlie our systems of meaning. It is therefore a highly transferable approach for the critical mind, and one that can make a significant contribution to our understanding of transitional justice. And yet this is not an approach that has so far been taken to the study of transitional justice. The use of post-structural theory to question the foundations of transitional justice is only beginning to emerge.

3.1 What is deconstruction?

'Deconstruction' is a word that evokes competing conceptions of the value of critical thought. For some, deconstruction can be criticised for failing to engage with important questions of justice and ethics.[3] For others, it is a necessary means of exposing the absence of secure foundation, of revealing the contingent nature of accepted values and beliefs. Deconstruction therefore means different things to different people.[4] By its very nature it defies institutionalisation in an authoritative definition. Derrida first outlined his concept of deconstruction in the context of language and linguistics,[5] exploring the interplay between language and the

3 Jacques Derrida, 'Force of Law: The Mystical Foundation of Authority' in Drucilla Cornell *et al.* (eds), *Deconstruction and the Possibility of Justice* (Routledge 1992) 1,7 (hereinafter 'Force of Law'). Derrida acknowledges how his texts can *seem* not to foreground these issues. See also Goodrich *et al.* (n. 2) 1.

4 Michael Rosenfeld, 'Deconstruction and Legal Interpretation: Conflict, Indeterminacy and the Temptations of the New Legal Formalism' in Drucilla Cornell *et al.* (eds), *Deconstruction and the Possibility of Justice* (Routledge 1992) 152.

5 Jacques Derrida, *Of Grammatology*, Gayatri Chakravorty Spivak tr. (Johns Hopkins University Press 1976) (hereinafter 'Of Grammatology').

construction of meaning. From this early work, and later works in which he has attempted to explain deconstruction to others,[6] it is possible to provide a basic explanation of what deconstruction is commonly understood to mean.[7] Three key features emerge from Derrida's work as making deconstruction possible. These are, first, the inherent desire to have a centre, or focal point, to structure understanding (logocentrism); second, the reduction of meaning to set definitions that are committed to writing (nothing beyond the text); and, finally, how the reduction of meaning to writing captures opposition within that concept itself (*différance*). These three features found the possibility of deconstruction as an ongoing process of questioning the accepted basis of meaning. Each will be explained in turn.

3.1.1 Logocentrism

Deconstruction is commonly associated with the identification and inversion of binaries, and revealing the way in which some groups, or some ideas, become subordinated to others. While this is a simplified, and incomplete, way of characterising deconstruction,[8] it is nevertheless a useful starting point from which to explore Derrida's understanding of the way in which meaning is constructed. Derrida takes as his starting point the assertion that modern Western philosophy is characterised by and constructed around an inherent desire to place meaning at the centre of presence. Put simply, philosophy is driven by a desire for the certainty associated with the existence of an absolute truth, or an objective meaning that makes sense of our place in the world. The clearest example of this dynamic occurs in religious thought. The Bible states that in the beginning there was The Word, and that the Word was God.[9] This statement confirms to the believer the existence of a higher authority that can, through the study of religious teaching, be discovered. The pursuit of 'The Word' therefore shapes the meaning of life for the religious believer. Termed 'logocentrism' by Derrida, when seen in broader terms this dynamic results in one particular term or concept being placed at the centre of all efforts at theorising or interrogating meaning. The term becomes the core around which meaning is constructed – the reference point that determines

6 Jacques Derrida, 'Letter to a Japanese Friend' in Peggy Kamuf and Elizabeth G Rottenberg (eds), *Psyche: Interventions of the Other Volume III* (Stanford University Press 2008) 1 (hereinafter 'Letter'); Jacques Derrida and John D Caputo, *Deconstruction in a Nutshell: A Conversation with Jacques Derrida* (Fordham 1997) (hereinafter 'Villanova Roundtable').

7 However, such explanation should be undertaken with caution, as Derrida himself was uneasy with applying a label to deconstruction. Simon Critchley, 'An Ethos of Reading' (2005) 129 *Radical Philosophy* 26. To apply a label is to risk belittling its complexities. Beardsworth (n. 2) xv. As Ramshaw notes, 'One may be obliged to employ such words when describing deconstruction, but the spectre of this warning necessarily haunts each use.' Sara Ramshaw, 'Deconstructing Jazz Improvisation: Derrida and the Law of the Singular Event' (2006) 2 *Critical Studies in Improvisation* 1, footnote 13.

8 Jacques Derrida, *Positions* (The Athlone Press 1981) 59 (hereinafter 'Positions').

9 The Holy Bible, King James Version (Cambridge University Press 1611).

all subsequent knowledge. In this way it becomes the foundational concept for the whole system.[10]

In the context of transitional justice, the reference point is 'justice'. The field depends for its existence on an abstract idea of justice that provides both the basis for its institution in law and policy and the standard against which efforts are judged. Without the existence of this abstract idea of justice, the field would be meaningless. Instead of a coherent field of activity, held together by a common claim to legitimacy,[11] transitional justice would exist simply as a fragmented series of initiatives, not held together by any common conceptual thread, but simply a range of different approaches driven by diverse motivations and judged according to different criteria. Justice is therefore the *logos*. Teitel's conceptualisation of the field of transitional justice, as discussed in Chapter 2, illustrates in practice how logocentrism works and how it shapes the ways in which transitional justice is given meaning in the present, in that it demonstrates the way in which one unifying concept, that of justice, can be used to narrate a coherent approach to transition.[12]

Having highlighted the existence of this trend towards logocentrism, Derrida explores the origin of the *logos*, and the way in which it becomes instituted into tangible form.[13] His work highlights how logocentrism assumes the existence of set and stable meanings that exist to be discovered.[14] The way in which this term – the *logos* – is made known is language, the translation into words of a concept or a way of thinking. Derrida describes this as the 'metaphysics of presence'[15] – the way in which we make present the objects of our thought. The *logos* represents nature, which is something different from the instituted form embodied in language or in text.[16] Crucial, therefore, is the idea of a rigid separation of the origin of meaning (the abstract idea of justice, for example) and the institutionalisation of that meaning in 'writing'.[17] Traditional philosophy relies on being able to maintain this distinction between nature and convention.[18] The written form – for example the Secretary General's Report on the Rule of Law and Transitional Justice in Conflict and Post Conflict States,[19] widely cited as the most authoritative

10 Of Grammatology (n. 5) 49. Derrida terms this dynamic within philosophy as a metaphysics of presence – as an acceptance of the existence of an external referent. This referent is the 'transcendental signified' – that which is to be captured in writing.

11 Bell (n. 1) 7.

12 For detailed discussion of this see Chapter 2.1.2.

13 Of Grammatology (n. 5).

14 Ibid. 47. Derrida describes logocentrism and the metaphysics of presence as the exigent, powerful, systematic and irrepressible desire for a transcendental signified, such as truth.

15 Ibid. 49.

16 Ibid. 13.

17 For Derrida, 'writing' refers to 'the disruption of the presence in the mark' and not the written form *per se*. Jacques Derrida, 'Signature, Event, Context' in Alan Bass tr., *Margins of Philosophy* (The Harvester Press 1982) 307 (hereinafter 'Signature, Event, Context'). However, in the current context I use written form to illustrate this relationship between nature and its institution.

18 Of Grammatology (n. 5) 13: 'Metaphysical roots require the separation of signifier and signified.'

19 United Nations, 'Report of the Secretary General on the Rule of Law and Transitional Justice in Conflict and Post Conflict Societies' (UN Doc. S/2004/616, United Nations 2004).

statement of the meaning of transitional justice – is preceded by the originary 'truth' that is external to it. The Report simply reflects the truth of the demands of justice in transition. Therefore, what is important is that, under traditional rules of philosophy, the act of writing does not create meaning, but rather is simply the institution of a meaning that already exists, that precedes its capture in written form.[20] Consequently, and to further reinforce the significance of this separation, the authority of writing is secured by the fact that it can appeal to this exterior force, this higher meaning, such as justice.[21] This is seen in Teitel's assertion that law in transition embodies principles of justice that are absent from domestic law.[22] The principles of justice – the *logos* – are what generate legitimacy for a reconceptualised model of law in transition precisely because they exist independently of that law.

3.1.2 Nothing beyond the text

However, for Derrida it is this logocentrism, and the idea of the exteriority of meaning, that opens up the possibility of deconstruction. Derrida examines how the natural 'origin' of meaning and its 'institution' in writing cannot be so easily separated. Rather than nature and institution existing independently of each other, what is being suggested is that nature itself is constructed only with reference to the institution.[23] They therefore depend on each other for their existence. This is a rejection of the rigid separation between the two that makes the quest for certainty possible. It destabilises the basic philosophical premise that institution simply reflects a prior natural origin. The origin is not something that is external to the institution, but is created at the moment of institution.

For Derrida, nature and institution exist in a relationship of oppositional hierarchy.[24] What this means is that rather than nature preceding the institution, and simply being reflected or enshrined in writing, the act of writing itself – of institutionalisation – subordinates nature to the institution. What Derrida suggests is that the process of institution itself, the process of writing, helps to shape meaning. By reading text or writing as reflecting or embodying a natural origin, what is ignored or concealed are all the other possible interpretations of nature that are not embodied or encapsulated in that text. In this way writing defines nature, as well as reflecting it. It subordinates nature to the interpretation captured in the institution, which itself becomes the dominant meaning. The process of institutionalisation therefore enshrines meaning by its privileging of one particular interpretation of nature, a privileging that was not possible except for its existence in writing.[25]

20 Of Grammatology (n. 5) 15 describes this as the text being secondary, preceded by truth, or a meaning already constituted and within the element of the *logos*.

21 Ibid. 15. The privilege of *logos* founds the literal meaning then given to writing.

22 See Chapter 2.1.2.2.

23 Of Grammatology (n. 5) 46.

24 Ibid. 13, 41–45. See also Positions (n. 8) 41.

25 Of Grammatology (n. 5) 109.

The point at which this particular interpretation is enshrined is the moment of origin of meaning. So to return to the case of transitional justice, despite the existence of a complex web of interrelated claims to the genesis and aims of transitional justice,[26] one overarching narrative has emerged dominant – that instituted in the Secretary General's Report, which casts 'justice' in transition as existing as a set of 'normative principles embodied in mechanisms such as trials, truth commissions and reparations'.[27] The encapsulation of this particular interpretation of justice in the written and extensively cited Report of the Secretary General shapes our understanding of what justice means, but excludes alternative interpretations through the privileging of one at the expense of the others.

For Derrida, the absence of another here and now, of another transcendental present or of another origin of meaning that also presents itself as natural, reveals the arbitrariness both of the way in which meaning comes to be instituted and, as a result, of the supposed opposition between nature and institution.[28] The idea of deconstruction is therefore concerned with countering the idea of a transcendental origin or natural referent.[29] It refutes the notion that it is possible to transgress the institution in order to discover something beyond – the existence of an independent origin such as a historical or a metaphysical reality that justifies the institution. This idea is famously encapsulated in the phrase, 'There is nothing outside of the text',[30] which is often used to summarise Derrida's work. While a pithy sound bite, the phrase embodies the spirit of deconstruction as a process that rejects the idea of a transcendental origin of meaning that exists independently of the way in which we translate that meaning and give it form. Rather it requires deeper interrogation of the interplay between the origin and the institution, and recognition of the ways in which the two are mutually constituted, each relying on the other for its meaning. This opposition opens up new possibilities for understanding meaning. Rather than relying on rigid distinctions and trying to work within the opposition, Derrida suggests that the relationship between the origin and the institution should be seen 'as an operation and not as a state, as active movement and not a given structure'.[31] The difference between nature and the institution can only exist if there is a 'condition outside', if one is regarded as being external to the other. It is this separation that Derrida critiques, and that deconstruction explicitly addresses. What is being deconstructed is the idea that

26 Catherine Turner, 'Deconstructing Transitional Justice' (2013) 24 *Law and Critique* 193.

27 Jelena Subotić, 'The Transformation of International Transitional Justice Advocacy' (2012) 6 *International Journal of Transitional Justice* 106, 120.

28 Of Grammatology (n. 5) 47.

29 'Transcendental' in this context is used to signify a standard that exists above the law.

30 Of Grammatology (n. 5) 158. The French original of this phrase is 'il n'y a pas de hors-texte'. Derrida suggests that this would be better translated as 'There is no outside text', removing the temptation to misinterpret the phrase as privileging writing, and emphasising the internal dynamics of the construction of meaning to which Derrida refers. It could also be noted that this debate illustrates very well Derrida's point about writing coming to determine meaning, rather than simply reflecting it.

31 Ibid. 51.

the origin of meaning and its institution exist as separate beings. In the context of transitional justice, this means questioning the way in which appeals to justice serve to legitimate claims in respect of the role of law in transition.

3.1.3 'Différance'

Derrida's approach takes as its starting point the existence of an oppositional structure to thought, in which two concepts, such as war and peace, are cast as different. However, rather than simply inverting the hierarchy or seeking to reverse the position of each of the concepts, what deconstruction does is to recognise that the difference between the two concepts, and the interplay between them, is crucial to determining meaning.[32] What this confirms is that, for Derrida, the origin does not exist independently of its institution, but exists only 'through its functioning within a classification and therefore within a system of differences'.[33] Derrida terms this phenomenon '*différance*', and it is this idea that forms the basis of deconstruction.[34]

Différance refers to the fact that meaning cannot be regarded as fixed or static, but is constantly evolving. Rather than pursuing the truth of a natural origin, what deconstruction requires is the interrogation of the 'web of interdependent contingent interpretations' that combine to produce individual legal and philosophical positions.[35] The act of institution – or writing – itself captures this constant competition between the differing possible interpretations of meaning within the institution. The effect of the translation of thought into language is therefore to inscribe *différance* into the structure of meaning. It simultaneously embodies the desired meaning as intended by the author, and the constraints placed on that meaning through the act of interpretation of the text.[36] In this regard, meaning is defined equally by what is included in the institution and what is not. At any one time, one concept will be dominant over the other, thus excluding the other. However, while the idea of exclusion suggests the absence of any presence of that which is excluded, in fact that which is instituted depends for its existence on what has been excluded. The two exist in a relationship of hierarchy.[37]

To return to the example of transitional justice, certain mechanisms, such as trials and truth commissions, are deemed legitimate by virtue of the fact that they are regarded as embodying principles of justice, as instituted in law and policy relating to transition. Other mechanisms, such as amnesties, are deemed illegitimate as they are regarded as conflicting with these policies, as

32 Ibid. 63.

33 Ibid. 109.

34 The term *différance* itself is an invention of Derrida's, intended to encapsulate the dual meaning of difference and deferral that combine to create difference. See Geoffrey Bennington and Jacques Derrida, *Jacques Derrida*, Geoffrey Bennington tr. (University of Chicago Press 1993) 71.

35 Ben Matthews, 'Why Deconstruction Is Beneficial' (2000) 4 *Flinders Journal of Law Reform* 105, 110.

36 Rosenfeld (n. 4).

37 Positions (n. 8).

embodying impunity, and by extension as being incompatible with the principles of justice. The determination of what is deemed legitimate and illegitimate represents the interplay of ideas in which legitimacy is defined both in terms of what it includes but also what it excludes. Legal mechanisms for accountability are deemed an appropriate response to conflict precisely because they combat impunity. Therefore, our understanding of transitional justice is conditioned not only on our understanding of the ways in which accountability in the form of trials or truth commissions embody the *logos* of justice, but also how impunity contradicts it. Both accountability and impunity are integral elements of our understanding of 'justice'. It is the ongoing process of negotiation over where the boundary between the two lies that gives rise to the instability of meaning.[38] This interplay also confirms the artificiality of the distinction between the origin and its institution. It is the interplay between the seemingly oppositional concepts of accountability and impunity that conditions our interpretation of justice, rather than a fixed meaning of justice that allows us to assess the relationship between accountability and justice, or impunity and justice. When seen in these terms, the oppositional structure of meaning is accepted, but what is suggested is that this opposition is something immanent to meaning, something productive rather than a state of affairs to be redressed. It is this interplay that Derrida terms *différance*.

In her commentary on deconstruction, Davies highlights the twofold nature of the idea of *différance*, made up of the distinct ideas of differing and deferring. She first emphasises that the idea of difference inherent in the term speaks to the fact that any system of meaning cannot be regarded as fixed, static or unchanging. This is a logical consequence of the rejection of the idea of a 'natural' origin that precedes the institution. If the idea of nature itself is rejected, it is no longer possible to rely on the existence of an idea in nature that can be simply instituted in writing. Rather than meaning being based upon an existing and stable set of criteria, for Derrida it is created by an ongoing and dynamic process of production through continual exclusion and setting up of differences. It is a process of constant negotiation of meaning, in which different opinions and interpretations of how the origin should be translated jostle for position.

The second element of *différance* follows on from the first. Given that it is not possible to identify one true origin or meaning, and that it is constituted through an ongoing process of negotiation, it cannot be said that meaning can be determined in the present. This point speaks directly to Derrida's identification of a metaphysics of presence whereby we make present, in the here and now, the objects of our thought. If the construction of meaning is a constant process of negotiation between the origin and the institution, then it will be impossible to ascribe fixed characteristics to meaning, as it is constantly changing in light of the shifting nature of the process. Meaning will always be constructed with reference

38 See, for example, early debates on whether truth, as instituted in the South African Truth and Reconciliation Commission (TRC) embodied or denied justice. This was discussed in Chapter 2.

either to what has preceded it or what is yet to come.[39] It will be interpreted and reinterpreted in light of shifting events and understandings, making it inherently unstable in form. Text has no inherent meaning, no one true meaning that exists to be discovered. Therefore, there is no 'outcome' to deconstruction, but rather an ongoing process of destabilisation through which systems of meaning are revealed. The aim of writing in these circumstances may be to attempt to reconcile difference, to reach an agreed version of the 'origin';[40] however, this is never wholly achievable.

This approach explicitly rejects a progressive, or genealogical,[41] reading of philosophy in which one arrives at true meaning at the end of a process of evolution. It therefore expressly engages with the dominant genealogical reading of transitional justice in which the current (legal) model is juxtaposed with earlier, failed, models tainted by claims of victor's justice, for example, or requiring political negotiation and compromise.[42] Traces of each of these earlier examples continue to be present within the current model, and it is the interplay between them that shapes our understanding of transitional justice rather than the location of current trends at the 'end of history', and therefore embodying a self-evident *logos* of justice. Having explained the basic premise of deconstruction, and how it can advance our understanding of transitional justice, the next step is to distinguish its operation from that of alternative methods more traditionally associated with the field of transitional justice.

3.2 Deconstruction 'happens'

The preceding section has outlined how deconstruction is concerned not with the discovery of 'truth' or of distilling correct conclusions, but rather with the process of questioning itself. It is characterised by an uncertainty, or indeterminacy, that stands at odds with many more traditional research methods. A brief survey of the literature on transitional justice reveals two distinct methodological approaches. The first is the study of mechanisms themselves. The rationale, the design and the operation of a wide range of transitional mechanisms, from the original work on trials to more recent work on reparations, forms the subject matter of a significant body of work in the field. The concern of these studies is with the effectiveness

39 Margaret Davies, 'Derrida and Law: Legitimate Fictions' in Tom Cohen (ed.), *Jacques Derrida and the Humanities: A Critical Reader* (Cambridge University Press 2002) 213. This means that how we understand a particular concept is determined not only by the past that gave rise to it, but also by how it is interpreted in the future. This is discussed in more detail in Chapter 5.

40 Rosenfeld (n. 4) 159, arguing that history is replete with examples of texts intended to reflect a 'concrete vision of the desired reconciliation between self and other'.

41 The term 'genealogical' is used here in reference to Teitel's famous 'Transitional Justice Genealogy' in which the origins of the field are traced from a historical and progressive perspective. Ruti Teitel, 'Transitional Justice Genealogy' (2003) 16 *Harvard Human Rights Law Journal* 69.

42 Ibid. See also Positions (n. 8).

of specific mechanisms, and they are framed as critical evaluations of the contribution of each of these to justice. The second significant approach is that of the case study. Work in this area focuses on detailed research of particular geographic case studies as a means of learning lessons for broader application to transitional justice. Whether single case studies or comparative approaches, the premise with this approach is that there are particular characteristics that can be distilled and applied in other contexts, representing a quest for objective factors that contribute to justice. While it is suggested that these approaches are driven by a desire to identify objective characteristics of justice, that does not mean that they are not critical. The engagement of feminist scholars with trials and truth commissions, for example, or post-colonial scholars on transitional justice in Africa, has produced significant critical insight into these particular examples.[43] Nevertheless, what unites these approaches is the aim of assessing how transitional justice mechanisms contribute to the achievement of the underpinning *logos* of justice.[44] This can be contrasted with the approach of deconstruction. The approach taken in this work is not to critique the mechanisms of transitional justice as a way of achieving justice, but rather to explore how our understanding of justice is constructed, and in turn how this impacts on our evaluation of how it is to be achieved.

3.2.1 Deconstruction is not a method

The most significant feature of deconstruction is that it is not a 'method', and it cannot be transformed into one.[45] This may appear to be an odd assertion, but it highlights an important feature that underpins the entire premise of the work. Deconstruction is not a method but rather a process. It does not consist of set rules, procedures, methods and accessible aspects.[46] One cannot 'apply' deconstruction to test a hypothesis or to support an argument.[47] Rather it is an ongoing process of interrogation concerned with the structure of meaning itself. Deconstruction as an approach follows from the identification of a twofold structure of *différance*. Derrida highlights how at any given time 'one of the two terms governs the other or has the upper hand'.[48] They are said to exist in a state of violent hierarchy. Therefore, the first task of deconstruction is to overturn the hierarchy. This, according to Derrida, is necessary in order to highlight the 'conflictual

43 See Chapter 2.3 for discussion.
44 Of Grammatology (n. 5) 103 discusses the acceptance of the separation of the origin and institution as allowing for 'methodology', understood as 'the scholar's right to employ methodological tools whose logical value is anticipated, and in a state of precipitation with regard to the "object", to "truth", etc.'
45 Letter (n. 6).
46 'Force of Law' (n. 3) 116.
47 Of Grammatology (n. 5) 103.
48 Positions (n. 8) 41.

and subordinating structure of opposition'.[49] It emphasises the dominance of one particular way of thinking over others, and belies the idea of fixed meaning, overturning, and therefore exposing, the existence of the binary and destabilising previously fixed categories of understanding. However, this is only the first stage. Derrida emphasises how to remain in this phase is to remain within the oppositional structure, allowing the hierarchy to re-establish itself. If deconstruction is limited to the simple inversion of binaries, then inquiry remains trapped 'within the closed field of these oppositions'.[50] What this means is that instead of making any real change to structural conditions, what we are doing is simply swapping the positions of dominant and subordinate, allowing the same conditions to persist. When thought of in terms of conflict and transition, if the only effect of transition is to reverse the positions of abused and abuser without addressing the structural conditions that allow abuse to happen, then no meaningful change will have been made.

In order to move beyond this dynamic, and to break open the structure itself, a second stage is necessary. This second stage is where the indeterminate element of deconstruction becomes visible. Rather than resting with the inversion of the binaries, and by extension accepting a different manifestation of fixed meaning, the second phase requires us to step outside the oppositions, to remain in search of new meanings,[51] not by repeating ideas but by analysing how ideas are framed, how arguments are made. Derrida describes this as searching for the 'tensions, the contradictions, the heterogeneity within [the] corpus'.[52] It is only through this element of endless analysis, criticism and deconstruction that we can prevent existing structures of dominance from reasserting themselves.[53]

When seen in these terms, it is clear that deconstruction cannot be described as a method or a methodology in the traditional sense of the word. However, Derrida also distinguishes it from other approaches, such as critique.

3.2.2 *Deconstruction is not critique*

Deconstruction is neither analysis nor critique.[54] It is not done with a particular aim. It is not a search for a 'simple element' or 'indissoluble origin'.[55] The consequence of this is that its value is not linked to any subsequent reconstruction. As discussed above, it does not exist to take apart one structure to replace it with another, but exists simply to reveal the inner logic of that structure so as better to understand it. The fact that it does not seek 'strategic engagement' such as that

49 Ibid.
50 Ibid.
51 Ibid. 59–66.
52 Villanova Roundtable (n. 6) 9.
53 Ibid. 42. This is discussed in greater detail in Chapter 4.
54 Letter (n. 6).
55 Ibid.

used by feminist scholars,[56] for example, means that it is not openly identified with advocacy and activism that pursues justice. Deconstruction differs from the other critical approaches discussed in Chapter 2 in that it does not promote definite political action, nor does it propose definite substantive outcomes. This is a logical response to the central premise of deconstruction, which rejects systems of thought that require determinate presence or truth.[57] This failure to take an overtly political stance on big questions led, in the early years, to a charge that deconstruction was an inherently unethical project that was at odds with a quest for justice.[58] Derrida is clear, however, that although deconstruction is not primarily concerned with advocacy or activism, neither is it nihilistic or anarchic. It does not reject the need for law and institutions, but rather seeks to work within those structures to reveal new possibilities.[59]

3.2.3 Deconstruction is not an act

Finally, deconstruction is not an act or an operation. Rather, it is something that happens, something that takes place.[60] It takes place everywhere. It does not require deliberation or consciousness, but rather its potential exists within our structures of meaning. It is interested in exploring and revealing the internal logic of ideas and meaning. It is concerned with opening up these structures and revealing the way in which our understanding of foundational concepts is constructed. This is internal to meaning itself, and not dependent on external factors.[61] What this suggests is that the possibility of deconstruction exists within the structure of meaning itself, within the structure of *différance*, and is not something to be found and applied from the outside. Therefore, to attempt to reduce deconstruction, which is concerned with the deeper interrogation of meaning, to a formalistic method would be to reduce its possibility.[62] It is primarily concerned with understanding ideas, not with their application.

Deconstruction does not aim to provide answers. It does not seek to prove an objective truth, or to support any one particular claim to justice over another. For this reason deconstruction itself is indeterminate, and therefore distinguishable from traditional 'methods' that apply a particular set of rules to test a hypothesis from which definite conclusions can be drawn. Derrida concedes that

56 Sari Kuovo, 'Review Essay: Feminism, Gender and International (Criminal) Law: From Asking the "Woman Question" in Law to Moving Beyond Law' (2014) 16 *International Feminist Journal of Politics* 669. The idea of strategic engagement is discussed in Chapter 2.3.1.1.

57 Rosenfeld argues that 'the ontological and ethical constraints imposed by deconstruction do not usually dictate a single determinate meaning'. Rosenfeld (n. 4) 165.

58 Goodrich *et al.* (n. 2) 9.

59 Villanova Roundtable (n. 6) 6.

60 Letter (n. 6); Villanova Roundtable (n. 6) 9.

61 For more detailed discussion, see section 3.1.

62 Letter (n. 6).

deconstruction is 'impossible'.[63] The 'happening' of deconstruction is not going to lead to a determinate outcome. It will not reveal the 'right' way to do transitional justice. It will not provide us with a definitive definition of the meaning of justice in transition that can be codified in a new UN toolkit. Rather, deconstruction requires first and foremost the relentless pursuit of the impossible. What is 'happening' is not the pursuit of an answer that marks the end of the inquiry, but rather the ongoing questioning that keeps our minds open to the idea that there may be alternative views and understandings of the meaning of justice in transition. When seen in these terms, it is not a method but simply a way of reading, writing, thinking and acting.[64] Rather than seeking an endpoint or a solid conclusion, the means cannot be distinguished from the end.[65] The ongoing process of questioning is the end in itself. It is about negotiating the impossible and the undecidable and, in so doing, remaining open to the possibility of justice.[66]

3.2.4 *Deconstructing transitional justice*

Herein lies the value of deconstruction for a project on transitional justice. Its possibility lies in the very fact that it does not seek to privilege one truth over the other, nor does it admit the possibility of a unitary truth. Rather, it works between irreconcilable positions to keep open the possibility of a new approach. To reduce it to a 'method' with set technical criteria and means would be to diminish the possibilities. To deconstruct the model of transitional justice is not an attempt to undermine or destroy the model. Deconstruction is not destructive, but rather an affirmative force.[67] It does not simply oppose institutions, such as the model of transitional justice, but neither does it simply repeat (or perpetuate) the given assumptions upon which the model is premised. This means that rather than accepting the established normativity or character of the field and replicating that logic, deconstructing transitional justice opens the model up to questioning, and so reveals new possibilities within the model.[68] It therefore works between the model as it currently exists and the future possibilities of the model. For Derrida, deconstruction consists of dismantling not institutions themselves, but rather 'structures within institutions that have become too rigid, or are dogmatic or which work as an obstacle to future research'.[69] Deconstruction therefore opens up possibilities

63 'Force of Law' (n. 3) 116. 'Impossible' in this context does not refer to the opposite of 'possible'. See Jacques Derrida, *Monolingualism of the Other: or, The Prosthesis of Origin*, Patrick Mensah tr. (Stanford University Press 1998). Rather, for Derrida, the structure of *différance* and the ongoing process of negotiation that it entails create the conditions for the possible. See Beardsworth (n. 2) 26.

64 Villanova Roundtable (n. 6) 32.

65 Gehring describes Derrida as balancing on the border between form and content, regarding deconstruction as procedure. Petra Gehring 'The Jurisprudence of the "Force of Law"' in Peter Goodrich *et al.* (eds), *Derrida and Legal Philosophy* (Palgrave Macmillan 2008) 55.

66 This is discussed in more detail in Chapter 6.

67 Villanova Roundtable (n. 6).

68 Ibid. 5–6.

69 Ibid. 8.

that have been suppressed by virtue of the dominance of one particular way of conceptualising transitional justice. The aim is not to destroy the model of transitional justice, but rather to rethink its philosophical foundations in such a way as to open up new possibilities.[70] Therefore, for the purposes of this book, a simple statement of the understanding of deconstruction that underpins the work is proposed. Deconstruction is not about answers, it is about questions. It is about recognising the ongoing process of negotiation between concepts. By requiring the interrogation of the structure of meaning, it provides a useful vehicle for exploring dominant discourses and ways of thinking. And in requiring a more self-reflective approach to the construction of meaning, deconstruction encourages a more open approach to questions of justice.

Derrida considered deconstruction to be a 'problematization of the foundation of law, morality and politics'.[71] It was therefore both 'foreseeable and desirable that studies of deconstructive style should culminate in the problematic of law and justice'.[72] Law, although not perfect, becomes the means by which justice is pursued.[73] Therefore, although Derrida came rather late to the idea of deconstructing law, and indeed to justice, his work raises significant questions in relation to law and legal practice. The question of law is addressed in a number of key texts in which he speaks to questions of the self-definition or limitation of the field of law,[74] its purported authority[75] and its character as an independent body of rules.[76]

3.3 Law and deconstruction

One of the core claims made in support of the rule of law is that law can be clearly distinguished from other fields of endeavour, notably those of politics, ethics or morality. This is equally true in respect of the role of law in transition as in a settled domestic regime.[77] A defining feature of law is that while it may at times internalise political or ethical values, it must remain separate from them.[78] It is this separateness that inscribes law with its authority, stemming both from the way in which law is created and the way in which it is maintained through the processes

70 Ibid. 12.
71 'Force of Law' (n. 3) 8.
72 Ibid. 7.
73 John McCormick, 'Derrida on Law: or, Post-structuralism Gets Serious' (2001) 29 *Political Theory* 395.
74 Jacques Derrida, 'Devant La Loi' in Alan Udof (ed.), *Kafka and the Contemporary Critical Performance* (Indiana University Press 1987) 128 (hereinafter 'Before the Law').
75 'Force of Law' (n. 3).
76 Jacques Derrida, 'Declarations of Independence' in Elizabeth Rottenberg (ed.), *Negotiations: Interventions and Interviews, 1971–2001* (Stanford University Press 2002) 46 (hereinafter 'Declarations of Independence').
77 See Teitel's assertion that law can transcend politics. Ruti Teitel, *Transitional Justice* (Oxford University Press 2000). This is discussed in Chapter 2.
78 Rosenfeld (n. 4) 170.

of interpretation and enforcement. It is also this element of separability that gives law its 'essentially deconstructible' character.[79]

Central to understanding Derrida's deconstruction of law is an appreciation of law as a closed system of rules. The character of law rests on a number of what Derrida terms 'axiomatic propositions' as to its nature.[80] These are underlying assumptions that are made about the nature of law, without which law could not function as a normative system of rules. Acceptance (even implicit) of these propositions is a necessary part of law's authority. These propositions are outlined by Derrida in 'Before the Law' and form the basis for his first explicit engagement with law itself. This section outlines common positivist understandings of law's authority, and explains how deconstruction provides an alternative lens through which to view law.

3.3.1 Axiomatic propositions of law

One of the core claims made by positivists, and indeed a claim central to law's continued existence, is that law can be clearly distinguished from other fields of endeavour, notably those of politics, ethics and morality. Although Derrida does not limit his study of law to the more formal or institutionalised form of law,[81] when he does turn his attention to 'law' as commonly understood, he chooses to focus on the positivist claims made in respect of law and its character.[82] This work examines positivist theories of law because of the increasing trend towards the codification of transitional justice in the 'toolkit' approach discussed in Chapter 2. While it is acknowledged that there are alternative views of the role of law and how it is framed, and indeed that law in transition is intended to address the rigidity of traditional legalism,[83] it is also suggested that conventional legalism is a dominant feature of current transitional justice law and policy.[84] This dominance justifies the characterisation of the 'rule of law' as a positivist enterprise and transitional justice as a legal institution. Law in transition, it has been suggested, provides a positive framework for the implementation of rights and enshrining principles of justice.[85]

The origin of the doctrine of rule of law, and of the objectivity of law, can be traced back to the legal positivism of the late nineteenth and early twentieth centuries. By this time, earlier ideas of natural law and natural rights had fallen from favour, replaced by an emphasis on legal rules whose authority derived not from their content but from their source.[86] Under such a conception, law and legal rules

79 Force of Law (n. 3).

80 'Before the Law' (n. 74).

81 In 'Before the Law', he also considers the laws of literature and of psychoanalysis. Ibid.

82 Davies (n. 39) 214.

83 See the discussion of Teitel in Chapter 2.1.2.

84 Kieran McEvoy, 'Beyond Legalism: Towards a Thicker Understanding of Transitional Justice' (2007) 34 *Journal of Law and Society* 411.

85 Teitel (n. 77) 21.

86 See Nicola Lacey, 'Modern Positivism: H.L.A. Hart and Analytical Jurisprudence' in James Penner *et al.* (eds), *Jurisprudence and Legal Theory* (Oxford University Press 2005) 143, 157.

can be regarded as descriptive, in that they describe objectively identifiable rules, rather than providing subjectively influenced prescriptions. Central to this school of thought, and underpinning the entire structure of positivism, is the belief that law (objective, descriptive) can be separated from politics or morality (subjective, prescriptive). For Hart, even where the content of legal rules and moral injunctions overlapped, they were not to be regarded as the same thing.[87] The purported objectivity of law ensures that law can provide justifiable solutions to normative problems.[88] Further, these solutions can be reached in a legally determined way, independent of political or moral considerations.[89] In this way legal formalism serves to legitimate claims of objectivity and neutrality in legal decision-making.[90]

It is this separateness of law – the fact that it can be regarded as independent of politics or morality – that ensures law's authority.[91] This separation of law and morality in particular is central to the positivist school of thought. Raz, for example, states that the separation of law and morality means that 'the validity of positive legal norms does not depend on their conformity with the moral order'.[92] The question of what determines the validity, and thus the authority, of law therefore rests solely on the source of the law and whether it has been posited in accordance with generally recognised rules, and does not depend on any calculation of value or justification.[93] In the positivist tradition this dynamic is clearly visible. The law is judged on its own terms and without recourse to any external validating standard such as justice.[94] Law is characterised as inward-looking, without any need to have recourse to external considerations.[95] This approach has, however, been subjected to critique. Even positivists acknowledge that there are times when the law as written will be inadequate to reach a clear decision. These so-called 'hard cases' present a challenge to law's authority, and to the assumption that a justifiable solution can be found from within the law itself. This is a challenge that has been raised most prominently by Ronald Dworkin, when he suggests that these hard cases expose the limits of positivism.[96] In such cases there will

87 Ibid. 157.

88 Martii Koskenniemi, *From Apology to Utopia: The Structure of International Legal Argument* (Cambridge University Press 2005).

89 Ibid. 24.

90 It should be noted, however, that positivism is not synonymous with formalism. See HLA Hart, 'Legal Positivism', *Encyclopaedia of Philosophy* (1967) vol. 4, 419.

91 Scholars have long sought to provide an adequate explanation for the authority of law. These range from Austin's Command Theory, through Hart's rules of recognition, to Kelsen's Pure Theory of Law. Modern jurisprudence has, however, sought to interrogate these claims rather than to attempt to provide a justification with modern resonance. See, e.g., Costas Douzinas and Adam Geary, *Critical Jurisprudence: The Political Philosophy of Justice* (Hart 2005).

92 Joseph Raz, *The Authority of Law* (Clarendon Press 1979) 133.

93 Ibid. 150.

94 While law may still be judged against standards of morality, this is not the same as allowing morality to determine the content of law.

95 See, e.g., Raz (n. 92) 53, stating that the content and existence of law is determined by reference to social facts and without relying on moral considerations.

96 Ronald Dworkin, 'Hard Cases' (1975) 88 *Harvard Law Review* 1057.

be need, according to Dworkin, to have recourse to considerations that cannot be said to derive their authority from a clearly defined and identifiable legal source.[97] This challenge, and the threat it poses to objectivity, is met by the doctrine of relative indeterminacy. Positivists, including Hart, acknowledge that at times there will be a need for judicial discretion in decision-making. However, to maintain the integrity of the positivist philosophy, such discretion must be presented as being exercised within the existing law.[98] This can be explained as simply the need to 'render vague standards determinate'.[99] This approach, in attempting to maintain the integrity of law, moves closer to an interpretivist approach, whereby a broader range of sources are brought within the scope of law and legal decision-making.[100] As such, this approach still seeks to provide a picture of a self-contained system of decision-making that does not need to make recourse to external considerations to justify a decision.[101]

This need to put flesh on the bones of vague legal standards has particular resonance in the field of transitional justice. In many cases, the international standards being relied upon provide no more than vague exhortations, which are subject to interpretation by a number of differing bodies. And yet these standards provide a legal framework within which decisions can be made. They provide positive, written obligations that can be relied upon without the need for recourse to more abstract (or politically contentious) concepts of right or justice to justify actions. The fact that law in transition is regarded as incorporating certain standards of justice neatly avoids the challenge that decision-making is rooted in political preference or on subjective assessments of the situation. The existence of an instituted model of transitional justice provides the objective standards necessary for a depoliticised process of reform. This reliance on written standards (as embodied in reports and toolkits, for example) brings transitional justice and rule of law reform within the parameters of positivist (or at the very least interpretivist) theories of law. The ability to rely on law, and to point to legal obligation rather than political preference or ethical necessity, has the effect of buttressing the legitimacy of the chosen course of action and excluding alternative options.

The challenge for law is that while it may at times internalise political or ethical values, it must remain separate from them.[102] It is this separateness that inscribes law with its unquestionable authority,[103] stemming both from the way in which law is created and the way in which it is maintained through the processes of interpretation and enforcement. In 'Before the Law', Derrida identifies a number of

97 Lacey (n. 86) 169.

98 Koskenniemi (n. 88) 34, referring to the use of the concept of equity *infra legem*.

99 Hart (n. 90) 132.

100 For an explanation of this approach to international human rights law, see Catherine Turner, 'Human Rights and the Empire of (International) Law' (2011) 29 *Law and Inequality* 313.

101 See in particular Ronald Dworkin, *Law's Empire* (Fontana 1986) on the manner in which principles and policies may legitimately influence legal decision-making.

102 Rosenfeld (n. 4) 170.

103 Davies (n. 39) 219.

axiomatic presuppositions, which are central to belief in a system of law. The first of these, and the one most clearly identified with legal positivism, is the necessary recognition that the text of the law has its own 'identity, uniqueness and unity'.[104] The legal personality of the text is established by the system of positive laws and conventions, which set the boundaries of the character and operation of law.[105] What is contained within the law and what remains outside the law must be clearly visible. This occurs when law is posited in accordance with agreed and legitimate law-making processes. This limitedness in turn provides the basis for the acceptance of the authority of law – the acceptance of the idea of law as objectively identifiable and neutral in its operation.[106]

Following on from his analysis that law must have its own uniqueness, unity and identity is Derrida's second axiomatic proposition – that law can be separated from its author. This relates to what Derrida terms the 'fictive narrativity' of law, the idea that law can – and indeed must – be separable from its author, that once it assumes the form of law that it transcends its origins.[107] This ability to separate the content of law from its author is crucial in any democratic system, where the identity of the party proposing the law ceases to be relevant once the law is passed in accordance with the recognised procedures. Once the law has been passed, all that remains is the law itself, divorced from its history and its author. Distinction is therefore drawn between the substantive content of law and the rules and conventions that exist to guarantee its existence as law – the form rather than the substance. This phenomenon is what Derrida identifies as the third axiomatic proposition of law. Once the law has been brought into existence, the ability to present itself as a unified and unique system of rules, guaranteed by prior conventions and narratives, is central to its ability to shield itself from challenge. This, for Derrida, is the narration of law. The embeddedness of law within existing narratives of the character of law ensures its recognition as law. It is therefore this narration that allows us to see and identify law as law. Even where these assumptions are not clear or evident, they nevertheless influence our perception of law and legal acts. The nature of law itself is bound up with a narrative about the creation and being law of law that helps to perpetuate our understanding of what law is and what it does. The existence of this narrative of law is therefore a 'conceptually prior condition of law, the limit of law which polices the boundary between law and non law'.[108] It is what enables us to distance the legal from the non-legal.

The nature of law, once established, is described by Derrida as 'intangible'. By this he means that it exists as sacrosanct – it is forbidden to change or disfigure it. In this way its form 'presents and performs itself as a kind of personal identity entitled to absolute respect'.[109] Once law has been named as law, that title 'names

104 'Before the Law' (n. 74) 129.
105 Ibid. 130.
106 Davies (n. 39) 222.
107 Declarations of Independence (n. 76).
108 Davies (n. 39) 220.
109 'Before the Law' (n. 74) 145.

and guarantees' its identity.[110] This is Derrida's fourth axiomatic proposition – that title guarantees the character of law. It is this title, external to the law, that locates the law within the prior narrative of the being law of law. The title itself precedes the law and simply vests it with its character. The process of designation as law is not tied up with the story of the law but rather is objectively determinable on the basis of existing conventional law. Put simply, where law exists, it should be able to be recognised and named as such. This does not depend on the substance of the law, but rather on our understanding of what law is and how it comes into being. This is an objective determination.

Each of these axiomatic propositions combine to create the framework within which law can operate as a self-contained system of rules whose authority derives from the closed nature of that system. What is critical, however, is the identification of law as exclusionary, as existing as something distinct from other factors. Having outlined his understanding of how law works, Derrida then demonstrates how a deconstructive reading of law helps us to better understand these processes. In so doing he reveals some of the uncertainties that remain within law.

3.3.2 The 'essentially deconstructible' nature of law

From the foregoing analysis of the nature of law, we see the dynamic emerge whereby law is defined partially with reference to what it is not. The existence of law, its meaning and its authority, depend on law being able to be distinguished from social and historical context, and from external values such as politics and morality. Law is law because it is not politics, because it is not simply morality. Law must possess its own unique characteristics in order to justify its normative claims. These characteristics are traditionally defined in opposition to the characteristics of politics or morality. The act of naming law as law serves to define its boundaries;[111] therefore, he or she who is vested with the power of legal decision-making also exercises the power of definition of the very boundaries of law itself. His or her charge is to determine what falls within the definition, and what remains without. Where this power is questioned, it is most commonly done from the perspective of whether external factors have unduly influenced a decision that should be based on pure legal reasoning and uncontaminated by external considerations.[112] This approach reinforces the accepted boundaries of the law and the idea that law is in fact separable from politics and morality. The way in which a Derridean interpretation of law differs from these more traditional explanations is in the way it highlights the traces of politics and morality that are inherent in the definition of law itself and which serve to construct our understanding of what law is through our appreciation of what it is not.[113] The idea of separability returns us to Derrida's challenge to the idea of exteriority discussed in section 3.1. The 'legal'

110 Ibid.
111 Ibid. 132.
112 See, e.g., JAG Griffiths, *The Politics of the Judiciary* (Manchester University Press 1977).
113 Douzinas and Geary (n. 91).

nature of law depends on its being able to be distinguished from external forces, such as politics and morality. These forces are deemed to exist outside of law, to be separate from law. Yet deconstruction of law reveals the relationship of mutual dependence between the two by demonstrating the ongoing negotiation between law and politics that shapes our understanding of the nature of law itself. Derrida sums this approach up in 'Before the Law' when he states that 'What remains concealed and invisible in each law is thus presumably the law itself, that which makes laws of these laws, the being-law of these laws'.[114] It is this characteristic that makes law inherently deconstructible. As law is founded on this distinction between legal and non-legal (or illegal), it is eminently suited to deconstruction.[115]

This power to set the boundaries of the definition of law also raises significant questions over who decides, and according to what criteria, the content or narrative of the law? Who sets the priorities? And what effect does this have on competing narratives? This critique is evident in Derrida's analysis of Kant's quest for morality within law.[116] If one accepts the premise of the positivist tradition – that law does in fact have its own identity and is separable from other forms of meaning – this by its very nature precludes further examination or questioning of the origin of the law or of its foundational authority. Derrida claims in 'Before the Law' that to be invested with its categorical imperative,[117] 'the law should be without history, genesis or any possible derivation'.[118] Yet to introduce the idea of a quest for morality into the operation of the law necessarily introduces both historicity and empirical narrativity.[119] Whether or not one is convinced by this apparent absence of historical origin, Derrida argues that the very act of accepting the command of the law – 'You must' or 'You must not' – requires the denial of historical origin,[120] regardless of what that origin may be.[121] It denies the subordination of politics and morality to the law at the moment in which law is created. There is therefore a tension that emerges between the ideal type of law whose authority exists independently of history or empirical narrative, and law as it actually exists and operates within society. One of the key questions to emerge from 'Before the Law' is whether or not it is possible to separate law from historical origin or from the narrative that has driven its creation. If one accepts that historical narrative

114 'Before the Law' (n. 74) 134.

115 Davies (n. 39) 228.

116 In 'Before the Law', Derrida discusses the way in which Kant appears to introduce morality into law. Kant speaks in particular of the maxim: 'act as if the maxim of your action were by your will to turn into a universal law of nature'. Derrida argues that the use of 'as if' in this maxim allows Kant's idea of practical reason to be reconciled with a teleology of history, and with the possibility of unlimited progress. However, in order to be invested with its categorical imperative, law should have 'no history, genesis or possible derivation'. In this way, Derrida critiques the internal contradiction of Kant's categorical imperative. See 'Before the Law' (n. 74) 133–134.

117 A nod to the language used by Kant himself. See Immanuel Kant, *To Perpetual Peace* (1795).

118 'Before the Law' (n. 74) 134.

119 Ibid. See also Davies (n. 39) 219.

120 'Before the Law' (n. 74).

121 Ibid. 138.

will always drive the impulse for progress, to strive towards moral imperatives, will history then always be present within the law?

Deconstruction of the apparent separability of law reveals the oppositional structure of meaning that underlies our understanding of the relationship between law and politics. In order for law to be law, it must suppress its history, the politics that gave rise to the need for law and the morality that drove competing positions in respect of law. Put simply, it must deny the existence of competing forces that were integral to its creation. These competing forces exist in a relationship of violent hierarchy, in which non-legal elements are subordinated to law, leaving an inside and an outside of law – the legal and the non-legal. Our understanding of law, and our ability to recognise it as such, depends on this subordination. And yet when the relationship between the two is deconstructed, what is revealed is not the absolute separateness of the two, but rather the continual negotiation that sets and resets the boundaries. The two therefore depend on each other for their existence. Where this becomes significant is where claims for the authority of law are made with reference to the underlying *logos* of justice.

3.3.3. Law as the means to justice (or why deconstruction is a valuable approach to transitional justice)

Law and justice are closely related in the popular imagination. When seen through the lens of traditional philosophy, justice is the natural origin that precedes law. Law is the instituted version of that natural origin. It embodies the principles of justice that drive law and legal reasoning. However, in the process of codification, in the writing of law, the law privileges its own version of justice over others that may exist in the realm of politics, ethics or morality. As such, it stands in a relationship of violent hierarchy to these excluded versions. Yet to be able to justify its authority, it must be seen to stand in a natural relationship to justice. The legal approach to transitional justice discussed above demonstrates the reliance on the form of positive law to avoid difficult and contested issues of politics and morality. It also ostensibly avoids any reliance on external standards of natural law or justice to ground the authority of law. And yet it is clear from the content of instituted standards that transitional justice is regarded as having a purpose beyond law – that it is regarded as being concerned with justice and as something that must be achieved. This in itself presents a tension – in that central to the very nature of positive law is the idea that it contains no trace of a 'beyond' to law, no question of there being a transcendental standard of right to which law must speak. Rather, the *logos* of justice is regarded as being embodied in the law.

Where a rule exists, questions of justice can be avoided through reliance on the rule,[122] and indeed its representation *as* justice. In this way, transitional justice

122 See Benedict Kingsbury, 'Legal Positivism as Normative Politics: International Society, Balance of Power and Lassa Oppenheim's Positive International Law' (2002) 13 *European Journal of International Law* 401, 421.

displays many of the key features of the positivist concept of the rule of law that are deemed to give law its distinctive quality that sets it apart from other disciplines. For example, the reduction of the requirements of transitional justice to writing, in reports and toolkits, increases certainty in what 'justice' is. The form and content of justice is no longer the subject of philosophical speculation. Justice is quantified in international instruments. The boundaries of the law are defined by criteria established by positive law and convention. As a result, law should be capable of providing justifiable solutions to the problem of transition. Courts can engage in interpretation of the precise scope and requirements of transitional justice.[123] In this way clarity and stability is ensured. Justice is no longer subject to political horse-trading or instrumental trade-offs, but is the subject of clearly defined legal obligations. Adjudication can be undertaken on the basis of a legally determined rule, independent of political influence. Finally, the separation of legal arguments from moral arguments is a way of overcoming disagreement.[124] Where there is a clash of competing conceptions of justice, that which is enshrined in law will prevail. Where balancing is required, this can be undertaken within the parameters of law itself, under the doctrine of relative indeterminacy. The simple fact of having to balance rights should not undermine the objectivity of the law *per se*. Law in transition is intended to transcend politics, fulfilling an important symbolic function.[125] Precisely because of the inevitable disagreement over the meaning of justice in most societies, law steps in to replace justice as the basis for authoritative decisions.[126] The formality of law and legal procedure facilitates the move towards a new form of governance, providing new sites of contestation, bounded by legality rather than physical violence. Law can also provide the means to confront injustice through the application of legal procedure to narrative forums. The apparent depoliticisation of law is a central feature of transitional justice.

And yet the question remains, is it ever possible for law to transcend politics completely? Or will the new law simply replicate the patterns it aims to replace? In particular, can the rigid adherence to law maintain objectivity in the face of historical and narrative claims? After all, much of this reasoning rests on the assumption that there is an objectively identifiable endpoint towards which transitional societies should be progressing. Underpinning this is a suggestion that what is legal can be equated with what is just. It is this collapsing of the boundaries between law and justice that deconstruction resists.

Deconstruction reveals the artificiality of the claim of law to represent justice in these circumstances. What it reveals is the way in which law violently subordinates alternative interpretations of justice.[127] In so doing, it highlights the mutual dependence of these concepts, and the way in which we understand law only with reference

123 See, for example, *Prosecutor v Kallon* SCSL-04-15-A.

124 Kingsbury (n. 122) 421.

125 Teitel (n. 77) 19; Colm Campbell and Fionnula Ní Aoláin, 'The Paradox of Transitions in Liberal Democracies' (2005) 27 *Human Rights Quarterly* 172, 188.

126 Kinsgbury (n. 122) 424.

127 'Force of Law' (n. 3) 23, where he states that the founding of law buries justice.

to what it excludes. We understand what law *is* by simultaneously understanding what it is not. Therefore, the trace of all of those other influences remains bound up within the structure of law itself. It is this structure of *différance*, the interplay of law with the excluded traces of politics, ethics and morality, that allows for the deconstruction of law and the questioning of its relationship to justice.

In 'Force of Law', Derrida writes that 'law claims to exercise itself in the name of justice, and justice is required to establish itself in the name of law that must be enforced. Deconstruction finds itself between these two poles.'[128] Rather than viewing law as giving effect to justice through its objective implementation of rules, Derrida sees law not as justice but as calculation.[129] The application of rules and programmes may be legal, but in Derrida's view it is not just.[130] Rather than seeking a definite outcome, the achievement of justice through law, what deconstruction requires is the ongoing questioning of the relationship between the two. Justice is not an endpoint, but rather exists in an *aporia* – suspended in the moment before a legal decision is made – the moment that separates law from justice.[131] It exists only as a possibility, as a hope, as something that will not ever be achieved in the present, but which we nevertheless continue to strive for. To say that law is not the same as justice is not to deny that law has any role to play. Rather, what is important is to recognise the risk that law, when viewed as a technical process of the application of rules, becomes reduced to a static and ultimately arbitrary standard.[132] If law is not subjected to ongoing questioning, then it can lose its ability to contribute towards meaningful change, and as a result towards justice. Placing too much faith in law as a means of achieving justice facilitates the masquerade referred to by Cornell, whereby violence and powerful interests are represented as the rule of law,[133] which is no longer subjected to critical engagement.

Critical engagement is the purpose of this work. It is suggested that the current model of transitional justice, and its application in practice, reveals the risk of stalemate inherent in a legal model that denies space for political and moral considerations. Rather than working within the existing model to try and identify elements of good or bad practice that might increase the success of transitional justice (in terms of achieving 'justice'), what deconstruction seeks to do is to interrogate the model itself to try and understand why stalemate occurs, and how we might rethink our understanding of transitional justice in a way that allows us to move beyond the oppositional hierarchies that currently dominate the field and that lead to stalemate.

128 Ibid. 22.
129 Ibid. 16.
130 Ibid. 23.
131 Ibid. 15. This is explained in more detail in Chapter 6.
132 Villanova Roundtable (n. 6).
133 Drucilla Cornell, 'The Violence of the Masquerade: Law Dressed Up as Justice' (1990) 11 *Cardozo Law Review* 1047.

3.4 Conclusion

The purpose of this chapter was to ascertain how theory can contribute to our understanding of transitional justice. The chapter has outlined the understanding of deconstruction that underpins the research. It has sought to highlight the indeterminate nature of the approach, and the fact that 'deconstructing' transitional justice involves introducing uncertainty into the model. Deconstruction does not aim to draw conclusions or make recommendations as to how we can achieve justice in transition, but rather is concerned with understanding the structure of meaning. It is worth reiterating that deconstruction is an affirmative force. It does not seek to undermine the idea of transitional justice, nor to dismiss the idea that justice is something for which we should strive. Deconstruction is concerned with the elements within structures and institutions that have become too rigid or dogmatic. It seeks to identify these elements so that they can be addressed. It was suggested in Chapter 2 that the institution of transitional justice into law and policy has resulted in the creation of a 'theatrical space' that has set clear boundaries on the field. If this 'theatrical space' becomes rigid and unresponsive to challenge and critique, then the transformative potential of transitional justice will be lost. Deconstruction seeks to introduce uncertainty into the rigid categories upon which the field is founded, and in so doing to bring new insight into the origin and the consequences of the oppositional structure of meaning. The purpose of this exercise is to encourage a deeper understanding of the core assumptions upon which the field is constructed, which should in turn lead to a more nuanced engagement with resistance and critique. Therefore, it is suggested that adopting a deconstructive approach is crucial to ensure the ongoing relevance of the field. Deconstructing transitional justice can help to explain why current models have resulted in stalemate and ongoing division rather than in the reconciled future promised by the rhetoric.

Exploring the way in which meaning is constructed also sets the scene for a more detailed examination of the negotiation between core underpinning assumptions of transitional justice. The relationship between violence and law is central to transitional justice. Challenging the idea that the two are distinct, with a clear dividing line between them, is the necessary first step in problematising a linear or progressive account of conflict and transition in which violence is replaced by law. This raises the important question of whether violence and law can be separated. Ultimately, understanding the relationship between violence and law is crucial if the role of law in transition is to be grasped. The following chapters will explore this relationship between violence and law. The discussion is contextualised by reference to the example of the transition in Northern Ireland. The purpose of this example is, first, to demonstrate the practical application of this theoretical approach, and second, to initiate a dialogue between the local and the global that can inform thinking in the field of transitional justice more generally.

Chapter 4

Violence

The first of the three key themes to be explored is that of violence. Central to understanding the critique of transitional justice being presented is an understanding of how violence is seen as relating to both law and justice in transitional contexts. This chapter asks whether violence and law can be separated. To do this it is necessary first to clarify what is understood by the term 'violence' and how it is applied in the current context. While transitional justice scholarship is tied up with the study of the relationship between violence and law, this analysis relates most commonly to direct physical violence, to the violence of insurgency or revolution or to that of overt state repression and the effect that this violence has on the law. In this way the field is concerned with the relationship *between* violence *and* law. What has been largely absent to date is any analysis of the violence *of* law itself. To interrogate more deeply the relationship between violence, law and justice in transitional contexts, and to deconstruct the opposition between war and peace upon which it is constructed, it is therefore necessary to move beyond the political critique and explore the more metaphysical concept of violence expounded by Derrida in 'Force of Law'.

Transitional justice, it is suggested, provides an exemplary case study through which to explore these ideas. Maley highlights how Derrida's work speaks most directly to 'limit cases' – those points at which the law threatens to unravel.[1] Examples of this include war crimes and genocide, where much larger and more important issues are brought to bear on the discourse of the law. These cases provide good examples of the ways in which law 'exposes its own constitution within a history of violence and mythology'.[2] They are also cases that are constituent of the field of transitional justice. Violence as a concept therefore has clear resonance in transitional justice. The field itself is premised on the need to move away from violence, whether in the form of war or of state repression and insurgency, towards a more peaceful future. In this regard the violence of open conflict is juxtaposed with peace, or the absence of violence, that is to be secured by transitional justice. War and peace become the central organising binary around which

1 Will Maley, 'Beyond the Law? The Justice of Deconstruction' (1999) 10 *Law and Critique* 49, 50.
2 Ibid.

transitional justice arguments are constructed. Of course this desire to replace violence with law is not unique to transitional justice. It is a desire deeply embedded in all democratic legal systems, reflecting the need to replace violent clashes of interests with the more civilised instruments of law.[3] However, in transitional contexts violence remains raw and visible, bringing into sharp focus the need or desire to found a new system of law that can mediate the violence. It will be argued in this chapter that the separation of the two concepts of violence and law is never as clear-cut as it first appears.

In 'Force of Law', Derrida seeks to move beyond a critique of violence which reveals the externally influenced and ideological superstructures of law towards a deconstruction of law which focuses on the intrinsic or internal relationship between violence and law through revealing the 'mystical foundation' of law's authority.[4] Inherent in this deconstruction is the idea that violence, far from being something separate from law, is in fact deeply implicated in law and therefore cannot fail to be implicated in any legal institution.[5] Thus, when we speak of violence in the context of deconstruction, it does not refer simply to overt physical violence, nor simply to structural violence that exerts an external force on law and legal adjudication, but rather of a conceptual violence, which can be used to explore the very nature and internal coherence of legal systems. What is required, according to Derrida, is a 'desedimentation of the super structures of law'.[6] Rather than seeing violence and law as separate phenomena that influence each other, violence and law are seen as integral to each other. This emphasis on the intrinsic relationship of violence to law is significant, for if the distinction between the two is revealed to be false, then the demand for the substitution of one with the other – replacing violence with law – loses its coherence. The risk that remains is that the 'rule of law' becomes no more than a mask for the rule of force.[7] The purpose of the critique of violence is therefore not simply to reveal its existence but rather to expound its relationship to law and justice. Every moment of founding law will be a moment of violence. While violence is commonly understood to have a negative connotation, as something wrong or illegitimate, for Derrida, violence has no intrinsic quality. He suggests that 'the concept of violence belongs to the symbolic order of law, politics and morals. And it is only to this extent that it can give rise to a critique'.[8] It is suggested that transitional justice also arises at the intersection of

3 Matthias Mahlmann, 'Law and Force: 20th Century Radical Legal Philosophy, Post Modernism and the Foundations of Law' (2003) 9 *Res Publica* 19.

4 Jacques Derrida, 'Force of Law: The Mystical Foundation of Authority' in Drucilla Cornell *et al.* (eds), *Deconstruction and the Possibility of Justice* (Routledge 1992) 1, 3 (hereinafter 'Force of Law'). See also Nancy Fraser, 'The Force of Law: Metaphysical or Political?' (1991) 13 *Cardozo Law Review* 1325; and Maley (n. 1) 53, naming the problem of telling the difference between law as force and the forces that appear to threaten law from the outside.

5 Fraser (n. 4) 1325.

6 'Force of Law' (n. 4) 13.

7 Mahlmann (n. 3) 20. See also Drucilla Cornell 'The Violence of the Masquerade: Law Dressed Up as Justice' (1990) 11 *Cardozo Law Review* 1047.

8 'Force of Law' (n. 4) 31.

law, politics and morals, and to this extent is a particularly suitable subject through which to explore the critique of violence. Inherent in the discourse of transitional justice is the contested use of law and violence. Ongoing negotiation of the legitimacy, acceptability or necessity of law and of violence provides the foundation for the discourse.

This chapter begins by revisiting the concept of deconstruction outlined in Chapter 3, building on the foundational concept of *différance* to explain Derrida's concept of violence that underpins the analysis presented in the rest of this chapter. The section thus outlines the economy of violence within which Derrida suggests law operates, and explores how each of these levels of violence is present in the context of transitional justice. In particular, it introduces the idea of the violence of reflection, by which the state is challenged. The chapter then moves on to consider in more detail the meaning of violence of reflection in this context, considering the ways in which opposition to the state is manifested, and how and where law and physical violence diverge. It explores the distinction that is drawn between legitimate and illegitimate uses of force, and how this shapes our understanding of the need for transitional justice. Finally, it considers the oppositional narrative that is created by the juxtaposition of violence and law in these contexts. It suggests that rather than viewing violence and law as separate concepts, the two are integral to each other and exist in a relationship of mutual contamination.

4.1 The economy of violence

Derrida's deconstruction of the relationship between violence and law is best understood in the framework of what he has termed the 'economy of violence' within which law is inscribed.[9] The term itself is taken from *Violence and Metaphysics*,[10] but the structure of this economy is outlined first in *Of Grammatology*.[11] While the concept initially arose in the context of language and linguistics, it has been read as equally applicable to a deconstruction of law as to that of language.[12] The basic premise of the 'economy of violence' is that all meaning is constructed on a tertiary structure in which meaning (or law) is founded in a moment of violence, in which one particular meaning emerges dominant (the violence of the origin); that violence is subsequently forgotten (the concealment of the origin); but excluded alternative meanings return to challenge the dominance of the law (the violence of reflection). This tertiary structure is used to explore the relationship between violence and law in transition.

9 Ibid. 14.

10 Jacques Derrida, 'Violence and Metaphysics' in Alan Bass tr., *Writing and Difference* (Routledge 1978) 117.

11 Jacques Derrida, *Of Grammatology*, Gayatri Chakravorty Spivak tr. (Johns Hopkins University Press 1976) 112 (hereinafter 'Of Grammatology').

12 See, for example, Leonard Lawlor, 'From the Trace to the Law: Derridean Politics' (1989) 15 *Philosophy and Social Criticism* 1, suggesting that it can be read as 'a movement from the philosophical to the political'.

Chapter 3 outlined the structure of *différance* that Derrida sees as underpinning meaning. Briefly, what is rejected is the existence of one fixed and objective meaning that can be discovered and translated into language or text. Derrida sees meaning as being constructed in the interplay between seemingly opposing concepts, such as war and peace, for example. In simple terms, this reveals the existence of a dominant meaning that by its existence excludes other forms of meaning. The effect is not simply to profess preference for one form of meaning or understanding over another in a way that acknowledges the existence and validity of competing interpretations, but rather to deny the existence of alternative forms of meaning altogether. This is the violent hierarchy in which these concepts exist.[13] And yet while one particular form of meaning will come to dominate others, this does not mean that alternatives cease to exist. Rather, they remain trapped within the concept itself, with the potential to reassert their presence and challenge the dominant order. Understanding meaning within the structure of *différance* allows its recognition as a process of negotiation rather than a fixed concept. When translated and applied to law, this dynamic can be seen in the moment in which law is made. This is the point at which one particular course of action is chosen at the expense of others, and enshrined in law. The starting point for any exploration of law's place within an economy of violence is therefore the idea that violence founds law, and that as a result all law bears violence at its heart.

4.1.1 The violence of the origin

The first stage of Derrida's economy of violence is that of the originary violence of naming.[14] Building on the discussion of the construction of meaning in Chapter 3, this chapter explores the violence of the origin of law – that is, the moment at which law subordinates alternatives and establishes itself as an independent, and indeed a dominant, force. As demonstrated by Derrida's work on violence and metaphysics, every act of positing law will entail some element of exclusion. It is in this element of exclusion that the originary violence of law exists. Chapter 3 outlined how positivist conceptions of the rule of law regard law's authority as deriving from its source rather than from its content.[15] If the 'being law of law'[16] is tied up with the source of law, then it is imperative to be able to identify the source of law, and consequently the legal obligation. What is at issue is the ability to distinguish between what is law and what is not. This leads us to the question of the origin of law from which this authority derives. As discussed in Chapter 3, Derrida rejects the idea that law somehow reflects or enshrines pre-existing principles of nature, but rather views law as something that occurs as

13 See Chapter 3.1.

14 Of Grammatology (n. 11) 112.

15 See Chapter 3.3.

16 Jacques Derrida, 'Devant La Loi' in Alan Udof (ed.), *Kafka and the Contemporary Critical Performance* (Indiana University Press 1987) 128 (hereinafter 'Before the Law').

a result of the act of the institution itself and the interplay between nature and its institution. Therefore, the moment of the institution of law is a moment of metaphysical violence, as it is the moment in which one interpretation of nature (of the requirements of justice, for example) is privileged over others.[17] This moment of metaphysical violence represents for Derrida the origin of law, the point at which its authority is established.[18]

Therefore, for Derrida the moment of founding of law will always be a moment of force, a rupture with the existing order and the institution of a new one.[19] This characterisation of the origin of law as a moment of rupture stands in direct contrast to the idea of law as reflecting a natural progression or an inevitable consequence of preceding circumstances. In the context of transitional justice, it speaks directly to the tendency to narrate transitional justice genealogically,[20] representing the quest for justice in a progressive reading of history in which war and injustice give way to peace and justice.[21] When the institution of law is seen as a rupture rather than as a progression, then the violence of the origin becomes clear. Derrida highlights how even where the founding of a new law, or a new legal order, presupposes certain conditions or conventions, this does not diminish the mystical limits of authority.[22] It is still not possible to point to a definite standard of justice, for example, that has simply been captured in legal form. So, for example, even where the passing of laws on transitional justice are framed with reference to international law frameworks in relation to human rights or rule of law, this does not alter the characterisation of the moment of the origin of law as being a moment of violence, a rupture from the preceding order.[23]

The act of founding an institution will always imply a break, and therefore some form of performative force or violence.[24] In this way, violence is implied in the very concept of law.[25] Some opinions will be reflected in law; others will be excluded – relegated to the realms of politics, ethics or morality – not deemed to have achieved the status of 'law'. As this element of founding or originary violence is inherent in the structure of law, it cannot be transcended. What is necessary, therefore, is that rather than trying to replace violence with law, the existence of law within an economy of violence should be recognised in order that it can be critiqued.[26] What is at issue here is not any external form of violence, such as war,

17 See Chapter 3.1.

18 'Force of Law' (n. 4) 6.

19 Ibid.

20 Ruti Teitel, 'Transitional Justice Genealogy' (2003) 16 *Harvard Human Rights Law Journal* 69 (hereinafter 'Genealogy').

21 See, for example, Claire Moon, 'Narrating Political Reconciliation: Truth and Reconciliation in South Africa' (2006) 15 *Social and Legal Studies* 257 for discussion of this tendency.

22 'Force of Law' (n. 4) 14.

23 To appeal to the higher authority of international law simply defers the problem of the origin. See 'Force of Law' (n. 4).

24 Ibid. 13.

25 Ibid. 14.

26 Ibid. 35.

revolution or insurrection, but rather a violence that is innate to law. The founding of law itself constitutes a moment of violence because at this moment boundaries are set that will determine the inside and the outside of law. Certain forms of thought and action will fall validly within the bounds of legality, and others will fall outside. This element of decision, the point at which the boundaries of meaning are set, constitute for Derrida a moment of violence in which alternative voices are subordinated in the name of the universality of law. In the context of transitional justice, the institution of a codified model of transitional justice reflects the emergence of one dominant understanding of transitional justice and its history.[27] The effect of this dominance is to effectively exclude and silence all competing accounts.[28] The 'violence' of metaphysics therefore exists in the exclusion of the 'other', reflected in the desire for objectivity. A deconstructive reading of this moment of the origin of law allows us to see the ways in which those excluded views, opinions and interpretations remain inscribed in law, and as such are fundamental to our understanding of what law is.

Turning to the example of Northern Ireland, the founding of the state by the Government of Ireland Act 1920 represented a performative act, a moment of originary violence. The establishment of the state of Northern Ireland could not be characterised as being 'inscribed in the homogenous tissue of history'.[29] It was, in the clearest sense, a rupture with the existing order. Direct physical revolutionary violence, actual and threatened,[30] had precipitated the founding of a new legal order. The result of this legal violence was the existence of a large Catholic minority within the new state of Northern Ireland, who were physically present within the territory but who felt excluded from the dominant political community. Once the law had been passed, political objections were subordinated to the fact of the existence of a new state with law-making authority. The law enshrined the view that conflict in Ireland would be best addressed through the partition of Ireland and the creation of two separate governments on the island. With the passing of the Act, this became the dominant narrative of the creation of the state. Competing interpretations of the necessity or desirability of this course of action were, at the moment of creation of the state, subordinated to this dominant narrative.

However, deconstructive reading of this originary violence reveals not only the dynamic of exclusion at play, but also the way in which the trace of the excluded becomes inscribed in the state itself. Rather than the state effectively transcending its origins, remodelling itself as a neutral, impartial and objective force or observer,

27 For discussion of this dominant model, see Chapter 2.1.

28 In this way, the existence of the current model reflects the tendency to narrate an 'end of history', in which current models represent the endpoint of a journey in which the limitations of prior models are overcome. See Genealogy (n. 20) on this temptation in the context of transitional justice. On the narration of an 'ideal', see Jacques Derrida, 'Spectres of Marx' (1994) 15 *New Political Science* 7 (hereinafter 'Spectres of Marx').

29 'Force of Law' (n. 4) 13.

30 See Chapter 1.3 for an overview of events leading to the establishment of Northern Ireland.

the 'otherness' of the excluded becomes entrenched at its very heart.[31] Alternative interpretations of the creation of the state did not simply disappear. Both historical and contemporary understandings of the nature of the Northern Ireland conflict are constructed not only on the dominant narrative of the partition of Ireland to avoid war, but also on the excluded interpretations of partition as a mistake, and as a political injustice.[32] The interplay between these two opposing views is what constitutes our understanding of the state and its identity. There cannot therefore be a rigid distinction between what is included and what is excluded. The essentially deconstructible structure of *différance* clearly exists within the law.

This dynamic neatly illustrates the interplay between the first stage of the economy of violence – the existence of originary violence – and the second stage, the necessary concealment of that violence.[33] In most cases, notwithstanding the violence of the origin, once the state has been created, legitimacy and legality become 'permanently installed', and the violence of the origin is forgotten.[34] This will be discussed in more detail below. The creation of the state of Northern Ireland by the Government of Ireland Act 1920 set the scene for ongoing contestation of the legitimacy of the state, the laws it enforced and, ultimately, the justifications used in relation to the use of force to maintain law and order. The idea of the economy of violence therefore reveals the artificial nature of claims to objectivity by demonstrating the ongoing and fluid relationship between the violence of the origin and the law that it created.

4.1.2 Reparatory violence (on the obliteration of the origin)

The first stage of the economy of violence is the violence that occurs at the moment when law is founded. However, this originary violence of the founding of law is not open and acknowledged. Rather, to maintain the authority of law that has been established in the originary moment, it is necessary that this violence be concealed. Derrida refers to this as the 'effacement and obliteration' of the violence of the origin.[35] Once the boundaries of inclusion and exclusion have been set by the legal system, they must then be legitimated by reference to the authority of law. The violence of the origin of law will be forgotten, and law will become the means by which permissible and impermissible conduct and belief is regulated.

31 See Margaret Davies, 'Derrida and Law: Legitimate Fictions' in Tom Cohen (ed.), *Jacques Derrida and the Humanities: A Critical Reader* (Cambridge University Press 2002) 213, 221.

32 These competing interpretations are evidenced, for example, in the Healing Through Remembering Initiative, which seeks to deal with the legacy of the 'conflict in and about Northern Ireland', acknowledging that there is no agreed position on the legitimacy of the state. See www.healingthroughremembering.org.

33 Of Grammatology (n. 11) 112.

34 Jacques Derrida, 'The Laws of Reflection: Nelson Mandela, In Admiration' in Jacques Derrida and Mustafa Tlili (eds), *For Nelson Mandela* (Seaver Books 1987) 18 (hereinafter 'Laws of Reflection').

35 Of Grammatology (n. 11) 112.

In most settled states, basic rules of recognition ensure that even where a law is unpopular, it is still regarded as legitimate.[36]

When read as concerned with the construction of meaning, of systems of thought or belief, the resonance of this stage of the economy of violence for law is clear. Law depends, for its existence and authority, on its having independent existence.[37] Principles of the rule of law require that law be objective, impartial and independent of politics, morality or other external influences. It is on this basis that the dominance of law is ensured. What this means, in simple terms, is that in order for law to establish its own authority, it must become separate from those who created it. It must be able to transcend the history and process that brought it into being, and to claim separate existence.[38] The violence of the origin must be concealed. Derrida subsequently explained this element of the economy of violence in terms of the law being 'bound up with the silence of its own force'.[39] While the originary violence of law sets up boundaries, in order to maintain its claim to authority it must transcend the empirical context that has created it.[40] The element of violence or exclusion must not be acknowledged. Corson suggests that the emergence of these orders is possible *because of* the denial of the originary violence of law and its constitutive 'injuries, injustices, reductions and blind spots'.[41] Therefore, to focus on an opposition between violence and the law that it creates, to treat them as separate and divisible phenomena, perpetuates the myth that law has an independent existence, and does not take into account the place of law within the economy of violence. Where the violence of the origin of the law is not fully concealed, it will remain visible, undermining the law's claim to authority. Transitional contexts often make this dynamic clearly visible. Where the founding of a state is particularly controversial, for example where it arises from war or is regarded as being founded on injustice, then it will be nearly impossible for the violence of the origin to be forgotten.[42] Where the legitimacy of the state is contested from the outset, the violence may be too great. In these contexts, as Derrida suggests, this violence 'cannot manage to have itself forgotten'.[43] Writing of the South African experience, Derrida highlights how the law will do no more

36 HLA Hart, *The Concept of Law* (Clarendon Press 1961). This is also discussed in Catherine Turner, 'Political Representations of Law in Northern Ireland' [2010] 3 *Public Law* 451.

37 For more detailed discussion, see Chapter 3.3.

38 See 'Before the Law' (n. 16); Jacques Derrida, 'Declarations of Independence' in Elizabeth Rottenberg (ed.), *Negotiations: Interventions and Interviews, 1971–2001* (Stanford University Press 2002) 46.

39 'Force of Law' (n. 4).

40 Derrida suggests that writing constitutes ideal objects by delivering them from the ties of spacio-temporal facticity. The condition of their ideality is their repetition through time and space, which depends on their inscription on a support that transcends empirical context. Richard Beardsworth, *Derrida and the Political* (Routledge 1996) 16.

41 Ben Corson, 'Transcending Violence in Derrida: A Reply to John McCormick' (2001) 29 *Political Theory* 866, 871.

42 Laws of Reflection (n. 34) 18.

43 Ibid.

than perpetuate the violence of the origin through propping up an unjust system through law and judicial pronouncement. The system breaks down where this violence of the origin is not effectively forgotten,[44] and the result will be ongoing challenge to the authority of the state.

This analysis of the ongoing violence of law also has clear resonance in the Northern Ireland context. From the moment that a new state was founded against the backdrop of political division and violence, it was going to be difficult for agreed authority to be established. It has been suggested that the new government of Northern Ireland could only maintain control of its territory through 'implicit and episodically explicit coercion'.[45] How this played out in practice is discussed in more detail below. For the purposes of illustration of the economy of violence, however, brief discussion of the events that led to the establishment of the Northern Ireland Civil Right Association (NICRA) in 1968 is useful.

Despite the stated commitment made to principles of tolerance, fairness and justice 'common throughout the British Empire' at the time of the establishment of the Northern Ireland state,[46] an examination of the administration of the new state demonstrates what Derrida describes as the attempt to legalise the violence of its origin, through laws designed to enforce and maintain the authority of the state.[47] Given that the state was founded in response to revolutionary violence, and against a backdrop of threats of further violence, it is unsurprising that emergency legislation should have been a significant feature on the legal landscape in Northern Ireland. McEvoy and Morrison describe how 'constitutional discourses in Northern Ireland have, since the formation of the state, been framed by the presence or threat of political violence'.[48] The Civil Authorities (Special Powers) Act (Northern Ireland) 1922, which curtailed basic civil rights such as fair trial rights, protection from arbitrary arrest and freedom from interference with privacy and home life,[49] marked only the beginning of a series of pieces of emergency legislation, each restricting civil liberties a little further, that would cast a long shadow over the law in Northern Ireland until the present day.[50] On each occasion that a new piece of legislation was

44 Ibid.

45 Graham Ellison and Greg Martin, 'Policing, Collective Action and Social Movement Theory: The Case of the Northern Ireland Civil Rights Campaign' (2000) 51 *British Journal of Sociology* 681, 684.

46 The need to uphold and protect these principles had been a central part of the Unionist claim for partition. See Thomas Hennessy, *A History of Northern Ireland 1920–1996* (Gill and Macmillan 1997).

47 Laws of Reflection (n. 34) 18.

48 Kieran McEvoy and John Morison, 'Beyond the Constitutional Moment: Law, Transition and Peacemaking in Northern Ireland' (2003) 24 *Fordham International Law Journal* 961, 970.

49 See Her Majesty's Stationery Office, 'Disturbances in Northern Ireland: Report of the Commission Appointed by the Governor of Northern Ireland' (Belfast, 1969) 12 (hereinafter 'Cameron Report').

50 Northern Ireland (Emergency Provisions) Act 1973; Northern Ireland (Emergency Provisions) (Amendment) Act 1975; Northern Ireland (Emergency Provisions) Act 1978; Prevention of Terrorism (Temporary Provisions) Act 1984; Northern Ireland (Emergency Provisions) Act 1987. The existence of this emergency legislation and its effects has been the subject of significant

passed, it was framed with reference to the 'emergency' and the need to protect the state against the threat of violence.[51] In addition to the direct curtailment of civil liberties by the emergency powers legislation, much more widespread allegations of discrimination were levelled against the Northern Ireland authorities. There were allegations of corrupt electoral practices that ensured Unionist domination of local councils,[52] discrimination in the allocation of public housing that not only gave preference to Protestant applicants, but also as a result ensured that voting majorities were protected,[53] and also discrimination in the allocation of public employment.[54] These practices created a strong sense of injustice and discrimination among the minority community, who viewed the operation of legislative power as perpetuating their position of disadvantage and exclusion. In fact it was a dispute over housing allocation that is widely cited as having sparked the Civil Rights movement.[55]

The fact that the Unionist government of Northern Ireland needed to establish authority against a backdrop of, at best, controversy over the origin of the state and its legitimacy highlights the point made by Derrida that where the violence of the origin of the state is not properly concealed, it will remain visible and will result in the state being unable to establish itself as a legitimate law-making authority in the eyes of the political community. In the case of Northern Ireland, this led to a spiral of political violence and state response in the form of emergency legislation. Whether or not perceptions and allegations of discrimination are well founded is irrelevant – what matters is the extent to which the law is regarded as legitimate by those subject to its authority.[56] In the case of Northern Ireland, the violence of the foundation of the state was never successfully forgotten. This gave rise to contestation and ultimately violent challenge to the legitimacy, legality and authority of the state that provided the backdrop for a new cycle of violence, both physical and conceptual.

academic scrutiny. See, for example, Kevin Boyle, Tom Hadden and Paddy Hillyard, *Ten Years on in Northern Ireland: The Legal Control of Political Violence* (The Cobden Trust 1980); Oren Gross and Fionnuala Ní Aoláin, *Law in Times of Crisis: Emergency Powers in Theory and Practice* (Cambridge 2006); Dermot Walsh, *The Use and Abuse of Emergency Legislation in Northern Ireland* (The Cobden Trust 1983).

51 For discussion see Cheryl Lawther, 'Securing the Past: Policing and the Contest Over Truth in Northern Ireland' (2010) 50 *British Journal of Criminology* 455.

52 See Campaign for Social Justice in Northern Ireland, *Northern Ireland: The Plain Truth* (Dungannon, 1964).

53 Historical literature on the consolidation of the state of Northern Ireland is replete with examples of this allegation. For an overview of these controversies and their veracity, see John Whyte, 'How Much Discrimination Was There under the Unionist Regime 1921–1968?' in Tom Gallagher and James O'Connell (eds), *Contemporary Irish Studies* (Manchester University Press 1983).

54 See Kieran McEvoy and Ciaran White, 'Security Vetting in Northern Ireland: Loyalty, Redress and Citizenship' (1999) 61 *Modern Law Review* 341.

55 Cameron Report (n. 49); Campaign for Social Justice (n. 52).

56 For discussion, see James Dingley and Jo Morgan, 'Job Discrimination in Northern Ireland in Relation to the Theory of Ethnic Nationalism' (2005) 7 *National Identities* 51.

4.1.3 The violence of reflection

The third and final stage of Derrida's economy of violence is the violence of reflection. For Derrida, this is the form of violence where the most commonly understood concept of violence is situated.[57] This is the level of violence that is most often associated with direct physical violence and with the legal mechanisms that provoke and accompany it. At this level consideration of the concept of violence begins to shift away from the metaphysical violence of the law *per se*, and towards direct physical violence. This violence – the violence of reflection – has been categorised as the return of that which has been excluded and repressed.[58] Discussed by Derrida in terms of 'bloodless' and 'blood letting' violence,[59] the violence of the originary founding of the state is, at least potentially, benign in its operation ('bloodless').[60] It is a necessary part of the formation of identity and meaning. With the operation of the secondary layer of violence that conceals the violence of the origin comes a quest for closure, for the impartiality and objectivity of law and authority. However, where the state is perceived to be founded on injustice, and as a result the violence of the origin cannot be properly concealed, the state can provoke violent opposition through its failure to acknowledge the violence of its origin ('blood letting').[61] It is at this level that the relationship between violence, law and justice begins to emerge. Whereas law has made claims to authority that remain the subject of challenge, violence at this stage of the economy of violence will often justify itself by an appeal to justice, in a call to overthrow and re-found law in the name of justice. Appeals to justice are therefore used in opposition to law, used to legitimise claims made against the state and its law-making authority, and ultimately to justify armed political struggle where the ends are deemed to be just.[62] In 'Laws of Reflection' Derrida speaks of the practice of reflecting law back upon itself – of reflecting back against the system the principles on which it purports to be based.[63] In this way, he highlights a paradox inherent in non-violent protest, whereby the law is the problem, but also the perceived solution.

By the late 1960s in Northern Ireland, a new dynamic of protest had emerged that represented itself as concerned not with the abolition of the state, but rather with reform within the existing constitutional structures of the state.[64] This led to the beginnings of non-violent protest, the playing out of which illustrates the

57 Of Grammatology (n. 11) 112.

58 Chung-Hsuing Lai, 'On Violence, Justice and Deconstruction' (2003) 29 *Concentric: Studies in English Literature and Linguistics* 23, 25.

59 'Force of Law' (n. 4) 52.

60 This is discussed in more detail in section 4.2 below.

61 Beardsworth (n. 40) 10 sums this up as 'procedures of truth are predicated on the disavowal of inscription'.

62 'Force of Law' (n. 4) 32.

63 Laws of Reflection (n. 34) 24.

64 See Northern Ireland Civil Rights Association, *We Shall Overcome: The History of the Northern Ireland Civil Rights Association 1968–1978* (Belfast, 1978) (hereinafter NICRA). The claim that the civil rights movement was concerned with reform within Northern Ireland, rather than being a veiled nationalist movement aimed at destroying the border, was accepted by Lord Cameron. Cameron Report (n. 49) 15.

concern of the state with maintaining its own existence. In the case of the NICRA, what was ostensibly being challenged was not the legality or the existence of the state, nor its law-making capacity, but rather the legality of the laws that were being passed and their impact on the minority.[65] In this way, in the language of justice and rights, the civil rights movement reflected back against the Northern Ireland state the principles of tolerance, fairness and justice that had been at the heart of Unionist demands for special treatment in 1920.[66] It is ultimately the way in which the state responds to this reflection that determines (or perhaps simply indicates) the extent to which the violence of the origin has been forgotten or remains an open sore. In the case of Northern Ireland, the response from the state, far from reassuring moderate nationalist concerns, served to exacerbate the tensions surrounding the violence of the origin of the state and the legitimacy of the legal order.[67]

One example serves to illustrate the dynamic of contestation that underpinned the NICRA marches. In August 1968 the Derry Housing Action Committee requested that a civil rights march be organised in the city.[68] However, when organisers notified the police of the proposed route, as they were required to do under the legislation, Unionist politicians objected on the grounds that the route would be 'offensive to a great majority of the citizens residing on the route'.[69] Threats of counter-demonstrations were also made.[70] The Minister for Home Affairs consequently prohibited the protesters from marching in certain areas of the city, resulting in serious violence and rioting on the streets during which a prominent Nationalist politician was injured. This decision brought the relationship between violence and the law into focus once again. The request had been made for a non-violent protest march to take place in central areas of the city of Derry. On the basis of objection from the majority community, the march had been prohibited under Public Order legislation. It was subsequently officially accepted that the effect of the prohibition of the march had been to transform the situation from one in which a small number of interest groups sought to protest against social conditions in Derry, to one where large numbers of the population felt aggrieved at the handling of the situation by the Minister.[71] The law was revealed not as facilitating impartial adjudication of conflict, but as playing a key role in conserving the state, thus recreating the violence of the origin.

65 NICRA (n. 64).

66 See Chapter 1.3.

67 A review commissioned by the Governor of Northern Ireland in 1969 presented a troublesome picture of the response of the state to the emerging civil rights movement. The Report highlights how legal powers, in the form of the Public Order Act (Northern Ireland) 1951, were used to prohibit non-violent protest, thus frustrating demands for a more inclusive Northern Ireland. Cameron Report (n. 49).

68 The route to be taken followed that used by Protestant or Loyalist marching organisations in the city. This, the organisers claimed, demonstrated the non-sectarian nature of the civil rights movement. Ibid. 25.

69 Ibid.

70 Ibid.

71 Ibid. 27. Thus Derrida's suggestion that the failure of law, in the form of scorn shown for citizens, can deprive the aggrieved of effective mechanisms for redress is borne out. Laws of Reflection (n. 34) 40.

This operation of the law was cited as exposing the myth of the separability of law and politics. In the introduction to their influential text on *Law and State*, Boyle, Hadden and Hillyard suggested, 'When the legality of law is attacked, when the basis of legitimacy is challenged, where there is a constitutional crisis and obligation to the law is denied, aspects of the legal order that are previously concealed become visible, the problematic nature of legal legitimacy is revealed.'[72] However, given the competing interpretations of the legitimacy of the state, it was inevitable that there would also be equally contested positions on the Civil Rights Association.[73] Division remains to this day over whether the NICRA simply 'reflected' the violence of the state in such a way as to highlight the grievances of the excluded, or whether the NICRA themselves caused conflict though political agitation.[74]

The discussion of Derrida's economy of violence so far demonstrates that violence can be conceptualised in a tertiary structure, each stage of which combines to create our understanding of what violence is. From the originary violence that founds the state, to the concealment of that violence (or the failure to adequately conceal it) and finally the violence of reflection in which the violence of the state is reflected back upon itself, each stage is integral to the overall 'economy' of violence. This section examined the first and second levels of this tertiary structure. The following section will explore in more detail the third level of the economy of violence, that of the violence of reflection, by considering the emergence of armed opposition to the state, the response of the state to that opposition and ultimately the ways in which this violence shapes calls for transitional justice.

4.2 Contested narratives and the turn to violence

In *Of Grammatology*, Derrida notes that the final stage of the economy of violence, that of the violence of reflection, is the level at which the common concept of violence is situated.[75] It is at this level that we see argumentation over law and the morality of transgression that underpins transitional justice discourses. Derrida suggests that this stage is the most significant of the economy of violence for it is only with reflection that the artificiality of the boundaries created by the originary violence of law is revealed. This type of violence therefore opens up closed

72 Kevin Boyle *et al.*, *Law and State: The Case of Northern Ireland* (University of Massachusetts Press 1975).

73 There was, at the time, among some in the Northern Ireland population (and government) a suspicion that the civil rights movement was simply a cover for Republican and nationalist movements. See Cameron Report (n. 49) 25. Demands for reform within the state were therefore read as a challenge to the state itself, when seen in the context of competing political aspirations that had the potential to undermine the existence of the state *per se.*

74 See Jennifer Curtis, *Human Rights as War by Other Means: Peace Politics in Northern Ireland* (University of Pennsylvania Press 2014) for discussion of how these competing views of the NICRA continue to underpin attitudes towards human rights today.

75 Of Grammatology (n. 11) 112.

systems and subjects them to interrogation. It challenges notions of impartiality and objectivity and reveals the contestation inherent within our systems of understanding.

In *Of Grammatology*, Derrida speaks of the 'proper name', which in the context of law can be translated as the 'system' established by the originary violence of law. This so-called 'proper name' is 'perceived by the social and moral consciousness as the proper, the reassuring seal of self-identity, the secret'.[76] Roughly translated, this means that the political community accepts the 'system'. Ordinarily the state will be regarded as the legitimate political and legal order. Its citizens will be united in their loyalty to the institution of the state, if not to a particular government. As noted, in a settled democratic state the authority of the law is guaranteed by rules of recognition that ensure that even where a law is not popular, it is still regarded as law, because the state is accepted as having legitimate law-making authority. In this way the citizens of the state are complicit in maintaining the violence of the origin of the state through their acceptance of its legitimacy and authority.[77] However, where there is challenge to the state, this violence of reflection 'breaks the secret of the proper name and the innocent complicity'.[78] The violence of reflection challenges the acceptance of the state as the 'proper' order. It reveals the violence of the state and the exclusions that have been created, thereby undermining the idea of a settled political community. In this way it renders open and acknowledged the violence of the origin that the state seeks (implicitly) to conceal. This is only possible, according to Derrida, through the violence of reflection, whereby the excluded 'other' reveals the violence of the origin that has been concealed.[79]

In transitional justice contexts, this excluded 'other' is most commonly a political opposition that challenges the idea of a homogenous and unified political community represented by the state by revealing the manner of its exclusion.[80] The reaction of the state to this violence of reflection will impact on whether or not this reflection remains in the realm of political and legal contestation, and therefore regarded as 'legitimate', within the bounds of the law, or whether it escalates into armed opposition and the type of violence deemed 'illegitimate'.[81] In Northern Ireland the events of the civil rights campaign provided a brief moment of reflection, the holding up of a mirror to the state, which was soon to be eclipsed

76 Ibid.

77 For analysis of how this impacts on the possibility of transitional justice, see Bronwyn Leebaw, *Judging State Sponsored Violence, Imagining Political Change* (Cambridge University Press 2011).

78 Of Grammatology (n. 11) 113.

79 Ibid.

80 However, the idea has broader resonance for contemporary debates on law and society, and on immigration in particular, in that Derrida characterises the other as a 'foreigner', meaning simply someone from outside the closed order who is thereby able to reflect the violence of the closed community back on itself. Ibid.

81 See Laws of Reflection (n. 34) 40, in which Derrida suggests that when non-violent protest is met with legal repression, the response is to meet (legal) violence with (physical) violence.

by the direct physical violence of the Irish Republican Army (IRA), and the violent response of the state, in both physical and legal terms. This would create a new cycle of violence, law and claims for justice that would eventually underpin the discourse of 'transition' in Northern Ireland.

4.2.1 Legitimate 'force' and illegitimate 'violence'

In crafting his deconstruction of violence, law and justice in 'Force of Law', Derrida draws heavily on Benjamin's 'Critique of Violence'.[82] In this critique, Benjamin seeks to distinguish two particular forms of violence – that which founds or preserves law (mythic) – and that which seeks to destroy it (divine).[83] For Benjamin, these two types of violence exist in opposition to each other. Indeed, his critique relies on the existence of this distinction.[84] The two types of violence can be distinguished by the way in which they relate to the ends that are to be achieved by the use of violence.

For Benjamin, where a state resorts to the use of force to quell insurrection or armed opposition, this use of force will be justified by reference to the end goal of restoring law and order, and is thus 'mythic' violence. Similarly, where physical violence is used to demand reform within the state, this violence will be mythic, for it has as its aim the re-establishment of law, albeit a different law.[85] This type of violence works *within* the established system and simply reinscribes the violence of the law. Violence is used instrumentally as the necessary means to a just end, whether reasserting the monopoly of force for the state, or opposing a repressive state. This can be contrasted with divine violence, which does not seek to re-establish law, but rather seeks to destroy the system altogether.[86] This is a form of anarchic violence in that violence is engaged for its own sake and does not depend on the justification of the end to be achieved.[87] It rejects the idea of improvement within the existing apparatus and calls for its overthrow.[88] Therefore, where violence is used in protest at the actions of the state, without regard to consequences or outcome, this is a form of divine violence. It does not seek to re-establish law and so therefore breaks free from the constraints of mythic violence. In this way, Benjamin juxtaposes the mythical violence of the state and the

82 Walter Benjamin, 'Critique of Violence' in Edmund Jephcott tr., *Reflections: Essays, Aphorisms, Autobiographical Writings* (Random House 1995) 277.

83 This distinction is explained by 'Force of Law' (n. 4).

84 See Maley (n. 1) 61.

85 This approach embodies the paradox identified by Derrida whereby law is simultaneously the problem and the solution. See Laws of Reflection (n. 34).

86 This form of violence is variably referred to as 'divine', 'mystical' and 'messianic'. In the interests of consistency, and drawing a clear semantic distinction with 'mythical' violence, I use the term 'divine' throughout.

87 This form of violence is also referred to as a 'violence of pure means', in that the means do not rely on the end to be achieved for their justification. See 'Force of Law' (n. 4) 49.

88 For further discussion of the distinction between these forms of action, see Laws of Reflection (n. 34).

divine violence that is used to resist it, and in so doing draws a distinction between violence and law, one being used either in support of, or opposition to, the other.

The distinction between these two forms of violence is illustrated in the early years of conflict in Northern Ireland. There are two distinct narratives in respect of the legitimacy of the use of armed opposition to the state. The first narrative, and that which was the dominant contemporaneous narrative of the Troubles, was that the IRA campaign was an illegitimate campaign of terrorist violence to which the state responded in order to defend itself.[89] Therefore, any use of force on the part of the state was a legitimate response, justified by the ends of upholding law and order. This is a form of mythic violence, concerned with the maintenance of law. The opposing narrative, espoused by Republicans, is that the state itself was illegitimate, and that physical force was the only means of effectively exposing the violence of the state.[90] This violence is a form of divine violence, in that it did not have as its aim, in the early years at least, the reconstruction of the Northern Ireland state, but rather its destruction.[91] The straightforward black-and-white nature of this opposition is complicated by the existence of a middle ground, whereby the legitimacy of violent opposition to the state was rejected, but the actions of the state in responding to this violence were challenged using political and legal methods. This arose initially with the NICRA and their demands for equality within the state, but was also maintained throughout the Troubles in the work of constitutional nationalist parties, human rights activists and NGOs who protested the actions of the state using legal and political means to reflect the violence of the state back on itself.[92] This section will explore the construction of these competing narratives, using the example of Northern Ireland to explore Derrida's deconstruction of the distinction between violence and law.

4.2.2 *The mythic state and the divine terrorist*

Any analysis of the relationship between violence and the law and Northern Ireland's Troubles must first be located within the tertiary structure of the economy of violence in which law is founded in a moment of violence, that violence is forgotten, but the excluded returns to challenge the dominant order. As discussed

89 For more detailed discussion of this narrative, see Kevin Hearty, 'A Shared Narrative? A Case Study of the Contested Legacy of Policing in the North of Ireland' (2014) 54 *British Journal of Criminology* 1047.

90 This attitude is reflected in Ellison and Martin's analysis of the NICRA and the state's response that where there is unwillingness to integrate excluded demands into the mainstream, campaigners will adopt a much more confrontational approach. See Ellison and Martin (n. 45) 685.

91 This is referred to (but not endorsed) by Boyle, Hadden and Hillyard as the 'political solution', whereby political violence could only be addressed by moving towards the reunification of Northern Ireland with the Republic of Ireland. See Boyle *et al.* (n. 50) 6.

92 Paul Mageean and Martin O'Brien, 'From the Margins to the Mainstream: Human Rights and the Good Friday Agreement' (1998) 22 *Fordham International Law Journal* 1498. See also Kieran McEvoy, 'What Did Lawyers Do During the War? Neutrality, Conflict and the Culture of Quietism' (2011) 74 *Modern Law Review* 350.

in section 4.1, the creation of the state of Northern Ireland was itself a moment of originary force (or violence). In the case of Northern Ireland, it is a well-rehearsed belief that life was good before the Troubles. People reminisce about how Protestants and Catholics used to live together peacefully, and how it was the outbreak of political violence in 1969 that created division.[93] This illustrates the dynamic that Derrida speaks of, whereby there is an acceptance, albeit unwitting, of the violence of the origin of the state and therefore complicity in the economy of violence that it creates. This is a crucial point and one determined largely by one's position on the legitimacy of the state and its law-making authority. One's position on the state will determine how one judges the use of force, either on the part of the state or against it. Significant cleavages in public opinion on the legitimacy of the state will inevitably lead to contested narratives of law and order, and on the legitimacy of the use of political violence.[94] This is seen particularly clearly in the use of the terms 'force' and 'violence' – one denoting legitimacy, the other illegitimacy.[95]

The summer of 1969 was a difficult one in Northern Ireland. It marked the culmination of tensions that had been steadily mounting around the civil rights campaign and was the year in which violence exploded – serious political violence that would last for the next thirty years. This period of the Troubles is the period of violence most commonly associated with Northern Ireland, and it is also the period from which it is in 'transition'. It is therefore the 'war' of the transitional justice 'war' and 'peace' binary. It is also the 'before' of the 'before and after' around which transitional justice is constructed. During this period the struggle over law played out primarily on the terrain of criminal law, with the relationship between law and direct physical violence remaining close to the surface and visible. From the outset, the distinction between mythic and divine violence was evident in the discourse on law and order in Northern Ireland. What was at issue was legitimacy of competing uses of violent force, starkly visible in the public realm. Protest against particular acts of government and the police manifested in severe rioting in the streets across Northern Ireland.[96] This violence was met by the use of force by the police and state forces to quell the riots.[97]

A direct comparison is therefore possible between attitudes towards the use of force by the state to uphold the law (mythic violence) and the use of violence to

93 See Kirk Simpson, *Unionist Voices and the Politics of Remembering the Past in Northern Ireland* (Palgrave 2009).

94 See generally Hearty (n. 89). See also Leebaw (n. 77) on the consequences of this.

95 In 'Force of Law', Derrida uses the terms violence and force interchangeably. However, it has been argued that the concept of 'violence' as used by Derrida should be understood as a generalised concept that includes legitimate force, coercion, power or authority. See Dominic LaCapra, 'Violence, Justice and the Force of Law' (1990) 11 *Cardozo Law Review* 1065, 1066. See also Sami Khatib, 'Towards a Politics of "Pure Means": Walter Benjamin and the Question of Violence' (2015) Anthropological Materialism http://anthropologicalmaterialism.hypotheses.org/1040, accessed 19 October 2015.

96 Cameron Report (n. 49).

97 Ibid.

oppose that law (divine violence). A rigid opposition existed between those who supported the state's right to use 'force' to protect itself, and therefore condemned anti-state 'violence', and those who advocated the use of violence to oppose an oppressive state, and therefore condemned the use of 'force' on the part of the state.[98] This opposition was constructed on a distinction between law and violence – either law as opposing violence, or violence opposing law. Boyle, Hadden and Hillyard note that the legal system by definition is committed to the protection of the state. Where a conflict is revolutionary, it is 'almost inevitable that the legal system will be seen as supporting one or other faction in the conflict'.[99] This was the case in Northern Ireland. The divisions that had been created by the creation of the state were replicated in the attitudes towards the legal system. In this phase, law was regarded as 'belonging' to the pro-state Unionists and as being used against, or marginalising, the Irish nationalist population. These dynamics of contestation are not unique to Northern Ireland.[100] Nor is analysis of the rhetoric of state versus freedom fighter a new invention in this context.[101] What they demonstrate, however, is the close interplay between violence and law.

During the 1970s, contestation moved gradually away from the raw and visible use of force on the part of the state that had characterised the early years,[102] and into the realm of contesting the legal response to anti-state violence. In particular, the question of the use of force by the state became subsumed to a much greater extent into the narrative of legality and the extent to which such force could be justified within a legal framework.[103] This was reflected in the move away from a military response to violence towards the use of the 'ordinary' criminal law.[104] Therefore, while force did not cease to be a key site of contestation, it became much more intricately linked with law from the early 1970s. As noted, from the creation of the Northern Ireland state, constitutional discourses in Northern Ireland have been framed by the threat or use of political violence.[105] This led

98 See, for example, contemporaneous reports on the violence commissioned by the British government that highlighted the existence of contested views of the legitimacy of the state and the role of this contestation in causing violence. See Cameron Report (n. 49); Her Majesty's Stationery Office, 'Report of the Tribunal of Inquiry on Violence and Civil Disturbances in Northern Ireland in 1969' (Belfast, 1972) (hereinafter 'Scarman Report').

99 Boyle *et al.* (n. 72) 2–3.

100 This is also reflected in Teitel's conceptualisation of transitional justice, in which she notes how the struggle for ownership of the law can be a key cause of conflict. See Ruti Teitel, *Transitional Justice* (Oxford University Press 2000) discussed in Chapter 2.

101 See Igor Primoratz, 'What Is Terrorism?' (1990) 7 *Journal of Applied Philosophy* 129; Jenny Teichman, 'How to Define Terrorism' (1989) 64 *Philosophy* 505; Conor Gearty, 'Terrorism and Morality' (2003) 4 *European Human Rights Law Review* 377.

102 For a general overview, see Cameron Report (n. 49).

103 See Fionnuala Ní Aoláin, *The Politics of Force: Conflict Management and State Violence in Northern Ireland* (Blackstaff Press 2000).

104 Her Majesty's Stationery Office, 'Report of a Committee to Consider, in the Context of Civil Liberties and Human Rights, Measures to Deal with Terrorism in Northern Ireland' (London, 1975) (Gardiner Report).

105 McEvoy and Morison (n. 48).

to the institution, from the early years of the state, of the legal framework of emergency powers. While these powers had existed in law since 1922, the period following the outbreak of violence was characterised by intensification in the use of emergency legislation to respond to political violence.[106] The way in which the cause of this violence was framed, and how blame was to be apportioned, was axiomatic to understanding the escalation of violence and the legal response thereto over the next ten years.

4.2.3 'Emergency' as an 'exceptional' state of affairs

The framework of 'emergency' assumed the existence of exceptional circumstances that justified an 'exceptional' legal regime, which allowed the state the flexibility to achieve desired outcomes in terms of responding to violent challenge while remaining within the bounds of legality.[107] The discourse of emergency was present not only in political narratives of violence, but was also reflected in law at multiple levels. At the national level, the period between 1970 and 1987 saw no fewer than five pieces of emergency legislation responding to 'terrorism' in Northern Ireland passed by the United Kingdom parliament.[108] This legislation was interpreted and applied by the courts in Northern Ireland.[109] And at the international level, the European Court of Human Rights (ECtHR) interpreted the requirements of the European Convention on Human Rights (ECHR) in light of the existence of the 'terrorist' threat in Northern Ireland.[110] The official use of this discourse gradually embedded the distinction between legitimate and illegitimate uses of force, thereby shaping public perceptions of the causes of the conflict and the state's response thereto, as well as dictating the consequences of engaging in actions deemed to be unlawful or illegitimate.

This dynamic is particularly well illustrated by the approach taken by the ECtHR to cases concerning the right to life enshrined in Article 2 of the Convention and the controversial use of lethal force by the state.[111] Article 2 guarantees the right to life. Its enjoyment is, however, subject to limitations. Article 2(2) provides that the

106 No fewer than five pieces of emergency legislation were passed in the years between 1973 and 1987. See n. 50 above. For discussion of the impact of this emergency legislation on the legal landscape in Northern Ireland, see McEvoy (n. 92).

107 For detailed discussion of the nature of emergency, see Gross and Ní Aoláin (n. 50).

108 See n. 50 above.

109 See, for example, *Ex Parte Lynch* [1980] NI 126, in which the court confirmed that the application of the label 'terrorist' was sufficient to legitimate an otherwise unlawful procedure. What was at issue was the disapplication of the normal rules of judicial review of detention in cases where a person was detained under the Prevention of Terrorism Act on suspicion of being involved in terrorist activity.

110 See, for example, the reasoning in *Brogan and Others v United Kingdom* [1988] 11 EHRR 177 and in *Brannigan and McBride v United Kingdom* [1993] 17 EHRR 539, in which the Court considered the scope of Article 5 of the ECHR and the derogation provisions contained in Article 15 that allowed the state to derogate from Convention guarantees in times of war or other public emergency.

111 For an overview of this particularly thorny issue, see Ní Aoláin (n. 103).

deprivation of life may be lawful if it is the result of a use of force that is no more than is 'absolutely necessary'.[112] Such force may be absolutely necessary where it is used in defence of any person from unlawful violence,[113] for example, or where it is used to quell a riot or insurrection.[114] These permissible limitations enshrine into law the distinction between legitimate and illegitimate uses of force. They set the boundaries of the lawful use of force, and they are the terrain on which contestation over the lawfulness and legitimacy of violence play out.

During the Troubles, a number of Article 2 cases failed to progress to a hearing before the Court as a result of determinations by the European Commission that the state had acted within the permissible limitations enshrined in Article 2.[115] The first Article 2 case to reach the Court was therefore *McCann and others v United Kingdom*,[116] which concerned the shooting dead of three IRA members. The three victims in this case were known members of the IRA who were present in Gibraltar. The army believed that they intended to carry out a car bomb attack on the territory and, as a result, the three were shot dead in disputed circumstances. What is interesting about this case for current purposes is the fact that by the time the case reached the ECtHR, there was little dispute as to the material facts. There was no ambiguity as to the status of the victims as members of the IRA, nor of their intention to engage in violence.[117] On the other side, there was no denial that state forces were responsible for the killing. What was at issue, therefore, was solely the *legality* of the killing by the state, when set against a backdrop of political violence. In this case the Court found that there had not been a violation of Article 2.[118]

This exposes the way in which notions of violence and law are constructed with reference to the purpose of the violence (in this case a lethal 'use of force' on the part of the state). What is beginning to be revealed is the way in which law maintains its own authority by suppressing alternative positions that have the potential to challenge the dominant order. As Campbell and Connolly note, 'In a

112 Specifically, Article 2(2) ECHR provides that 'deprivation of life shall not be regarded as being inflicted in contravention of this Article when it results from the use of force that is absolutely necessary'.

113 ECHR Article 2(2)(a).

114 ECHR Article 2(2)(c).

115 See in particular *Stewart v United Kingdom* App. no. 10044/82 (ECHR, 1984), in which the Commission determined that soldiers had acted in a manner that was 'absolutely necessary' to quell a riot, in the course of which a young boy was shot and killed. See also *Kelly v United Kingdom* App. no. 17579/90 (ECHR, 4 May 2001), in which the Commission declared the case inadmissible on the grounds that soldiers who had shot and killed the driver of a stolen car, which had failed to stop at an army checkpoint, had acted within the limits of Article 2.

116 *McCann and Others v United Kingdom* [1995] 21 EHRR.

117 The precise timing of the attack, however, was misjudged. The army had believed that the attack was imminent. However, after the shootings it was discovered that the bomb had not yet been moved in to place. Ibid.

118 While a finding of no violation was made, *McCann* introduced a procedural requirement to Article 2, discussed in more detail in Chapter 6.

democracy, law is not "outside" the conflict; rather it provides one site on which the conflict can be conducted, and is thus partly constitutive of it.'[119] In Northern Ireland, as in all transitional societies, the law and its constituent exclusions were integral to the conflict. The critique of the failure of law to adequately address the conflict emerged both at the domestic level, in terms of analysis of confidence in the law in Northern Ireland itself, but also touched on the limitations of international law. The ECtHR was robustly criticised for its systematic failure to address the perceived gap between law and justice that had opened up in the course of the Northern Ireland conflict.[120] The approach of the ECtHR to the Article 2 cases emanating from Northern Ireland arguably represented a particularly cautious approach, in which strict legalism was used to avoid becoming involved in political issues.[121] From a legal point of view, the 'mythic' violence of upholding the law was prioritised over the 'divine' violence that opposed the law. This force was permitted in order to protect the system from violent challenge.[122] Therefore, if one accepts the legitimacy of the state as the guardian of law and order, then the use of lethal force in responding to violence that challenges the existence of the state or the security of its citizens is a perhaps regrettable, but nevertheless justified – both legally and morally – course of action.

This lawfulness also colours moral perceptions of law and transgression. For the state, the use of force is a means of responding to a particular threat or attack, as well as a means of serving the broader purpose of protecting the values of the rule of law *per se*. Those who use violence to challenge the state are challenging the so-called 'proper name'. Therefore, while violence used against the state violates law, the act of killing the 'enemy' is a means of reinstating law.[123] Those who use violence to challenge law have placed themselves outside law. In taking the lives of others, their own lives are no longer guaranteed.[124] The consequence of transgressing the social order is potentially death. And this death will be legal; it will occur within the law. In this way, the character of the 'rule of law' is guaranteed

119 Colm Campbell and Ita Connolly, 'A Model for the "War Against Terrorism"? Military Intervention in Northern Ireland and the Falls Curfew' (2003) 30 *Journal of Law and Society* 341, 348.

120 See in particular Oren Gross and Fionnuala Ní Aoláin, 'To Know Where We Are Going, We Need to Know Where We Are: Revisiting States of Emergency' in Angela Hegarty and Siobhan Leonard (eds), *Human Rights: An Agenda for the Twenty First Century* (Cavendish 1998) 79 on the systemic failure of the ECHR to exercise effective oversight of the existence of public emergency and the need for derogation.

121 On this as a general strategy in relation to violence in Northern Ireland, see McEvoy (n. 92).

122 This reflects the underlying purpose of the ECHR as a legal order to maintain effective political democracy and protect human rights, itself bound up with transition from war and abusive regimes. See Michael Hamilton and Antoine Buyse, 'Introduction' in Antoine Buyse and Michael Hamilton (eds), *Transitional Jurisprudence and the European Convention on Human Rights* (Cambridge University Press 2011) 1.

123 Derrida notes how state power and sovereignty are marked by the right of life and death over its citizens. Jacques Derrida, *The Death Penalty, Volume 1*, Peggy Kamuf tr. (University of Chicago Press 2014) 5.

124 Ibid. 14.

not only at the domestic level, but also regionally through the enforcement of the 'legal order' created by the Convention itself. Crucial to this narrative of legitimate use of force to uphold the law is the acceptance of the state as the legitimate and lawful authority. From this perspective, the role of the security forces, including the army and the police, is not only to protect civilian life, but also to protect the state itself from violent challenge. Assessment of the 'necessity' of the use of force will be framed with reference to the need to protect the state.[125]

While this dynamic is clearly visible in relation to the use of physical force by the state, it operates equally in respect of the force of law. In addition to the cases brought before the ECtHR under Article 2 of the Convention, a series of cases challenging the operation of emergency legislation, and in particular the provisions on detention, were also brought.[126] It is suggested that these cases are interesting in that they relate not specifically to the distinction between legitimate and illegitimate uses of physical force – and therefore the distinction *between* violence *and* law – but rather they deal more specifically with the violence *of* law and how it responds to challenge. These cases also illustrate the interplay between the domestic and international jurisdictions, and the ways in which law appeals to prior conventions in order to guarantee its authority.[127]

In the case of *Brogan and Others v United Kingdom*, the applicants had been arrested and detained under the Prevention of Terrorism Act 1984. While there was no dispute that the arrest and detention were lawful under the provisions of Northern Ireland's law,[128] the applicants claimed that this lawfulness was not enough to meet the requirements of the Convention. The European Commission initially accepted the government's reasoning that a certain degree of flexibility was required when interpreting the scope of a Convention right in order to take account of the terrorist threat, and on this basis determined that there had been no violation of the applicants' rights. However, the Court rejected this reasoning. Upholding the applicants' case, the Court confirmed that whether an arrest or detention could be regarded as lawful should be determined not only with reference to domestic legislation, but also in light of both the text of the Convention and its underlying legal principles.[129] The government had argued that the provisions were necessary

125 This position has been altered since *McCann*, with the evolution of a strong procedural element to Article 2, whereby the state is required to conduct an effective investigation into any controversial killings as a means of establishing whether or not it was in fact absolutely necessary. See, e.g., *McKerr v United Kingdom* [2002] 34 EHRR 20.

126 These cases were brought under Article 5 of the Convention. See *Brogan and Others v United Kingdom* [1988] 11 EHRR 177; *Brannigan and McBride v United Kingdom* [1993] 17 EHRR 539.

127 'Before the Law' (n. 16).

128 *Brogan* (n. 126) para. 49. The Prevention of Terrorism Act provided that, where a person was suspected of being involved in terrorist activity, they could be arrested. This arrest was not subject to the normal rules of judicial review of detention under the Magistrates Court (Northern Ireland) Order 1981, meaning that those detained were not subject to the rules and safeguards normally applied to those arrested. In *Ex Parte Lynch* [1980] NI 126, the court in Northern Ireland confirmed that the application of the label of 'terrorist' was sufficient to legitimate this otherwise unlawful procedure.

129 *Brogan* (n. 126) para. 65.

to protect the community as a whole from terrorism. While the Court accepted that this could be regarded as a legitimate aim that was being pursued, they concluded that it was not on its own sufficient to ensure compliance with the specific requirements of Article 5 of the Convention.

While this decision may initially be read as a victory for justice over the law, the reaction of the government adds a further layer of complexity to the relationship between the two at the international level. Article 15 of the Convention provides that states may derogate from their Convention obligations during a public emergency that threatens the life of the nation.[130] The language of this article, and the opt-out clause that it provides, enabled the government to enter a derogation covering specifically the issue raised in *Brogan* – namely the arrest and detention of terrorist suspects. In a statement made by the Home Secretary at the time announcing the derogation, specific reference was made to the background of the terrorist campaign and the overriding need to bring terrorists to justice.[131] This derogation led to a very different decision in the subsequent case of *Brannigan and McBride v United Kingdom*.[132] In this case the Court accepted the reasoning of the government that the situation in Northern Ireland fell within the scope of the meaning of an emergency threatening the life of the nation under Article 15. The existence of the derogation therefore legitimated action that had been found to be a violation in *Brogan*. These cases lead us back to the essentially deconstructible nature of law, and Derrida's critique of the separation of the two concepts of violence and law that forms the basis of Benjamin's critique. It exposes the oppositional nature of the rhetoric of violence and law, whereby law, and legal amendment, was necessary to oppose political violence.

4.3 The mutual contamination between violence and law

For Derrida, wherever concepts are set up in opposition to each other, they are essentially deconstructible.[133] Exposing the binary system of opposition allows a deconstructive reading that reveals the interplay between the two concepts. This reveals the artificiality of the distinction drawn by Benjamin between violence and law. In 'Force of Law', Derrida highlights the mutual contamination between the foundation of law and its ongoing conservation, which complicates the straightforward opposition between violence and law.[134] Returning to the economy of violence, whereas the moment of the founding of law can be regarded as a moment

130 This article therefore provides for a short-term response to exceptional challenge. For critique, see Fionnuala Ní Aoláin, 'Transitional Emergency Jurisprudence: Derogation and Transition' in Antoine Buyse and Michael Hamilton (eds), *Transitional Jurisprudence: Transitional Justice and the ECHR* (Cambridge 2011) 24.

131 As cited in *Brannigan* (n. 126) para. 54.

132 [1993] 17 EHRR 539.

133 A concept is 'essentially deconstructible where it is founded on interpretable textual strata, or where its ultimate foundation is by definition unfounded'. 'Force of Law' (n. 4) 14.

134 Ibid. 40.

of originary violence, each time that law is interpreted with the aim of maintaining law and order, the violence of the origin is repeated. This in itself is a form of violence – a law-conserving violence.[135] The element of mutual contamination relates not only to the direct reassertion of the authority of law through legal decision-making (mythic violence) but also exists in the relationship between physical (divine) violence and law. Whereas Benjamin regards divine violence as existing in opposition to law, to destroy law, Derrida suggests that all violence will have as its outcome the re-establishment of law,[136] and therefore the distinction between the two forms of violence cannot be maintained. Law and violence are connected in a cycle of violence whereby law is destroyed and re-founded with each legal decision. However, this violence does not have any intrinsic quality. At the moment that law is founded it cannot be said to be either 'just' or 'unjust'.[137] It cannot be said at the time at which it is happening that the violence of the founding of law is either 'good' or 'bad'. It is only with the passage of time that the moment of the founding of law comes to be either accepted or rejected as a source of legitimacy. In particular, it depends on the extent to which the violence of the origin is successfully concealed.[138] Our interpretation of law therefore depends both on the past that has given rise to the law, and on the way in which that law is subsequently interpreted. Law thus relies on a *post hoc* legitimation of its origin in order to secure its authority. It cannot be given fixed meaning in the present. Derrida sums this up when he suggests that law belongs to 'an order of right that does not yet exist'.[139] Our understanding of law and its legitimacy arises from the perpetual state of negotiation between violence, law and justice. Recognising the existence of this dynamic is an important element of the critique of violence, and therefore also of transitional justice.

In this context the Northern Ireland cases, both in the House of Lords and the ECtHR, provide a clear illustration of the immanence of violence to law. Each time the state responded physical to violence with a new piece of emergency legislation, the metaphysical violence of the founding of law was repeated. However, rather than acknowledging the violence of the institution of emergency legislation, the decision-making of the courts was dressed up as legality, as the fairness and impartiality of law, in contrast to the arbitrariness of terrorist violence.[140] In the case of Northern Ireland, the framework of emergency became the single lens through which the conflict was refracted, underpinning the reasoning of the courts in respect of the government's response to violence. The courts, both domestic and international, adopted a broad reading of emergency powers on the basis that 'exceptions from established principles were necessary in the conflict

135 Ibid.
136 Ibid. 35.
137 Ibid. 13.
138 See section 4.1 for discussion.
139 'Force of Law' (n. 4) 35.
140 For discussion of the difficulties of challenging this narrative, see McEvoy (n. 92) 380.

situation in Northern Ireland'.[141] With each decision that referred to the need to combat the terrorist threat, the originary violence of the creation of the law was repeated. Whether or not measures taken that were 'exceptions' to established principles were adjudged to be reasonable or proportionate was interpreted in light of the security context. As Livingstone suggested, 'such questions call for an examination of facts, circumstances and perceptions.'[142] Where there are competing narratives over what exactly the security context is, and where the illegitimate violence emanates from, it is inevitable that at the moment of legal decision a moment of violence will occur, whereby one narrative is chosen over the other.

During the Troubles, it was an oft-cited criticism that the House of Lords, when asked to adjudicate conflict-related cases from Northern Ireland, regularly constructed the context from 'the perspective of the security forces and the dangers they face'.[143] This approach failed to take account of competing perspectives that could have provided a different way of constructing context. Through its operation, law set up exclusions and determined the boundaries of good versus bad citizens.[144] By accepting one narrative and reinforcing that view of the context through legal decision-making, the law effectively silenced those with competing political opinions of violence and law. In this way, the violence of the origin of the law was repeated with each decision that upheld exceptional emergency measures, reinstating the boundaries of inclusion and exclusion that had been set with the institution of that particular law.[145] Further, not only was one narrative privileged over others, the legal character of the decision also effectively eliminated the basis for any (legitimate) contestation of the law.[146]

The extent to which the idea of an emergency, created by a terrorist threat to the existence of the state, created an interpretive framework is clearly visible. The judgments are clearly framed with reference to the need to uphold the law against violent challenge. In this way they refer back to the past that gave rise to the law – the existence of a terrorist threat, often manifested in a particular act of violence. As the excluded trace remains inscribed within law, the effect of the political violence, far from destroying law, was to establish new law. In this way, violence and law are two sides of the same coin.[147] Violence, rather than being something separate from law, is the 'other' to which the law must respond in order to reassert its authority. The political trace – that which is excluded from the dominant narrative

141 See Stephen Livingstone, 'The House of Lords and the Northern Ireland Conflict' (1994) 57 *Modern Law Review* 333, 344.

142 Ibid. 350.

143 Ibid.

144 For the most authoritative account of the effect of the emergency legislation, see Paddy Hillyard, *Suspect Community: People's Experience of the Prevention of Terrorism Act in Britain* (Pluto Press 1993). This study demonstrates the ways that the legislation operated, not only in a narrow or technical legal manner, but how its social implications exceeded its technical aspects.

145 'Force of Law' (n. 4) 43. 'Iterability requires the origin to repeat itself … [it] inscribes conservation in the essential structure of foundation.'

146 For discussion of the role of decision-making, see William Sokoloff, 'Between Justice and Legality: Derrida on Decision' (2005) 58 *Political Research Quarterly* 341.

147 'Force of Law' (n. 4) 54.

of emergency and security – remains bound up within the structure of the law. Similarly, each time a legal decision is made that upholds the need to protect the state and safeguard the rule of law, the law is interpreted as requiring a particular course of action. The meaning of the law, and its legitimacy, rather than having fixed meaning in the present, is constructed with reference to both its past and its future. Seen in these terms, the state and its laws continue to be haunted by the violence of the origin, and by the excluded other.[148]

Law, through legal decision-making, determines what falls within the law, and is therefore legitimate, and what falls outside the law, and is therefore illegitimate. Each time the interpretive framework of emergency was accepted and applied, it reinforced the system of legal reasoning and strengthened the validity of the framework, thereby perpetuating the violence of the origin of the law through the ongoing interpretation of violence and the state's response to it. It did so not only in its attempts to delegitimise the use of political violence and any narrative of grievance that may have underpinned it, but also in suppressing alternative voices on the legitimacy or indeed morality of the state's response to this challenge. This gave rise in some quarters to an unwillingness to accept human rights arguments in respect of the operation of the emergency legislation. This was evidenced not only in decisions of higher courts such as the House of Lords and the ECtHR, but also more pervasively in political attitudes towards human rights that were infused with deep suspicion as to the motives of those making human rights arguments.[149] For example, pro-state constituencies regarded human rights as a challenge to the authority of the state, and being in sympathy with the (illegitimate) violence of the IRA.[150] As noted in Chapter 3, meaning is constructed through the interplay of seemingly oppositional concepts that exist in a state of violent hierarchy. During the period of the Troubles, the narrative of the state response to violence as an abuse of human rights was subordinated to that of the necessity of the security response. The concept of emergency, underpinned by security concerns, was the dominant narrative of the law during this time, with narratives of either political grievance or human rights concerns as the excluded trace.

Thus law established the dominant narrative on violence. It also constructed the binary oppositions that are evident in transitional justice. For example, the operation of emergency legislation defined right and wrong and with it set the category of (innocent) victim and perpetrator. This particular binary is one that continues to play out in Northern Ireland's transition and is discussed in detail in Chapter 6. What this demonstrates is that the way in which these oppositions are

148 On the concept of 'haunting', see Spectres of Marx (n. 28).

149 See famously the statement of Nobel Peace Prize Laureate David Trimble that human rights groups were complicit in murder. Giles Tremlett, 'Human Rights Groups are Complicit in Murder, Says Trimble' *The Guardian* (London, 29 January 2004) www.theguardian.com/uk/2004/jan/29/northernireland.humanrights, accessed 19 October 2015.

150 For example, Ian Paisley described the language of rights as 'fancy non-partisan jargon' and 'well-known shorthand for Republican supremacy'. Ian Paisley, 'Peace Agreement – or Last Piece in a Sellout Agreement?' (1998) 22 *Fordham International Law Journal* 1273.

constructed during conflict will continue to dominate how discourse of justice in transition and its inclusions and exclusions are constructed.

4.4 Conclusion

This chapter asked whether violence and law can be separated. If the two can be separated then a progression between the two – from violence to law – is possible. However, if the separation is revealed to be false, then the possibility of a linear progression between violence and law becomes problematic. Derrida's economy of violence has demonstrated that every moment of founding law will be a moment of metaphysical violence. However, while violence is commonly understood to have a negative connotation, as something wrong or illegitimate,[151] for Derrida it has no intrinsic quality. At the point at which violence happens, it has no intrinsically good or bad quality. Judgment on its use comes only after the fact. Benjamin similarly observes that the violence that creates law does not, at the moment at which it is used, have to be 'legitimate'. It only has to be victorious.[152] There is no means of establishing before the fact whether the violence used is legitimate or not. Rather, this determination will depend on the subsequent legitimation, through the law, of those actions.[153]

Those who engage in revolutionary violence therefore take a risk. If they succeed in their aims, the violent means used will be retrospectively legitimated in the way in which the story of the conflict is told, subsumed into a 'revolutionary philosophy committed to the infinite task of redeeming the past'.[154] Violent opposition will be characterised as an unfortunate but necessary response to injustice, as a struggle for social and legal transformation.[155] But this is only possible where violence has been victorious. In short, the means will be justified with reference to the ends. If the campaign does not succeed, however, then the use of violence will remain condemned – a violence deemed as unjust,[156] for any use of physical violence will be condemned in the first instance.[157] At the point of its occurrence, violence will be regarded as 'illegal, brutal, evil'.[158] It is only with victory that it will begin to be legitimised.[159] Because violence is justified on the basis that it aims to enact a new and more just legal order,[160]

151 This reflects its status as something traditionally pushed out of public discourse.
152 Mahlmann (n. 3) 22.
153 See Elizabeth Frazer and Kimberly Hutchings, 'Remnants and Revenants: Politics and Violence in the Work of Agamben and Derrida' (2011) 13 *British Journal of Politics and International Relations* 127, 128.
154 Robert Sinnerbrink, 'Deconstructive Justice and the "Critique of Violence": On Derrida and Benjamin' (2006) 16 *Social Semiotics* 485, 491.
155 Costas Douzinas, 'Violence, Justice and Deconstruction' (2005) 6 *German Law Journal* 171, 175.
156 'Force of Law' (n. 4) 6.
157 Sinnerbrink (n. 154) 486 suggests that legitimate force can be used by law, and it is inextricably bound to our legal and moral sense of justice. Force without law, however, is sheer violence that we rightly condemn as unjust.
158 Douzinas (n. 155).
159 Ibid.
160 Maley (n. 1) 61.

the struggle for the law is no less political than the use of violence that precedes it. In 'Force of Law', Derrida suggests that 'all revolutionary situations, all revolutionary discourses ... justify recourse to violence by alleging the founding, in progress or to come, of a new law'.[161] In this way law finds its place within the cycle of justification that relies on recourse to history as a means of legitimising the past.[162] Violence will be understood as necessary to achieve progress, a break from a conflicted past that can be contrasted with the new and more just order that has been founded.[163]

This suggests that although violence itself has no intrinsic quality, a value judgement is nevertheless possible on the use to which violence is put. This is particularly true in respect of state versus non-state violence. Discourses of human rights and transitional justice are founded on the position that law-conserving violence used on the part of the state is inherently wrong. Therefore, the fact that a state has an interest in preserving not only its existence but also its monopoly on the use of violence within its borders is viewed as problematic. By implication, the state will be susceptible to violent opposition, as political opponents seek to engage the violence of reflection against the state, justified by the need to re-found the state. However, given that all law is founded in a moment of violence, it is not simply a matter of disaggregating the law that conserves the authority of the state from that which is used to challenge it. What is necessary is to recognise that violence forms part of a circular logic whereby protest against law has as its aim the re-founding of law, thereby perpetuating the cycle of violence. This cycle of overcoming law by simply re-establishing it demonstrates that there is something fundamentally 'rotten' in the law.[164] All attempts to challenge law depend on the articulation of a new law that simply perpetuates the circular logic.[165]

Deconstruction of the violence of law therefore reveals the interdependence of violence and law. The two cannot be separated, but remain trapped within a cycle of violence. This raises a further question for transitional justice research. If metaphysical violence is immanent to law, can law adequately address deep-rooted political conflict? To address this question it is necessary to move beyond an oppositional conceptualisation of violence and law and to take seriously the inexorable relationship between the two.[166] This requires a greater acknowledgement of the dynamics that underpin legal reasoning and legal decision-making. The following chapter will explore the way in which attempts to transcend violence with law in transitional contexts operate within the economy of violence. It will demonstrate how the metaphysical violence that is immanent to the law replicates the violence of open conflict, and asks whether in this context law can contribute towards justice.

161 'Force of Law' (n. 4) 35.

162 Petra Gehring, 'The Jurisprudence of the "Force of Law"' in Peter Goodrich *et al.* (eds), *Derrida and Legal Philosophy* (Palgrave Macmillan 2008) 55, 61.

163 Douzinas (n. 155).

164 See 'Force of Law' (n. 4) 14.

165 See Frazer and Hutchings (n. 153) 130.

166 See Roberto Buonamono, 'The Economy of Violence: Derrida on Law and Justice' (1998) 11(2) *Ratio Juris* 168, 171.

Chapter 5

Law

In 1998, following thirty years of violence on the streets of Northern Ireland, the Belfast Agreement was signed.[1] The Agreement followed years of negotiations among all parties to the conflict, including the British and Irish governments, local political parties and representatives of armed paramilitary groups. It was widely heralded as a new beginning for politics in Northern Ireland,[2] and as marking the end of the Troubles.[3] It also marked the beginning of the period of 'transition'.[4] The previous chapter demonstrated how, during the Troubles, human rights claims were subordinated to security concerns, as the concept of 'emergency' established itself as the dominant force in law and politics. In recent years, however, as the language of human rights is increasingly relied upon to frame political demands in respect of dealing with the past, as well as issues such as identity, language and culture, the opposition between security and human rights that characterised the Troubles has been exposed. The increasing prominence of the concepts of human rights and transitional justice has destabilised what were previously fixed understandings of the causes of the conflict and are arguably becoming the dominant discourses in which legal and political demands are made and assessed in Northern Ireland. The language of transition is pervasive among the legal academic and policy communities who seek to influence government policies in

1 Belfast (Good Friday) Agreement (1998) (hereinafter 'Agreement').

2 See ibid. Declaration of Support.

3 1998 also saw the second IRA ceasefire, followed by a similar declaration by Loyalist paramilitaries. While the Agreement did not mark the end of conflict or 'struggle' in Northern Ireland, it was intended to mark the beginning of a new phase in which politics would be conducted by exclusively legal means. See Gerry Adams, 'To Cherish a Just and Lasting Peace' (1998) 22 *Fordham International Law Journal* 1179.

4 In 2003 Campbell, Ní Aoláin and Harvey published an article in which they suggested that the framework of 'transition' was the most appropriate within which to analyse the legal changes brought about by the Agreement. This article is the first sustained engagement with the language of transition in the Northern Ireland context and the first attempt to reconceptualise the effect of the Agreement in legal and policy terms. See Colm Campbell, Fionnuala Ní Aoláin and Colin Harvey, 'The Frontiers of Analysis: Re-framing the Transition in Northern Ireland' (2003) 66 *Modern Law Review* 317. This is discussed in more detail in section 5.2.1.

this area.[5] It has brought to the forefront the terminology of 'dealing with the past' and established as a matter of legal imperative the question of accountability for past abuses.[6] This relates not only to the high-profile 'use of force' cases, but is also increasingly evident in legal and political discourse on economic, social and cultural rights in Northern Ireland.[7]

The period from 1998 until the present day is therefore marked not by direct physical violence, as the preceding thirty years had been, but rather by legal contestation over the status of the Agreement and the meaning to be given to its terms. While the Agreement was signed amid an atmosphere of great optimism for peace in Northern Ireland, recent years have seen divisions sharpen over key aspects of the Agreement, and indeed over key transitional justice mechanisms, such as institutional reform and dealing with the past. Of particular note is the ongoing contestation over accountability for state violations of human rights, in particular for controversial killings for which no responsibility has been accepted.[8] However, while the involvement of the state in these controversial killings represents the sharp end of claims in respect of the past, there is also significant and growing unrest over the way in which the law is being interpreted. Central issues in the most recent round of negotiations included the flying of flags and the regulation of Loyal Order parades, both issues that have been subject to contested interpretation since the Agreement.[9]

The previous chapter demonstrated the interdependent relationship between violence and law. It raised the question of whether law can adequately address deep-rooted political violence. Building on the analysis of the metaphysical violence of law presented in the previous chapter, this chapter asks whether the framework of 'transition' is any less violent than the framework of 'emergency' that it replaced. The signing of the Agreement, and its passing into law – under, most notably, the Northern Ireland Act 1998 – represented a moment of originary violence. It represented a rupture from the legal order that had preceded it and the creation of a new legal order. Seen in these terms, this is the re-founding

5 For example, see the submissions made to public consultations on dealing with the past that draw extensively on the language and conceptual architecture of transitional justice to frame recommendations. See, for example, Kieran McEvoy *et al.*, 'Dealing with the Past in Northern Ireland: Amnesties, Prosecutions and the Public Interest': Written Submission to Dr Richard Haass and Dr Meaghan O'Sullivan and the Panel of Parties in the Northern Ireland Executive (Belfast, 2013) http://blogs.qub.ac.uk/amnesties/files/2013/11/Amnesties-Prosecutions-and-Public-Interest-Submission-to-Haass-talks.pdf, accessed 19 October 2015. See also Northern Ireland Human Rights Commission, *Dealing with Northern Ireland's Past: Towards a Transitional Justice Approach*' (Belfast, 2013).

6 This is discussed in more detail in Chapter 6.

7 Discussed in Section 5.2.3.

8 During the course of the Troubles, state forces were responsible for 367 deaths. See David McKittrick *et al.*, *Lost Lives: The Stories of the Men, Women and Children Who Died as a Result of the Northern Ireland Troubles* (Mainstream Publishing 1999) 1476. While there have been public inquiries held into some of these, others remain unresolved.

9 See Stormont House Agreement 2014.

of law that follows revolutionary violence.[10] However, as discussed in the previous chapter, this is only the first stage of an economy of violence within which the new law must be located. It is worth reiterating in this context that violence, in the metaphysical sense, is not necessarily negative. All violence, at the time at which it occurs, is neither inherently 'good' nor 'bad'.[11] That determination comes only with time. Therefore, rather than viewing the use of the term 'violence' as making negative comment on the Agreement, it should be understood in its metaphysical sense, as concerned with differential force within society.[12] Understanding it in these terms helps to locate the Agreement and the increasing resistance it faces within an economy of violence within which violence and law are co-implicated. Understanding the unrest evident in Northern Irish political life is a necessary first step to addressing the bigger question of 'why' resistance to transitional justice arises. In particular, it requires deeper scrutiny of the role of law in transition and the way in which it creates and perpetuates sites of silence and exclusion.

This chapter explores the way in which the discourse of human rights began to assert itself as the dominant language in which resistance to the state and its laws was expressed. It then locates the Agreement itself against a backdrop of political violence, and considers the terms of the Agreement and the way in which it was envisaged at the time as marking a break, and a new beginning, for Northern Ireland. In this way it reveals the originary force of the Agreement. Section 5.2 moves on to explore the idea that has gained significant policy traction – that Northern Ireland should be regarded as being in 'transition'. It begins by exploring the origins of these claims and considering the application of the framework of 'transition' as an exceptional measure. The section then moves on to examine in detail the way in which the Agreement has been interpreted by the courts in light of the requirements of 'transition' and the constitutional status ascribed to it. In so doing, the idea of a linear progression from past to present is problematised, and the ongoing conserving violence of the law is highlighted. Finally, the chapter highlights the way in which the violent hierarchy has been inverted in the case of Northern Ireland. It suggests that the Agreement is subject to the same dynamics of contestation as the emergency legislation that preceded it. It concludes by suggesting that the increasing resistance and challenge to the Agreement, and the legal framework of transition that it introduced, represents the third stage of the economy of violence – that of the violence of reflection. In this way it demonstrates the circular nature of the relationship between violence and law. The chapter is concerned with the metaphysical violence of law. By exploring the way in which the Agreement has created a powerful legal context within which politics

10 Discussed in Chapter 4.

11 Jacques Derrida, 'Force of Law: The Mystical Foundation of Authority' in Drucilla Cornell *et al.* (eds), *Deconstruction and the Possibility of Justice* (Routledge 1992) 1, 13 (hereinafter 'Force of Law').

12 Ibid. 7.

in Northern Ireland takes place, it demonstrates the oppositional structure within which law operates, and ultimately how this impacts on the possibility of transitional justice. Rather than moving from violence to law, or from conflict to peace, the chapter demonstrates the circular logic of this relationship.

5.1 The violence of the origin

5.1.1 Shifting means of resistance: the Armalite and the ballot box

As discussed in the previous chapter, during the course of the Troubles resistance to the state manifested in both political violence and in legal contestation. During this period the language of human rights was used to 'reflect' the way in which the emergency legislation that dominated the legal landscape in Northern Ireland had suppressed legitimate challenge to the actions of the state. The relationship between the two strategies of political violence and legal contestation is illustrative of the complex relationship between violence and law – and whether or not the two can be regarded as separate phenomena. In the early years of the Troubles, those who advocated the use of physical violence did so as an explicit rejection of law as a means of effectively challenging the state.[13] Those who engaged in human rights advocacy and non-violent protest did so as an explicit rejection of violence as a legitimate means of doing politics. A clear distinction was therefore drawn between violence on the one hand and law on the other. However, as discussed in the previous chapter, the two cannot be so easily separated.

For Derrida, all revolutionary violence will have as its ultimate end the re-establishment of law.[14] In Northern Ireland, the Republican approach to violence and law gradually began to shift. Whereas in the early years violence had as its aim the destruction of the state, gradually it came to be acknowledged that legal strategies that challenged the state could also contribute to political ends.[15] What was necessary was to effectively challenge the legitimacy of the framework of emergency in order to appeal to a broader constituency.[16] Law therefore adopted a much more central role in Republican strategy from the mid-1980s,[17] with human rights creeping into the political discourse of Sinn Fein.[18] During the 1980s and 1990s, a legal strategy was adopted that sought to highlight human rights issues – such as prison conditions, controversial killings and fair trial

13 See Jacques Derrida, 'The Laws of Reflection: Nelson Mandela, In Admiration' in Jacques Derrida and Mustafa Tlili (eds), *For Nelson Mandela* (Seaver Books 1987) 18 (hereinafter 'Laws of Reflection').

14 'Force of Law' (n. 11). This is discussed in Chapter 4.

15 For a comprehensive analysis of this strategy, see Kieran McEvoy, 'Law, Struggle and Political Transformation in Northern Ireland' (2000) 27(4) *Journal of Law and Society* 542.

16 This change in tactic was famously summed up in the statement that the IRA would use 'the Armalite and the ballot box' to oppose British rule in Northern Ireland. Ibid.

17 Kieran McEvoy and John Morrison, 'Beyond the Constitutional Moment: Law, Transition and Peacemaking in Northern Ireland' (2003) 24 *Fordham International Law Journal* 961.

18 See Sinn Fein, *Towards a Lasting Peace in Ireland: Sinn Fein Manifesto for the Westminster Election* (Belfast, 1992).

rights – not only domestically, but also on the international front.[19] The purpose of this strategy was to counter the delegitimising effect of the dominance of the emergency discourse and its condemnation of violence.[20] This represented the beginning of a shift towards a revolutionary violence that could be justified by the promise of a new and more just legal order.[21] Is also reflected a pragmatic acceptance of 'mythic' (law-creating) violence in contrast to the earlier engagement of 'divine' (law-destroying) violence,[22] and began to shape the narrative of the causes of the conflict, which would in turn shape the Agreement and its implementation.

It was at this time that talks began that would eventually lead to the Agreement. Whereas in the past those who engaged in violence had been systematically excluded from negotiations, from the mid-1980s there was a change in approach. The first evidence of an official acceptance of competing narratives of the state in Northern Ireland came in 1985, with the Anglo-Irish Agreement.[23] This was followed by a series of Joint Declarations made by the British and Irish governments in which the rhetoric moved away from that of terrorism and security and towards a more conciliatory rhetoric based on human rights and shared understandings of the future of Anglo-Irish relations.[24] Gradually the subordinated discourse of human rights began to assert its presence against the dominant narrative of security and emergency powers. At the time, the Declarations were criticised by Unionist politicians as being taken from the lexicon of nationalism[25] and as being extracted by violence and the threat of violence.[26] This reflects the oppositional nature of contestation whereby the law was seen as belonging to one side at the expense of the other.[27] The rhetoric of security implicitly favoured Unionist interpretations of law and violence,

19 See, for example, *McCann and Others v United Kingdom* [1995] 21 EHRR; *Brannigan and McBride v United Kingdom* [1993] 17 EHRR 539. See also Amnesty International, *United Kingdom: Killings by Security Forces in Northern Ireland* (New York, 1986).

20 See Kris Brown, 'Rights and Victims, Martyrs and Memories: The European Court of Human Rights and Political Transition in Northern Ireland' in Antoine Buyse and Michael Hamilton (eds), *Transitional Jurisprudence and the ECHR: Justice, Politics and Rights* (Cambridge University Press 2011) 52.

21 See McEvoy (n. 15) on the dual use of violence and law. While the use of law increased during this time, McEvoy is clear that this should not be read as a linear progression away from violence and towards legal contestation. The two remained linked and used simultaneously as the 'struggle' demanded, each influencing the other.

22 'Force of Law' (n. 11). See Chapter 4.2.2 for explanation of these terms.

23 Agreement Between the Government of the United Kingdom of Great Britain and Northern Ireland and the Government of the Republic of Ireland (Cmnd.9657, 1985). This agreement dealt specifically with legacies of division, including discrimination and the relationship between the security forces and the community, in Northern Ireland.

24 See The Joint Declaration by An Taoiseach Mr Albert Reynolds, TD and the British Prime Minister, The Rt Hon. John Major, MP (Cm. 2442, 1993). See further A New Framework for Agreement [1994] 34 ILM 946.

25 Ian Paisley, 'Peace Agreement – or Last Piece in a Sellout Agreement?' (1998) 22 *Fordham International Law Journal* 1273.

26 Ibid.

27 See Chapter 4.

representing violence as illegitimate and the security response as necessary to uphold the rule of law. Human rights claims, with their emphasis on state wrongdoing, presented a direct challenge to established narratives of law and order within the state. The shift towards the rhetoric of human rights evident in these Declarations was therefore in direct opposition to established Unionist positions and, as a result, seen as favouring nationalist interpretations of the conflict.[28] This was particularly marked in the context of the provisions on changes to policing and security that had been some of the most contentious issues throughout the Troubles, and which were at the very heart of divisions over questions of violence, law and justice within Northern Ireland.[29] The language of human rights challenged the dominance of the framework of emergency, and the effect of this challenge was to expose the relationship of violent hierarchy that existed between the two. The increasing prominence of human rights created a new political context within which negotiations took place. The following section will discuss how this new context was reflected in the terms of the Agreement itself.

5.1.2 Framing the Agreement

The Agreement has been celebrated for the extent to which it places human rights at its heart.[30] This relates not only to the human rights provisions that are enshrined in the text itself, but also in relation to the way in which the Agreement can be read as acknowledging past abuses.[31] In the Declaration of Support that opens the Agreement, the parties acknowledge the legacy of suffering and dedicate themselves to 'the achievement of reconciliation, tolerance, and mutual trust, and to the protection and vindication of the human rights of all'.[32] In this way the document falls within the definition of 'transitional, in that it is both forward and backward looking, speaking to the injustices of the past while attempting to articulate a more just future'.[33]

Central to the Agreement is the creation of democratic institutions in Northern Ireland.[34] The text of the Agreement makes specific reference to the need to provide

28 Paisley (n. 25).

29 See Cheryl Lawther, 'Securing the Past: Policing and the Contest Over Truth in Northern Ireland' (2010) 50 *British Journal of Criminology* 455 for discussion.

30 For discussion see Paul Mageean and Martin O'Brien, 'From the Margins to the Mainstream: Human Rights and the Good Friday Agreement' (1998) 22 *Fordham International Law Journal* 1498.

31 Ibid.

32 Agreement (n. 1) Declaration of Support.

33 It therefore speaks directly to Teitel's conception of transitional justice. Ruti Teitel, *Transitional Justice* (Oxford University Press 2000).

34 Agreement (n. 1) Strand One. This point appears contradictory in light of the fact that Northern Ireland was, before the Agreement, part of a liberal democracy in which period elections did occur. However, it speaks to the 'conflicted' nature of that democracy and the need to address perceptions of the illegitimacy of the existing structures. See Colm Campbell and Fionnuala Ní Aoláin, 'The Paradox of Transitions in Liberal Democracies' (2005) 27 *Human Rights Quarterly* 172.

'safeguards to protect the rights and interests of all sides of the Community'.[35] Safeguards in this context are interpreted as including the incorporation of the European Convention on Human Rights (the Convention) into domestic law, the creation of a Bill of Rights for Northern Ireland and the establishment of a Human Rights Commission to oversee the new arrangements.[36] These terms are supplemented by the specific inclusion of rights, such as the right to free political thought and the right to equality of opportunity in all social and economic activity.[37] These terms are simultaneously forward- and backward-looking. Their inclusion in the Agreement is framed with reference to the 'recent history of communal conflict',[38] but they provide a forward-looking guarantee of a more just order in which different political beliefs and traditions are given equal respect. Similarly, while not making specific reference to 'dealing with the past', the Agreement also contains provisions on the reform of policing and justice. These are also both backward- and forward-looking, in that in proposing reform they are framed, albeit implicitly, as responding to past failures. For example, the Agreement requires the removal of emergency powers for Northern Ireland.[39] Reforms arising from the Agreement have also included the transformation of the Royal Ulster Constabulary (RUC – a police 'force') into the Police Service of Northern Ireland (PSNI – a police 'service') under the auspices of the Patten Report;[40] the establishment of a Northern Ireland Human Rights Commission and the presentation of a draft Bill of Rights to Westminster;[41] and the appointment of numerous statutory bodies, including the Equality Commission[42] and more notably the Parades Commission – established to decide on the legality and re-routing of mainly Loyalist parades.[43]

All of these changes have been part of a radical package that has ostensibly set about examining the operation of law in Northern Ireland.[44] Each of these bodies has its origin in the Agreement and each frames its activities with reference to the need to give effect to its terms and mark a break from the past.[45]

35 Agreement (n. 1) Strand One, Art. 1.
36 Ibid. Section 5(b) Safeguards.
37 Ibid. Strand One.
38 Ibid. Art. 1.
39 Ibid. Strand One, 'Rights, Safeguards and Equality of Opportunity', 'Security' Art. 2(iii).
40 Independent Commission on Policing for Northern Ireland, 'A New Beginning: Policing in Northern Ireland' (Belfast, 1999). In this report, the Commission explicitly locates its work in the context of giving effect to the Agreement. The recommendations of the report were given statutory footing in the Police (Northern Ireland) Act 2000.
41 'A Bill of Rights for Northern Ireland: Advice to the Secretary of State for Northern Ireland' (Belfast, 2003) www.nihrc.org/uploads/publications/bill-of-rights-for-northern-ireland-advice-to-secretary-state-2008.pdf, accessed 19 October 2015.
42 Established under the Northern Ireland Act 1998.
43 Formally established by the Public Processions (Northern Ireland) Act 1998.
44 For discussion, see Catherine Turner, 'Political Representations of Law in Northern Ireland' [2010] *Public Law* 451.
45 Gordon Anthony and Paul Mageean, 'Habits of Mind and "Truth Telling": Article 2 ECHR in Post-Conflict Northern Ireland' in K McEvoy *et al.* (eds), *Judges, Transition and Human Rights* (Oxford University Press 2007) 181, 187.

Each also provides an ostensibly non-political body tasked with making impartial decisions on contentious political issues.[46] These types of reform are not unique to Northern Ireland, but increasingly represent the type of 'rule of law' reform that will be required of any transitional society, as the requirements of transitional justice have in recent years crept further towards systemic constitutional reform as a means of addressing legacies of injustice.[47] In this way Northern Ireland is an early, but by no means unique, example of reforms that seek to institutionalise political debates.[48]

However, the Agreement, while including strong human rights provisions, makes no specific reference to what we now understand as typical transitional justice mechanisms. There is no requirement that an institution, whether criminal or civil, be established to ensure accountability for the past.[49] Nor is the language of truth or reparation evident in the text. While reconciliation is included as something to which the parties strive, it does not ground the Agreement, nor does it provide a framing reference point.[50] At the time that the Agreement was signed, the compromises it included were the result of political negotiation, framed by international law and best practice. It was not dictated by a normative framework of 'transition'.[51] However, the language of human rights did provide a shared vocabulary. For nationalists, the inclusion of guarantees of safeguards could be read as an acknowledgement of the failings of the Stormont government and an acceptance of their human rights claims, particularly in respect of discrimination.[52] They also pointed to international law as the standard to which the Agreement should aspire in terms of human rights compliance.[53] Unionists were also able to locate the Agreement within a broader national and international

46 Ibid., identifying these reforms as being at 'the heart of the practical process of transition in post-conflict Northern Ireland that was thought would characterize the bedding down of the Agreement'.

47 See Catherine Turner and Ruth Houghton, 'Constitution Making and Post Conflict Reconstruction' in Matthew Saul and James Sweeney (eds) *International Law and Post Conflict Reconstruction* (Routledge 2015).

48 See Jelena Subotić, 'The Transformation of International Transitional Justice Advocacy' (2012) 6 *International Journal of Transitional Justice* 106.

49 This has led to criticism that efforts to deal with the past have been, at best, 'piecemeal'. See Christine Bell, 'Dealing With the Past in Northern Ireland' (2002) 26 *Fordham International Law Journal* 1095.

50 Agreement (n. 1) Declaration of Support.

51 It has been suggested that this was a deliberate omission, due to the position of the UK government that the conflict was an internal matter. Bell (n. 49).

52 See, for example, Agreement (n. 1) Strand One, Annex A, which sets out the Ministerial Pledge of Office, requiring all Ministers in the new institutions to promote equality and prevent discrimination.

53 Other international legal developments also served to ground the Agreement, including developments on self-determination and minority rights (see Christine Bell and Kathleen Kavanaugh, 'Constructive Ambiguity, or Internal Self Determination? Self Determination, Group Accommodation and the Belfast Agreement' (1998) 22 *Fordham International Law Journal* 1345) and the emergence of a fundamental rights jurisprudence in the European Court of Justice, cited by David Trimble, 'The Belfast Agreement' (1998) 22 *Fordham International Law Journal* 1145, 1148.

context. At the time the Agreement was being negotiated, moves were underway within the UK to incorporate the provisions of the Convention into domestic law. The inclusion of human rights provisions that mirrored those protected by the Convention therefore allowed Unionist politicians to accept human rights as part of broader constitutional reform within the UK and to assert their belief that 'the legal protection of human rights was an indispensable part of any agreement'.[54]

In this way, the Agreement and the parties responsible for 'selling' it to their respective constituencies drew on international standards and international comparison as a means of legitimising the inclusion of strong human rights provisions.[55] The Agreement was therefore framed in the language of transcendence,[56] whereby internationally validated human rights provisions could be used to externalise and transcend difficult political issues that might have prevented agreement from being reached. While not directly using the language of transition, the sentiment is the same. As discussed in Chapter 2, Teitel's conceptualisation of the role of law in transition draws heavily on the transcendent quality of international law, whose incorporation of principles of justice allow it to transcend domestic politics.[57] The language of the Agreement similarly speaks of a desire to reach agreement on principles that could be agreed by both sides.[58] The Agreement therefore represented the promise of a new order, of a reconciled politics *within* Northern Ireland. This shifted the focus of the constitutional question away from the status of Northern Ireland as a part of either the United Kingdom or a united Ireland and placed it squarely on the jurisdiction of Northern Ireland. Any future decision over the status of Northern Ireland would be made by the people of Northern Ireland themselves.[59] This principle marked a break from the previous constitutional order, created by the Government of Ireland Act 1920. The Agreement specifically refers to the past, and to its own role in marking a break from that past, to ensure a new start for politics in Northern Ireland. This suggests a linear progression, in which the injustice of the past gives way to the future. When seen in these terms, one flows naturally from the other.

However, while the Agreement can be narrated as 'progress' away from violence towards peace, a Derridean reading of the Agreement problematises this linear

54 Trimble (n. 53).

55 See Mageean and O'Brien (n. 30) on the international context within which the Agreement was located.

56 See in particular Kate Fearon and Monica McWilliams, 'The Good Friday Agreement: A Triumph of Substance over Style' (1998) 22 *Fordham International Law Journal* 1250 on the adoption of an interest-based negotiating position by the Women's Coalition – focusing on the language of rights rather than on divisive constitutional politics.

57 See Chapter 2.1.2.3

58 See Barry Collins, 'The Belfast Agreement and the Nation that "Always Arrives at Its Destination"' (2002) 20 *Penn State International Law Review* 385.

59 This is known as the 'consent' principle, contained in the Agreement (n. 1) Declaration of Support, 'Constitutional Issues', Art. 1(1). This was accompanied by the removal of a territorial claim to Northern Ireland enshrined in the Constitution of the Republic of Ireland, which was amended to recognise the principle of consent. Nineteenth Amendment to the Constitution Act 1998.

characterisation. Rather than viewing the Agreement as 'a moment inscribed in the homogenous tissue of a history',[60] it becomes what Derrida terms a 'rupture' – a break from the past that introduces a new system.[61] In short, the moment of the signing of the Agreement was a moment of originary violence in which the legal order was simultaneously destroyed and re-founded.[62] This was the moment in which the framework of 'emergency' gave way to that of 'human rights' and subsequently 'transition'. Seeing the moment of the Agreement as a rupture, rather than simply a step in a natural progression, has implications for how we interpret both the past and the present. While human rights were enshrined at the heart of the Agreement, different parties had different reasons for their inclusion. The following section will discuss how this difference in understandings of the role and significance of rights led to competing interpretations of the Agreement and the need for legal reform.

5.1.3 The Agreement as a constitutional moment

By definition, peace agreements that give rise to transitions from war to peace will be framed against a backdrop of contestation over the legitimacy of the state and the legality of the prior regime and its laws.[63] However, the idea of law representing a natural progression is one that is of interest in the context of revolutionary violence and transition. History is replete with examples of hard-won political concessions being enshrined in law. From the Magna Carta to the Universal Declaration of Human Rights, war or revolution are inevitably followed by the declaration of a new legal order. The violence that preceded the law is absorbed into a progressive account of the move from the state of war to that of peace founded on law. The moment in which the Declaration is made, and the concessions achieve legal form, is a constitutional moment – the moment in which a new institution is created. In the modern context of transitional justice, the peace agreement fulfils this role of moving a state from the unmitigated violence of war, conflict or repression, to peace.[64] The signing of a peace agreement will represent a rupture with the existing order. It will be the moment that marks a break from the past and institutes a new order. While peace agreements take many disparate forms, and are intended to fulfil different roles at different stages of transition, the fact that they are intended to mark at least the beginning of new order means that

60 'Force of Law' (n. 11) 13.

61 Margaret Davies, 'Derrida and Law: Legitimate Fictions' in Tom Cohen (ed.), *Jacques Derrida and the Humanities: A Critical Reader* (Cambridge University Press 2002) 213, 226.

62 'Force of Law' (n. 11).

63 The field had its origins in the examination of how successor regimes chose to deal with an abusive prior regime. See Neil J Kritz (ed.), *Transitional Justice: How Emerging Democracies Reckon with Former Regimes* (United States Institute of Peace 1996) vols 1–3.

64 The majority of 'transitions' are now brought about by negotiated settlement rather than outright victory, thereby making the peace agreement an integral aspect of the study of transition and transitional justice. See Christine Bell, *Peace Agreements and Human Rights* (Oxford University Press 2000).

they have increasingly been characterised as having constitutional form.[65] This was the case in Northern Ireland, where the Agreement represented for some 'a new constitutional beginning for resolving a historic problem'.[66] The Agreement '[laid] down the terms upon which people in Northern Ireland, from all communities, [were] willing to be governed'.[67] As such it has been interpreted as a constitutional moment, whereby the Agreement and its implementing legislation were 'constituent acts in the establishment of a new polity'.[68] The aim of the Agreement, according to one central figure, was to create unity from diversity.[69] When seen in these terms, the Agreement founds both a new legal order and a new political order.[70]

As discussed in the context of the Belfast Agreement, the peace agreement must be both backward- and forward-looking. It must speak to past injustice while also crafting a new future for the state. This backward-looking element will respond directly to the perceived injustices of the past (and by extension to the illegitimacy of the previous regime) and, in this way, is firmly rooted in ideas of justice and moral progress. The new order is expressly juxtaposed with the past – the binary of before and after – the 'before' of illegitimacy and conflict juxtaposed with the 'after' of legitimacy and peace. When seen in these terms, the Agreement is no different from the revolutionary Declarations that have preceded it. Throughout history, revolutionary declarations have drawn on the language of transcendence to guarantee their authority. From the 'self-evident truths' of the American Declaration of Independence, to the values of '*liberté, égalité, fraternité*' that underpinned the French Declaration, appeals are made to a higher authority in order to legitimise the violence of revolution and the re-founding of legal order. This appeal to higher principles suggests that the new law, rather than representing a violent rupture, simply embodies and gives effect to (natural) principles of justice that precede the law.[71] In so doing, it seeks not only to legitimate the physical violence that has led to the re-founding of law, but also to conceal the violence of the declaration itself. It masks the history of violent contestation that has given rise to the declaration, presenting instead a unified set of principles (of justice or equality, for example) upon which the new legal order will be founded. It is this narrative of progress towards law that Derrida seeks to problematise in his essay, 'Declarations of Independence', in which he addresses the linearity of the

65 Christine Bell, 'Peace Agreements: Their Nature and Legal Status' (2006) 100 *American Journal of International Law* 373.

66 McEvoy and Morison (n. 17) 964.

67 Ibid. 969.

68 Ibid. This interpretation of the Agreement as a constitutional moment was subsequently confirmed by the House of Lords in *Robinson v Secretary of State for Northern Ireland* [2002] UKHL 32.

69 John Hume, 'Ireland – The Healing Process' (1998) 22 *Fordham International Law Journal* 1171.

70 This is described by Campbell, Ní Aoláin and Harvey (n. 4) 327 as a 'fluid and reconstituted political space'.

71 See Jacques De Ville, 'Sovereignty without Sovereignty: Derrida's Declarations of Independence' (2008) 19 *Law and Critique* 87.

constitutional moment.[72] Derrida's analysis is significant for transitional justice because it reveals the way in which contestation is masked and one particular view is made to appear the impartial or 'correct' view of the declaration and its requirements.

The previous section discussed how there were differing interpretations of the significance of the human rights provisions of the Agreement. This flows from the fact that Northern Ireland was a 'conflicted democracy' in which there were sharply divided opinions over the use of violence and the need for legal reform.[73] The nature of 'justice' is not accepted as self-evident in this case.[74] This exposes the oppositional structure in which debates over the role and significance of human rights occur. Where a distinction is drawn between a natural order and a positive legal order, the question to be asked is whether the declaration, by drawing on transcendent values, simply declares the existence of these values (natural law) or whether the act of making the declaration creates them (positive law). In other words, does law precede violence or does violence precede law? This distinction also bears on the authority of the declaration itself. Where 'natural' principles of justice and truth are relied upon to ground the declaration, the declaration can be read as law-preserving, in that it gives effect to, and guarantees, existing principles of natural law.[75] However, if the existence of transcendent standards is rejected, the declaration is seen not as a law-preserving act, but as a law-creating, or 'positive', act. Rather than declaring the existence of values, the effect of the declaration is to bring those values into being by virtue of their promulgation in law. This leads to two clearly defined and competing philosophical positions on the legitimacy of the declaration. It is the clear distinction between the two that Derrida seeks to destabilise.

As discussed in Chapter 3, the separation between nature and its institution is an artificial one for Derrida. Rather than trying to distinguish values existing outside of the law from those created by law, Derrida sees law as arising as the result of the constant negotiation between these two positions.[76] It is, therefore, not possible to draw a rigid distinction between the two concepts, but rather it is necessary to recognise the relationship between them and how this shapes our understanding of law. Reverting to Derrida's original example – that of a declaration of independence – Derrida highlights the paradox of this approach: 'One cannot decide … whether independence is stated or produced by this utterance.'[77] There

72 Jacques Derrida, 'Declarations of Independence' in Elizabeth Rottenberg (ed.), *Negotiations: Interventions and Interviews, 1971–2001* (Stanford University Press 2002) 46 (hereinafter 'Declarations of Independence').

73 Campbell and Ní Aoláin (n. 34).

74 This is largely due to the fact that the transition is negotiated rather than arising from outright revolution.

75 See De Ville (n. 71), suggesting that this incorporates self-evident matters of justice and rights that had previously been lacking.

76 See Chapter 3.

77 Declarations of Independence (n. 72) 49.

are traces of both present in the Declaration.[78] This dynamic is also visible in the context of the Agreement. The question that 'Declarations of Independence' raises in respect of the Northern Ireland example is whether, at the time of the Agreement, the parties were united in support of (transcendent) human rights values, support of which was simply being declared in the Agreement, or whether human rights and equality, and the unity in diversity that they created, were produced by the Agreement. By exploring this question, we begin to reveal the negotiation between competing positions, and the way in which law relies on the subordination of alternative views to ensure its own dominance. The following section will therefore discuss competing interpretations of the significance of human rights, and how they reveal the paradoxical nature of the Agreement itself.

5.1.4 Declaring or creating unity?

The language of the Agreement is much more cautious than that of revolutionary declarations. It is, of course, a negotiated settlement that recognises, rather than denies, the existence of competing political views and aspirations. Nevertheless, the paradoxical nature of the Agreement as a foundational document remains. There are two possible, and competing, explanations for the inclusion of human rights and equality in the Agreement. The first is that it was simply giving effect to existing values of international law. In dissolving the existing political bond, that of the Government of Ireland Act 1920 and the specific political community that it had created, the Agreement draws on the language of human rights – the existence of which is a fact to be recognised.[79] Human rights and the entitlement to respect are not values that are being created by the Agreement, but rather their existence is being reflected in the Agreement. When seen in these terms, the text of the Agreement institutes in the new legal order principles and values that precede it. Those responsible for negotiating and drafting the Agreement simply 'represent' an existing constituency or 'people' that has given them the authority to act on their behalf in instituting these principles in law.[80] This element of representation of a community is further rubber-stamped by seeking the consent of the people by referenda.[81] Therefore, when seen in this light, the Agreement reflects transcendent international values of human rights that were simply consigned to writing by those who drafted the Agreement and given authority through the referenda.[82] The Agreement therefore does not create anything new but simply institutes

78 For more detailed discussion of this dynamic, see Chapter 3.1.

79 Agreement (n. 1) 'Rights, Safeguards and Equality of Opportunity'.

80 In this way the role of the 'people' is broadly analogous to the idea of the nation that has in the past been the foundational origin of law. See Collins (n. 58) 386.

81 Referenda on the Agreement were held in both Northern Ireland and the Republic of Ireland, as required by the Agreement. Agreement (n. 1) 'Validation, Implementation and Review' S 2.

82 See Declarations of Independence (n. 72) 48 where Derrida suggests that the author of the text simply represents those who have delegated to him the task of drawing up what they *knew* they wanted to say. This interpretation of the Agreement as reflecting existing principles is also evident

and guarantees values that already exist – namely international law standards of human rights.[83] In this way the Agreement can be regarded as a law-preserving act. This interpretation is significant because it regards human rights as normative, and as such non-negotiable, commitments. There is some support for this position in the fact that both nationalist and Unionist politicians were able to see benefit to themselves in supporting the use of the language of human rights to frame the Agreement.[84]

The alternative position is that the Agreement, rather than reflecting the existence of consensus on the values of human rights and equality, actually created these new norms. When seen in these terms, the values of human rights and equality that underpin the Agreement are read not as transcendent standards that precede the law, but as the legal results of a process of political negotiation in which parties reached agreement on how competing aspirations should be guaranteed. This would cast the Agreement as a performative act – one that produces a new community and a new legal order. In this light, the political community and its values do not exist before the Agreement is signed, but rather are created by the act of signature.[85] Rights, when seen from this position, are political – the subject of negotiation rather than pre-existing normative commitments. There is certainly evidence for this reading of the Agreement. The fact that the text of the Agreement itself speaks of the existence of different political aspirations appears to acknowledge the attempt to create unity rather than to reflect it. Research also suggests that the Agreement was regarded by those who drafted it as a political, rather than a legal, document that created a space within which difficult issues could be addressed.[86] The way in which the Agreement is crafted also carefully speaks to each side of the community, allowing them to support it for their own reasons rather than on the basis of a transcendental standard of right that is simply being reflected.

To read the Agreement from a Derridean perspective, however, requires that we resist the urge to try and characterise the Agreement as *either* a constative (law-preserving) *or* a performative (law-creating) act and to justify that conclusion. Rather, a Derridean reading requires that we recognise the relationship of mutual contamination between the two.[87] The moment at which the Agreement was

in Mageean and O'Brien's analysis (n. 30) of the way in which human rights advocacy underpinned the substantive provisions of the Agreement.

83 For discussion of the importance of locating the Agreement in international law, see John Morrison and Marie Lynch, 'Litigating the Agreement: Towards a New Judicial Constitutionalism for the UK from Northern Ireland' in Kieran McEvoy *et al.* (eds), *Judges, Transition and Human Rights: Essays in Memory of Stephen Livingstone* (Oxford University Press 2007) 105, 106.

84 This dynamic is referred to as 'constructive ambiguity', whereby particularly contentious issues were left deliberately vague in order to secure agreement. For discussion see David Mitchell, 'Cooking the Fudge: Constructive Ambiguity and the Implementation of the Northern Ireland Agreement, 1998–2007' (2009) 24 *Irish Political Studies* 321.

85 Declarations of Independence (n. 72) 49.

86 Morrison and Lynch (n. 83) 115.

87 'Force of Law' (n. 11) 40.

signed contains both law-creating and law-preserving elements, and the two cannot be separated out into a neat narrative of cause and effect. The Agreement was both constituted by and constitutive of a new human rights and equality agenda.[88] This means that our understanding of the Agreement is constructed not on fixed positions but rather on the relationship between two competing interpretations of human rights as either normative or political.[89]

Whether the Agreement declared or created a new legal order, what remains clear is that once it was signed and instituted in law, the previous constitution was destroyed and a new one founded.[90] This, for Derrida, is the outcome of all revolutionary violence. From the point that the Agreement was signed and ratified, it was guaranteed as a new order that had been created and therefore must be protected by law.[91] The Agreement, as a foundational document, claims its authority by virtue of the break that it marks with the past, in the way in which the order that it creates can be distinguished from the conflicted past.[92] When read in the light of Derrida's economy of violence, the originary aspect of this moment of re-founding law becomes clear. By definition, there will be (at least) two opposing sides in any violent conflict. The moment at which the Declaration is founded is therefore a moment of violence. It is the point at which one side emerges dominant and subordinates its opposition. In more practical terms, the Declaration marks the point at which violence gives way to law and the point at which the *means* of revolutionary violence potentially become justified by the *end* of a more just order.[93] However, for Derrida it is not possible, *at that moment in time*, to judge whether the 'end' of the new legal order justified the violent 'means' that led to it.[94] Nor is it possible to judge at the moment of origin whether or not the new legal order will be capable of establishing legitimacy or authority.[95] This happens only through the ongoing process of negotiation between two opposing positions,[96] and the emergence of one position as dominant over the other, thus subordinating it in a violent hierarchy of meaning. The moment of founding law

88 In these terms it can be characterised as a performative act that supposes anterior conventions. Ibid. 27.

89 This is discussed in more detail in Chapter 6.

90 'Force of Law' (n. 11).

91 Declarations of Independence (n. 72) 51.

92 In these terms the Agreement can be read as what public lawyers term a 'critical juncture' in which the constitutional moment provides a new and different foundation for the constitution. For discussion in context see Morrison and Lynch (n. 83).

93 Derrida describes the assumption that 'just' ends, determined by reference to natural or transcendental standards, will ultimately justify the means (violence) as a common presupposition of natural and positive law. 'Force of Law' (n. 11) 32.

94 Ibid. 36. This for Derrida is a moment of 'non' law. This also reflects his rejection of the 'metaphysics of presence' discussed in Chapter 3.

95 And whether or not it will succeed in legitimising the violence that led to its institution. On this dynamic see Costas Douzinas, 'Violence, Justice and Deconstruction' (2005) 6 *German Law Journal* 171.

96 'Force of Law' (n. 11) 36. 'Only the yet-to-come (*l'avenir*) will produce intelligibility or interpretability of this law.'

is a moment of metaphysical violence that will ultimately become the new source of authority of the law. Yet at the moment in which it is founded, it is neither legal nor illegal.[97] This means that although we speak of the violence of law when we speak of the Agreement, this violence also has no intrinsic quality. While there were those who supported the Agreement and those who opposed it, on the metaphysical level the Agreement itself was neither 'good' nor 'bad'. This judgment comes only afterwards, and depends on how the Agreement itself is interpreted and how well the violence of the origin is concealed.

How violence, both political and metaphysical, is interpreted in the post-Agreement phase depends on the interplay between past, present and future. For example, a decision that the Agreement requires significant reform of the police force carries with it an implicit acceptance of the human rights narrative and a rejection of the security narrative. The moment of decision is a moment of metaphysical violence in which the security narrative is violently subordinated to that of human rights. Over time this will colour our interpretation of the past. If the law declares that those who opposed the state were the victims of abuse of their human rights, this lends legitimacy to the use of violence and calls into question the authority of the previous legal order. This can be contrasted with the effect of a judgment that confirms the restriction of fair trial rights as necessary to counter a terrorist threat, the effect of which is to delegitimise the use of violence and uphold the authority of the law. With each decision that accepts the human rights discourse, the use of political violence appears incrementally more justified as a necessary means towards a just end, even if the suffering caused along the way was regrettable.[98] In this way the law is violent, because it is complicit in the privileging of one particular interpretation at the expense of the other. This represents the force *of* law – violence in the metaphysical sense.

What we have seen is that there were competing understandings of the significance of human rights in the Agreement. Our assessment of the Agreement, and the legal order that it created, is constructed on the interplay between these oppositional positions in which one will ultimately subordinate the other. However, in order to ensure its own authority, the new legal order must conceal the history of violent contestation from which it emerged.[99] The following section will discuss how the violence of the origin of the Agreement has been concealed, and how one particular account of the significance of human rights has become established as the dominant account. This is particularly interesting as it reveals the way in which the terms of contestation over law have been set, and how this has had the effect of creating new sites of silence and exclusion.

97 Ibid. 14.

98 This reflects Derrida's suggestion that interpretive models give sense, necessity and above all legitimacy to the violence that has produced, among others, the interpretive model in question. 'Force of Law' (n. 11) 36.

99 Jacques Derrida, *Of Grammatology*, Gayatri Chakravorty Spivak tr. (Johns Hopkins University Press 1976) (hereinafter 'Of Grammatology').

5.2 Concealing the violence of the origin

5.2.1 Northern Ireland in 'transition'

In 2003 it was argued that analysis of the Agreement should be 'sited in an emerging field of legal scholarship, that of "transitional justice"'.[100] Transitional justice, it was argued, 'demands engagement with the specific legal imperatives operative in the case of societies in transition'.[101] By advocating the re-framing of the Agreement as a transitional justice measure, this analysis sought to shift the primary site of engagement with the Agreement away from established UK constitutional law and towards the emergent legal framework of transition. This analysis firmly locates Northern Ireland as undergoing a 'move away from violent conflict to political contestation', placing it firmly within the parameters of the new 'conceptual space' of transitional justice.[102] The benefit of adopting this lens through which to view the Agreement, it was argued, was that it could act as both a 'mediating paradigm and a prescriptive framework'.[103] In particular, the flexibility of the framework of transition would allow for a transformative approach to the interpretation and implementation of the Agreement. This would help to mitigate the risks of a clash of the 'distinct logics of law and politics' that would inevitably occur when the political gains of the Agreement were subjected to legalistic (and, by implication, conservative) interpretation.[104]

A further effect of adopting the framework of transition was to expose post-Agreement legal reform in Northern Ireland to the closer application of international law, and in particular to the emergent international standards of transitional justice. In 2004 the Report of the Secretary General on the Rule of Law and Transitional Justice in Conflict and Post-Conflict Societies elaborated a legal framework of transition, emphasising legal rule of law imperatives for post-conflict societies.[105] This international framework compensated for the absence of any strong transitional justice provisions in the Agreement itself, and provided an additional source of law to which parties could have recourse when making political demands. In particular, the international law framework of transition provided legal standards in relation to dealing with the past, most notably in terms of a 'right to truth', a right to a remedy and guarantees of non-repetition of human rights abuse.[106] These provisions had been absent from the negotiated settlement of the Agreement, yet were to prove central to the way in which public discourse around the past developed. While there are a number of competing conceptual and legal frameworks within which the Agreement and

100 Campbell, Ní Aoláin and Harvey (n. 4) 318.

101 Ibid.

102 Ibid. 319. For discussion of the 'conceptual space' of transitional justice, see Chapter 2.1.

103 Campbell, Ní Aoláin and Harvey (n. 4) 326.

104 Ibid. 324.

105 United Nations, 'Report of the Secretary General on the Rule of Law and Transitional Justice in Conflict and Post Conflict Societies' (UN Doc. S/2004/616, United Nations 2004).

106 These are discussed in more detail in Chapter 6.

its conceptual significance are analysed,[107] the one that has come to dominate is that of transition.

Derrida identifies a dominant discourse as arising when three key tiers of society combine – namely the political, the media and academic spheres.[108] According to Derrida, dominance occurs where all three 'communicate and co-operate toward producing the greatest force with which to assure the hegemony [of that discourse]'.[109] The effect of this co-operation is to produce a discourse founded in the 'incontestable self-evidence' of the truths it proposes.[110] In the case of Northern Ireland, there is strong evidence to suggest that the combination of political discourse,[111] media reporting[112] and academic intervention[113] in the peace process has in recent years shifted the debate firmly onto the terrain of transitional justice.

5.2.2 Dominant and subordinate accounts of conflict

Arguments in favour of framing the Agreement within the conceptual space of transition arise from the existence of conflicting interpretations of why the Agreement was necessary and what it was intended to achieve. The way in which the Agreement and its requirements would be interpreted therefore very much depended on how those responsible for its interpretation and implementation viewed its purpose. The argument in favour of adopting the lens of transitional justice through which to view the Agreement is explicitly rooted in the concern that a conservative interpretation that remained centred in UK constitutional law would not give effect to some of the more far-reaching political demands that had underpinned the Agreement, particularly in respect of human rights.[114]

107 See Morrison and Lynch (n. 83) 108–109.
108 Jacques Derrida, 'Spectres of Marx' (1994) 15 *New Political Science* 7.
109 Ibid.
110 Ibid. Obradović-Wochnik also notes this trend in transitional justice in Serbia, where she suggests that society has been constituted through an alliance between NGOs and academics. J Obradović-Wochnik, 'The "Silent Dilemma" of Transitional Justice: Silencing and Coming to Terms with the Past in Serbia' (2013) 7 *International Journal of Transitional Justice* 328.
111 As evidenced in the Stormont House Agreement.
112 See, for example, the participation of Desmond Tutu on a BBC Northern Ireland series of programmes on 'Facing the Truth', aired in 2006, in which victims and perpetrators were brought face-to-face with each other. More recently, the BBC in Northern Ireland has begun to put pressure on non-state actors in respect of the past.
113 In this context, this refers not particularly to the contribution of academic analysis, but to the way in which academics have teamed up with policy organisations to influence the way in which demands are made. See, for example, Committee on the Administration of Justice, *Mapping the Rollback: Human Rights Provisions of the Belfast/Good Friday Agreement 15 Years On* (Belfast, 2013), presented in partnership with both Queen's University Belfast and the University of Ulster. See also Bridge of Hope's 'Transitional Justice Grass Roots Toolkit', developed with the University of Ulster's Transitional Justice Institute.
114 Committee on the Administration of Justice (n. 113).

The framework of transition takes as its starting point that law in the past has been problematic.[115] As law itself has been partly responsible for the problem, any use of law will also risk perpetuating the violence of law. Law in transition must therefore be 'both the subject and object of change'.[116] What this suggests is that by viewing law as flexible, and as being able to adapt to a unique political context such as transition, that law can break free from its abusive past to become a new agent for change.[117] This is the 'imperative of normative discontinuity' that characterises the role of law in transition.[118] It is for this reason that the focus is relocated away from established domestic law towards international legal standards, which are viewed as being both independent of the parties to a conflict and also as providing comparative reference points that can help to shape the justice debate.[119] This largely involves adopting a strongly normative approach to the role of human rights. The framework of transition is itself regarded as an exceptional measure.[120] The emergency legislation and derogation from human rights obligations that punctuated the legal landscape during the Troubles were represented as exceptional and short-term measures designed to ensure the restoration of the rule of law. Similarly, the framework of transition is regarded as a regime of exceptionality whereby there is divergence from established models of legality, but this is justified by the ends of re-establishing the integrity of the rule of law.[121]

While arguments in favour of the application of the framework of transition are framed in the language of transcendence, they represent a deeply political choice. By asserting as a matter of fact that the starting point for analysis of the Agreement should be that there were systematic institutional failings in Northern Ireland, and that law itself had been implicated in causing and sustaining the conflict, a substantive statement is being made on where the responsibility for the conflict lies and how that should be addressed. For some, this choice also makes an implicit statement on the legitimacy or otherwise of the violence that preceded the Agreement. While the language of 'transition' is absent from the Agreement, it has been suggested that it envisaged a 'context of transition'.[122] Characterising Northern Ireland as being 'in transition' therefore also represents

115 Campbell, Ní Aoláin and Harvey (n. 4) 334, stating that 'Typically, one of the products of extended conflicts is the use and abuse of legal form'.

116 Ibid.

117 For detailed discussion of the claims made in respect of the role of law in transition, see Chapter 2.

118 Teitel (n. 33) 224.

119 Campbell, Ní Aoláin and Harvey (n. 4) 334.

120 For discussion of the exceptional temporality of emergency and transition, see Fionnuala Ní Aoláin, 'Transitional Emergency Jurisprudence: Derogation and Transition' in Antoine Buyse and Michael Hamilton (eds), *Transitional Jurisprudence: Transitional Justice and the ECHR* (Cambridge 2011).

121 For discussion of the tension between differing modes of legality in respect of transitional justice, see Ruti Teitel, 'Transitional Justice Genealogy' (2003) 16 *Harvard Human Rights Law Journal* 69 (hereinafter 'Genealogy'). See also Teitel (n. 33) 224 where she justifies departure from conventional legality in terms of democratic consolidation.

122 Anthony and Mageean (n. 45) 181, 200.

a further moment of violence, in that one particular account of the causes of the conflict in Northern Ireland was privileged and inscribed into the legal framework. Competing accounts of conflict, and of the role of human rights, were thereby subordinated in the violent hierarchy of meaning. The concept of 'transition', bringing with it its own specific legal imperatives, provides an interpretive framework that will sustain the law and colour subsequent interpretations of the Agreement and its purpose. This is not a disputed aim of the application of the framework of transition.[123] In casting the role of law in transition as being both backward- and forward-looking, the model assumes that law will be used to achieve specific political outcomes, and that this sometimes stands contrary to established notions of legality.[124]

What is not acknowledged in this discourse, however, is the way in which, in seeking to move away from violence, the legal framework of transition captures violence at its heart. This violence consists of the manner in which the Agreement and the framework of transition themselves both shape and constrain permissible accounts of what the conflict was about and how it should be resolved. The narrative that has emerged dominant is the one according to which the conflict was about human rights and equality within Northern Ireland. The 'normative' interpretation of human rights has been privileged at the expense of the 'political' interpretation. This does not mean that other interpretations do not exist, but rather that they have been subordinated by the 'normative' approach that analyses legal and political reform in the objectively framed language of human rights.[125] It then follows that if the problem is defined as one of legal shortcomings, it can be resolved by law and legal guarantees. The effect of the post-Agreement framework of transition is therefore that all accounts of the conflict, and indeed of post-conflict politics, must be articulated in the language of 'law' and 'transition'.[126] The creation of this powerful interpretive context has implications for how the debate is shaped. For example, transitional justice traditionally focuses on abuses committed by the state. The dominance of this framework means it is less easy to accommodate competing demands for truth and accountability from non-state actors.[127] Similarly, those who choose not to engage are themselves marginalised and silenced.[128] Their voice is no longer one among equals, but rather

123 See Campbell and Ní Aoláin (n. 34) on the politics of the label of transition in conflicted democracies.

124 Genealogy (n. 121).

125 For discussion, see Jennifer Curtis, *Human Rights as War by other Means: Peace Politics in Northern Ireland* (University of Pennsylvania Press 2014).

126 For further discussion, see Catherine Turner, 'Deconstructing Transitional Justice' (2013) 24 *Law and Critique* 193.

127 Colm Campbell and Catherine Turner, 'Utopia and the Doubters: Truth, Transition and the Law' (2008) 23 *Legal Studies* 374; Kieran McEvoy, 'Human Rights, Humanitarian Interventions and Paramilitary Activities in Northern Ireland' in Colin Harvey (ed.), *Human Rights, Equality and Democratic Renewal in Northern Ireland* (Hart 2001) 215.

128 This is discussed in more detail in Chapter 6.

is subordinated in the violent hierarchy of meaning that has been created by the transitional framework.

Returning to the tertiary structure of the economy of violence, it has been demonstrated how the Agreement represents a moment of originary violence, in which the law is destroyed and re-founded. This first stage of the economy is the moment of constitution of a new order, framed as a 'transition' from conflict to peace. The second stage of the economy is that of reparatory violence, in which the violence of the origin is concealed. As discussed in Chapter 3, this concealment is a necessary part of the establishment of the authority of law. If the Agreement is successful, then gradually the history of division and violence that gave rise to it will be forgotten, and the violence of the law concealed.[129] The success of the idea of 'transition', and the extent to which the Agreement can be read as having created an interpretive framework that at once upholds and conceals the violence of the law, can be seen in the way in which its terms have been interpreted in the courts.

5.2.3 Litigating the Agreement (and concealing the violence of the origin)

A central conceptual element of transitional justice is the use of law to mediate political decisions. By removing particularly contentious issues from the realm of politics, it is suggested that law in transition can secure meaningful change. In the context of the Agreement in Northern Ireland, it is clear how the rationale, if not necessarily the language, of transition has been adopted. Underpinning a transitional justice approach is a purposive approach to the interpretation of the Agreement, one that recognises the Agreement as playing a role in responding to a legacy of past injustice. However, rather than viewing this as a purely political task of redressing past imbalances, the application of the lens of transition casts the task as a legal one. The narrative of transition, to be successful, must be constructed on the idea of consensus. It is presented as a normative (and, as such, objective) regime that provides a framework for political reconciliation.[130] It is with this process that the violence of the origin of the law is concealed.

The Agreement, a political document, was given legal form primarily in the Northern Ireland Act 1998. It was this legislation that transformed the political undertakings of the Agreement into law in Northern Ireland.[131] With this came

129 Jacques Derrida, 'Devant la Loi' in Alan Udof (ed.), *Kafka and the Contemporary Critical Performance* (Indiana University Press 1987) 128, 134 (hereinafter 'Before the Law'). Law should be without history, genesis or any possible derivation. 'To enter into relations with the law which says "you must" or "you must not" is to act as if it had no history, or at any rate no longer depended on its historical presentation.'

130 Catherine Turner, 'Flag Protests, Politics and Transition in Northern Ireland' (2013 Critical Legal Thinking) http://criticallegalthinking.com/2013/02/04/flag-protests-politics-and-transition-in-northern-ireland/, accessed 6 August 2015.

131 Specific measures were also introduced by separate legislation. See, for example, Northern Ireland (Sentences) Act 1998; Police (Northern Ireland) Act 2000; Justice (Northern Ireland) Act 2002; and, more recently, the Victims and Survivors (Northern Ireland) Order 2006.

a new constitutional context, as well as the potential for subsequent legislation and political decisions to be subjected to judicial review on the basis of a range of grounds of competence, not least human rights and equality.[132] These competences created an interpretive context for law in post-Agreement Northern Ireland that was evidenced in the decisions of the domestic courts and continues to shape the way in which 'transition'-related arguments are made.

The first and clearest example of the courts accepting the constitutional nature of the Agreement came in the case of *Robinson v Secretary of State for Northern Ireland.*[133] *Robinson* concerned a challenge by the Democratic Unionist Party to the legality of the election of a First Minister and Deputy First Minister, on account of the fact that it had taken place outside the time frame for elections specified in the Northern Ireland Act. While concerned with a technical point, the *Robinson* case is significant because of the way in which it constructs the Agreement and its implementing legislation. The judgment is clear that the Court regards the Act as having constitutional status, and that it explicitly accepts the Agreement as marking a new constitutional beginning for Northern Ireland.[134] This, according to the Court, is the new context in which the Agreement should be interpreted, with the majority considering that the 'relevant statutory provisions should be read in the light of the context set by the Belfast Agreement'.[135] Once this context had been recognised, the Court confirmed that the Act should be interpreted 'generously and purposively', in light of the 'values which the constitutional provisions are intended to embody'.[136] The reasoning of the Court is also resonant of the underlying rationale of transitional justice, namely that some flexibility in legal interpretation may be required to give effect to transitional aims. Lord Bingham suggests that 'where constitutional arrangements retain scope for the exercise of political judgment, they permit a flexible response to differing and unpredictable events in a way which the application of strict rules would preclude'.[137]

Beyond *Robinson*, there is further evidence in the case law of the Northern Ireland courts that the judiciary has accepted the rationale of a 'new beginning' and of a post-Agreement 'context' within which decisions are to be made. This includes the Court upholding a claim challenging the oath of allegiance required for elevation to the senior bar in Northern Ireland,[138] giving the newly created Northern Ireland Human Rights Commission the right to intervene as a third party in the litigation of human rights issues,[139] and confirming that taxi licensing

132 Morrison and Lynch (n. 83).
133 [2002] UKHL 32.
134 *Robinson* (n. 68) Per Lord Hoffmann para. 25.
135 See Gordon Anthony, 'Judicial Review in Northern Ireland – A Guide to the "Real" Devolution Issues' (2009) 14(3) *Judicial Review* 230, 232.
136 *Robinson* (n. 68) Per Lord Bingham para. 11.
137 Ibid. per Bingham LJ para. 12.
138 *In Re Treacy's and Another's Application for Judicial Review* [2000] NI 330.
139 *In Re Northern Ireland Human Rights Commission (Northern Ireland)* [2002] UKHL 25. This was subsequently confirmed in legislation in the Northern Ireland Act 1998 s 69.

regulations should also be read in light of the Agreement and in particular should not disadvantage former prisoners on account of conflict-related convictions.[140]

More recent case law has confirmed the way in which the Agreement has provided a legal 'context' within which legal argument and decision-making takes place. In the 2011 case of *Re Colaiste Feirste*, the applicant sought judicial review of the decision by the education authorities not to provide dedicated transport for pupils attending an Irish language-medium secondary school in Belfast.[141] In arguments on behalf of the applicant, reference was made to the Agreement, and specifically to the economic, social and cultural rights provisions therein. The applicant highlighted the undertaking made by the parties to the Agreement to facilitate and encourage the use of the Irish language and asserted that this should be regarded not merely as an aspirational principle, but as a legal duty.[142] In accepting the applicant's arguments, the Court confirmed that the statutory duties placed on the education authority must be construed in light of the Agreement.[143] Similarly, in the 2015 case of *Re CAJ* the Court accepted arguments that the failure of the government to publish an anti-poverty and social exclusion strategy amounted to a breach of obligations arising from the St Andrews Agreement 2006.[144] The reasoning in this case was based on the principle of equality that underpinned the Agreement. Section 28(E) of the Northern Ireland Act 1998, which had its origins in the St Andrews Agreement, required the government to 'adopt a strategy setting out how it proposes to tackle poverty, social exclusion and patterns of deprivation based on *objective need*'.[145] The applicant in this case interpreted the criteria of 'objective need' as central to tackling discrimination in the allocation of resources and, as such, as an 'important milestone in the development of equality law in Northern Ireland'. The Court, finding that the government had failed in its statutory duty, accepted this reasoning.[146]

The interpretive 'context' set by the Agreement therefore has force well beyond the relatively narrow band of 'dealing with the past' cases that are most commonly associated with transitional justice. The cases discussed speak to a much broader and more holistic interpretation of the requirements of transition and the role of law in facilitating the redress of past injustices.[147]

140 *In the Matter of an Application by Damien McComb for Judicial Review* [2003] NIQB 47.

141 *In the Matter of an Application by Colaiste Feirste for Judicial Review of a Decision of the Department of Education Relating to School Transport* [2011] NIQB 98.

142 This assertion was based on the Education (Northern Ireland) Order 1998 Art. 89, which required the government to facilitate and encourage the development of Irish medium education.

143 *In the Matter of an Application by Colaiste Feirste* (n. 142) para. 16.

144 *Re Committee on the Administration of Justice (CAJ) and Another's Application for Judicial Review* [2015] NIQB 59.

145 Northern Ireland Act 1998 s 28E(1). Emphasis added.

146 While the government was found to have failed in its statutory duty, the discussion of the meaning of 'objective need' was obiter, and as such, lacking binding legal effect for the time being.

147 For a good discussion of the role of courts and judges in distinguishing present from past, see Christiane Wilke, 'Enter Ghost: Haunted Courts and Haunting Judgments in Transitional Justice' (2010) 21 *Law and Critique* 73.

The way in which the Court interprets the Agreement, as having created a particular context that should guide future decision-making, is an integral element of the concealment of the originary violence of the Agreement. For Derrida, the idea of context as a means of grounding legal interpretation and decision-making is problematic.[148] The way in which the Agreement is framed as having set a context within which decisions should be made assumes that we can ascribe fixed and immutable intention to those who signed the Agreement. It assumes that there is one definite (and identifiable) context, and that if that context is appropriately respected, a 'correct' answer to the political or legal problem can be ascertained. In particular, it appears to support the idea that the inclusion of human rights in the Agreement was based on 'normative' rather than 'political' considerations. However, this belies the range of different positions, interests and intentions that combined to create the Agreement. For Derrida, context is never absolutely determinable.[149] The very essence of writing – of committing ideas to text – is that that text should be able to be understood in the absence of its author.[150] This may mean in the physical absence of an author – someone who has died, for example – or it may also mean in the event that the author ceases to support its provisions. The act of writing itself is characterised by the possibility of being repeated.[151] The text therefore breaks free from the context in which it was created.[152] What this means in practical terms is that, rather than there being one singular and fixed 'context' that must ground subsequent interpretation of the text, each time the text is interpreted a new context is generated.[153] The context does not precede the decision, but rather is (re)constituted by it. By representing the decisions of the Court as an exercise in purposive legal interpretation, determined by context and thereby denying the political and essentially contested nature of the decision being made, the violence of the origin of the law is repeated.[154] And yet this decision is presented as the impartial operation of the law.

This leads us back to the economy of violence. From the examples cited, it is clear that legal decision-making, both legislative and judicial, is now framed by the Agreement and the need to give effect to its (normative) terms. As discussed in Chapter 4, our understanding of key concepts, such as where the boundary

148 Jacques Derrida, 'Signature, Event, Context' in Alan Bass tr., *Margins of Philosophy* (The Harvester Press 1982) 307 (hereinafter 'Signature, Event, Context').

149 Ibid. 310.

150 Ibid. 320.

151 Derrida cites, by way of example, the use of citation. The ability to cite is an inherent quality of writing. Derrida asks: 'What would a mark be that one could not cite?' Ibid. 321. Subotić (n. 48) also notes that this is a key feature of the new transitional justice toolkit approach.

152 Signature, Event, Context (n. 148) 320.

153 The fact that writing can be cited, put between quotation marks, suggests that it can 'break with every given context, and engender infinitely new contexts in an absolutely nonsaturable [*sic*] fashion'. Ibid. 320.

154 'Force of Law' (n. 11). The moment of decision is both law-preserving, in that it confirms law as the basis on which decisions are made, but also law-destroying, in that with each decision the old law is destroyed and a new one constituted.

between legal and non-legal and indeed legitimate and illegitimate, is drawn depends not on a fixed and immutable standard but rather on the interplay between the different opposing positions. And yet this political dynamic of adjudication is not open and acknowledged, but is concealed behind legal form.[155] In the act of decision-making, the authority of the law is reasserted and simultaneously concealed. This has implications for the possibility of resistance and articulating an alternative reading of the law.

The cases cited demonstrate that the application of the framework of transition has, in some ways, been empowering. The existence of international law standards has been used to lend authority to demands for reform. But in other ways it has been disempowering, in that it has restricted the permissible demands to those that can be framed in law, and in particular those that are recognised as being 'legitimate' transitional justice demands. The gradual change in terminology is significant in that the use of these terms in judgments of the higher courts serves to inscribe the political struggle over the causes and responsibility for the conflict into law.[156] This in turn 'intrinsically [defines] the possibilities of elaborating a historical narrative'.[157]

As a result, the idea of transition, and the constraints that it has placed on political contestation in post-Agreement Northern Ireland, has also been divisive. The effect of the dominance of law is to silence those who oppose the rhetoric of transitional justice. For example, the acceptance of 'transition' as the appropriate framework for analysis of the Agreement largely excludes not only Unionist narratives of the conflict, rooted in terrorism and security,[158] but also those of Republicans, now commonly referred to in a pejorative sense as 'dissidents', who do not recognise the narrative of human rights and equality within Northern Ireland as being the aim of the 'struggle'.[159] These alternative positions on the causes of the conflict and the legitimacy of the Agreement are largely suppressed in current political discourse. The language of legal imperative leaves little room for negotiation or compromise.[160] In establishing its own authority, the legal order created by the Agreement relies on the exclusion of all competing narratives. This moment of originary violence is perpetuated by the context-driven approach to legal interpretation outlined. While it is by no means the case that all political

155 'Before the Law' (n. 129) 145. 'Law is intangible, it is forbidden or illicit to change or disfigure it, or to touch its form.'

156 See Alejandro Castillejo-Cuéllar, 'Historical Injuries, Temporality and the Law: Articulations of a Violent Past in Two Transitional Scenarios' (2014) 25 *Law and Critique* 47, 53.

157 Ibid.

158 Kirk Simpson, 'Untold Stories: Unionist Remembrance of Political Violence and Suffering in Northern Ireland' (2008) 3 *British Politics* 465.

159 For discussion, see Curtis (n. 125).

160 See, for example, McEvoy *et al.*, who criticise the community relations approach as ignoring the fact that human rights and equality 'legislation is based upon binding international legal standards, which cannot simply be abolished'. Lesley McEvoy, Kieran McEvoy and Kirsten McConnachie, 'Reconciliation Is a Dirty Word: Conflict, Community Relations and Education in Northern Ireland' (2006) 60 *Journal of International Affairs* 81.

questions that come to be decided under the Agreement or the Northern Ireland Act are reinterpreted as legal questions, or as questions in which the courts should diverge from established legal principles,[161] the Agreement nevertheless profoundly shapes legal discourse and the way in which political demands are framed. The struggle for ownership of the language of transition is no less political than the violence that preceded it. And yet the use of legal form shields decisions from challenge. It is here that the violence of the law lies. Rather than acknowledging the existence of alternative interpretations, competing narratives are subordinated to the dominant account of human rights and transitional justice as a normative framework within which decisions are to be made. The violence of this hierarchy is not open and acknowledged, but is denied as the necessary means by which law establishes its own authority.

From the preceding discussion it can be seen how law-making and legal decision-making in the transitional phase mimic that criticised during the Troubles. Whereas during the Troubles the legislature and the courts accepted the security rationale and the need for emergency legislation to combat a terrorist threat,[162] in the transitional phase the courts are guided by the values of the Agreement, thus implicitly accepting human rights and equality-based arguments for legal reform.[163] The way in which the story of the conflict is told begins to be shaped by the interpretive framework of transition, inherently privileging one side over the other. In this way it can be seen how, in subordinating the narrative of security to that of human rights, the hierarchy has been exposed and largely reversed. Each time a decision is made that reaffirms the centrality of human rights and equality, the violence of the origin is repeated and alternative positions on the requirements of the Agreement are silenced. However, the silenced positions do not cease to exist. Rather, they remain trapped as the excluded trace within the law.[164] As discussed in Chapter 4, where the violence of the law is improperly concealed or where the state fails to acknowledge the place of law within an economy of violence,[165] this can give rise to challenge. This is the third level of the economy of violence, that of the violence of reflection. In Northern Ireland, protest over some aspects of the Agreement and legal reform have begun to spill over into physical violence on the streets. This is the case in respect of two particular issues – those of flags and parades.

5.3 The violence of reflection – flags, parades and the past

While the Agreement continues to be the primary reference point for legal decision-making in Northern Ireland, cracks have appeared that are beginning

161 See Anthony (n. 135).

162 Stephen Livingstone, 'The House of Lords and the Northern Ireland Conflict' (1994) 57 *Modern Law Review* 333.

163 Brice Dickson, 'The House of Lords and the Northern Ireland Conflict – A Sequel' (2006) 69 *Modern Law Review* 383.

164 Jacques Derrida, *Positions* (The Athlone Press 1981) (hereinafter 'Positions').

165 Laws of Reflection (n. 13).

to make visible the violence of the origin of the new legal order. As discussed in section 5.1, the purpose of the Agreement was to attempt to create a new polity in Northern Ireland. This polity would be characterised by its respect for diversity and its commitment to human rights and the rule of law. In order to do this, it was necessary to project an image of unity. However, as Collins suggests, deconstruction 'reveals the way in which the act of constituting the nation in legal discourse is also an act of excluding those counter-discourses that challenge the nation's unitary character'.[166] While it is not argued, either here or in political discourse in Northern Ireland, that the Agreement sought to either declare or create a unified 'nation', the idea that the Agreement could create a new polity, unified in its respect for diversity,[167] does suggest that the use of law and legal discourse mimics this trend. The new boundaries that were set were those of 'pro-' and 'anti-Agreement'. One was either for the Agreement or against it. Rather than transcending opposition, this simply shifted the boundaries.

There are three key pinch points around which opposition to the Agreement, and the idea of 'transition', are coalescing. These are flags, parades and the past. Each represents a particularly fraught political issue where law has been unable to accommodate the competing demands being made. Each demonstrates the exclusionary nature of the discourse of transition and the use of law to further the aims of transition. The first two issues, of flags and parades, together present an example of where the interpretive context of the Agreement is deemed to have gone too far and has begun to create a new sense of grievance and marginalisation among some Unionist communities. In respect of the third example, that of the past, transitional justice is deemed not to have gone far enough. The inherent limitations of law and the division that it creates have prevented any meaningful progress on the past from being made. The remainder of this chapter will consider the issues of flags and parades, while the past and efforts to 'deal' with it will be the subject of the next chapter.

5.3.1 Flags

One of the core values that underpins the Agreement is that of equality. Speaking directly to a history of discrimination in the past, the Agreement has been central to the articulation of demands for economic, social and cultural rights. While in some cases the Agreement has been used successfully to campaign for increased recognition of these rights, in other cases it has been used to strike down measures that were deemed to be essentially political. This has caused problems for the apparent impartiality of the Agreement and the idea of transition, particularly for the Unionist and Loyalist communities. Whereas judicial review has been successfully used in furtherance of what would be perceived as 'nationalist' demands,[168] it has been perceived as being biased against Unionist

166 Collins (n. 58) 389.

167 Hume (n. 69).

168 For examples see section 5.2.3.

demands. For example, an application for judicial review of a policy requiring that recruitment to the new Police Service of Northern Ireland (PSNI) be done on a 50:50 Catholic/Protestant basis was rejected.[169] Similarly, the appointment of an Interim Victim's Commissioner, nominated for the post by a Unionist political party, was overturned as a result of judicial review.[170] One of the reasons given for the decision in the High Court was that the appointment was politically motivated,[171] and therefore in breach of the provisions of the Northern Ireland Act that outlawed discrimination, giving legal effect to the commitment made in the Agreement to strengthen anti-discrimination legislation.[172] In another case the appointment of two members of Loyal Orders to the Parades Commission was ruled unlawful.[173] While these decisions are based on the need to ensure that public appointment procedures are conducted on the principle of merit and appointing the best candidates for the job, and are mostly decided on very technical points of public law rather than on broad 'context' considerations, the *perception* created by these decisions is that the law leans against Unionists, and in favour of nationalists, where the interpretation of the Agreement is concerned.[174] This is part of a broader problem whereby human rights and equality are traditionally associated with nationalist and Republican narratives of the conflict rather than those of Unionists,[175] which is in turn consolidated by the acceptance of the narrative of transition. This has created an opposition that continues to dominate legal argumentation in the post-conflict environment.[176]

This dissatisfaction was made visible to the world in December 2012, following a decision of Belfast City Council to restrict the number of days that the Union flag could be flown over City Hall. This decision was justified with reference to the equality and parity of esteem provisions of the Agreement,[177] and sparked weeks

169 *Re Parsons* [2004] NI 38. The purpose of the 50:50 rule was to redress the balance in the police force and make it more representative of the community, and therefore more acceptable. However, the effect was that it was made difficult for Protestant applicants to gain positions within the police, resulting in allegations of discrimination in favour of Catholic applicants. The measures were found to be proportionate on the grounds that they were time-limited.

170 The position of Victim's Commissioner was also created to give effect to the terms of the Agreement in relation to the needs of victims. Ibid. s 6 paras 11–12.

171 The candidate had been nominated by the Democratic Unionist Party, which at that time was opposed to the Agreement and had refused to participate in government.

172 *Re Downes' Application* [2009] NICA 26, para. 47. The decision in the House of Lords was, however, reached on a very technical ground that did not speak to the context.

173 *Re Duffy's Application* [2008] UKHL 4.

174 For discussion, see Roger MacGinty and Pierre Du Toit, 'A Disparity of Esteem: Relative Group Status in Northern Ireland After the Belfast Agreement' (2007) 28 *Political Psychology* 13.

175 See Mageean and O'Brien (n. 30). See also Morrison and Lynch (n. 83) on the role of lawyers in advising Sinn Fein on the Human Rights, Equality and Safeguards provisions of the Agreement.

176 For discussion of this, see Catherine Turner, 'The "Right" to Protest on Northern Ireland's Streets' (Human Rights in Ireland, 20 January 2013) http://humanrights.ie/civil-liberties/turnerresponse/, accessed 14 August 2015.

177 For a detailed analysis of these protests, see Paul Nolan *et al.*, *The Flag Dispute: Anatomy of a Protest* (Queens University Belfast 2014).

of protest, some of which turned violent. The violence of these protests returns us to Derrida's economy of violence, whereby the violence of reflection is that stage of the economy most commonly associated with physical violence.

The eruption of violence in the context of the flag protests represented a much deeper disillusionment with post-Agreement politics, namely a perception that the law is being used unfairly against Unionist and Loyalist communities.[178] The physical violence of the protests therefore reflects back the metaphysica violence of the origin, revealing the manner of the exclusion of these groups from the dominant political community.[179] The problem is not necessarily the fact of the decision to restrict the flying of the flag. Rather, it exists in the feeling that the law belongs to one community at the expense of the other. The violence of the law exists in the way in which debate is constrained by the terms of the rhetoric of the Agreement and its institution in legal form. The dominance of one particular way of understanding the Agreement and the significance of the human rights and equality provisions, and its representation as objective law, means that alternative views will necessarily be subordinated in the violent hierarchy of meaning.[180] Whereas the language of human rights and equality contained in the Agreement and incorporated into law in the Northern Ireland Act provide a legitimising legal framework for political reforms, those who seek to maintain the status quo or to oppose reforms for valid political reasons have no such means of opposition. To oppose human rights and equality, or even to challenge the interpretation of what human rights and equality requires, is to appear reactionary, to risk having oneself branded as a bigot and having one's opinion dismissed as irrelevant, or as attempting to drag Northern Ireland back into the past.[181] The dominance of the Agreement and the narrative of transition – the progress away from past and towards the future – create a profoundly uneven playing field on which these debates must play out.

When seen in the context of transitional justice, this is problematic. The justification given for having a distinct conceptualisation of the rule of law in transition is that it can help to transcend political divisions. However, when analysed through the lens of the economy of violence, what these most recent protests demonstrate is that oppositional structures have not been transcended. Rather, the opposition has been reversed, laying bare the continued existence of a binary structure and a relationship of violent hierarchy between the two. The protests reflect the metaphysical

178 Ibid.

179 Ibid.

180 Positions (n. 164).

181 For another good example of this, see the debate between Traditional Unionist Voice MLA Jim Allister and Sinn Fein MLA Daithi McKay on the Special Advisor Bill in Stormont. This bill sought to prevent those with serious criminal convictions from being employed as special advisors to MLAs. During this debate, no fewer than 107 references were made to the Agreement and the need to prevent Northern Ireland from going back to the flawed justice systems of the past. The Official Report of the Debate is available at www.niassembly.gov.uk/globalassets/documents/official-reports/plenary/2012-13/revised-daily-part-3-june-2013.pdf, accessed 21 March 2016.

violence of this hierarchy, making it visible through physical violence.[182] Therefore, the violence of the protests can be read as a demand for equality – as a demand to have one's voice heard – that simply reflects back the principles of the Agreement, most notably that of parity of esteem.

5.3.2 *Parades*

A similar demand is made in respect of the restriction of Loyal Order parades. The years since the early 1990s have seen a resurgence in conflict surrounding parades, with increasing numbers of protests against the particular routes that parades take.[183] These protests have been framed as human rights protests, demanding in particular the 'right' to be free from sectarian harassment.[184] This has resulted in some high-profile parades being restricted or re-routed away from what were traditional routes. Following the signing of the Agreement, as part of the reform of legal administration, an independent statutory body (the Parades Commission) was established to adjudicate on parades and make determinations where routes were disputed.[185] The aim of this was to place mediation and consensus at the heart of the process.[186] However, the reality has been a little different. One particular example serves to illustrate the conflict that now surrounds Parades Commission determinations.

In July 2013 a North Belfast Lodge notified the Commission of a proposed parade along an arterial route from North Belfast into the City Centre and home again that evening.[187] The proposed route passed a strongly Republican residential area, and residents also notified the Commission of a counter-protest. This parade took place in the context of a history of violent clashes at this particular location, which lies in one of the most volatile and divided areas of Belfast. The Parades Commission allowed the parade to pass on the outward route subject to restrictions, but determined that it should not pass the flashpoint on the way home. Enforcement of this determination resulted in serious violence and rioting, during which a prominent Unionist politician was injured.[188] The site at which the

182 Laws of Reflection (n. 13).

183 For background, see Democratic Dialogue, *Politics in Public – Freedom of Assembly and the Right to Protest* (Belfast, 1998).

184 This is not a right reflected in any existing convention.

185 Public Processions (Northern Ireland) Act 1998.

186 This aim is repeated in determinations made by the Commission. See, for example, the 2013 determination on one of the most contentious parade routes: Determination Made in Relation to the Ligoniel True Blues LOL 1932 Parade Notified to Take Place in Belfast on Friday, 12 July 2013, www.paradescommission.org/fs/files/det-ligoniel-true-blues-lol-1932-12july-2013.pdf, accessed 16 March 2016.

187 Ibid.

188 M McHugh and L McKeown, 'DUP MP Nigel Dodds hit by brick during north Belfast Twelfth riot' (*Belfast Telegraph* 13 July 2013) www.belfasttelegraph.co.uk/news/northern-ireland/dup-mp-nigel-dodds-hit-by-brick-during-north-belfast-twelfth-riot-29417638.html, accessed 19 October 2015.

parade was stopped has remained a protest site and focal point for the increasing disillusionment of this community with the new legal order that has been created in Northern Ireland. In publishing its determination on the parade, the Parades Commission justified the restriction in light of statutory duties imposed by Northern Ireland-specific legislation, the Human Rights Act 1998 and the Convention.[189] This therefore clearly made it a legal determination set against a context of human rights and competing claims in terms of what rights should be be protected.[190]

Chapter 4 discussed how the restriction of a civil rights march in Derry in 1969 led to a more general sense of grievance in respect of the law and how it operated.[191] Clear parallels can be drawn between that march and the 2013 parade and the way in which protest has developed since then. In the immediate aftermath of the parade, Unionist politicians claimed that the anger and frustration that the community felt towards the Parades Commission was justified, and indeed that the Parades Commission bore responsibility for the violence that was the inevitable result of its determination.[192] The Parades Commission has become the specific focus of a more general sense of marginalisation that has led protesters and their political supporters to draw analogies between their own 'struggle' and that of the US civil rights movement.[193] The language of civil rights is once again being engaged as a means of articulating political isolation and making demands for a voice to be heard.

While there are clearly competing versions of this story and where the responsibility for violence lies, what this example demonstrates is the way in which opposition has become reinscribed in Northern Ireland. In the 1970s there was a community that felt alienated, felt that the state did not adequately meet their political and social aspirations, and felt that the law and the agents of its enforcement were biased against them.[194] Now the hierarchy has been inverted and it is the previously dominant community that is feeling alienation and powerlessness. While it is easy to dismiss this as 'justice' or simply 'sour grapes' on the part of the Loyalist communities in particular, to do so is foolhardy in light of the consequences of failing to adequately address political grievance in the 1970s. It is for this reason that to invert the hierarchy is not enough without also addressing the structures

189 Parades Commission (n. 186).

190 For detailed discussion of this theoretical debate, see Michael Hamilton, 'Freedom of Assembly, Consequential Harms and the Rule of Law: Liberty Limiting Principles in the Context of Transition' (2007) 27 *Oxford Journal of Legal Studies* 75.

191 See Chapter 4.1.3.

192 Comments of the First Minister Peter Robinson published in the *Belfast Telegraph* (n. 189).

193 This analogy is not new in this context, but has been being drawn by Unionist politicians since the Agreement came into force. See Gregory Campbell, 'The Peace Process and the Protestants' in Dominic Murray (ed.), *Protestant Perceptions of the Peace Process in Northern Ireland* (Cain 2000).

194 As documented in K Boyle *et al.*, *Law and State: The Case of Northern Ireland* (University of Massachusetts Press 1975). I originally made this comparison in 'The "Right" to Protest on Northern Ireland's Streets' (n. 176).

that give rise to conflict. Without addressing structures, the cycle of violence will simply re-establish itself.

5.4 Conclusion – the hierarchy inverted

For Derrida, the inversion of violent hierarchies is the necessary first step in deconstruction.[195] The reversal of the binary of emergency and human rights was necessary in order to highlight the 'conflictual and subordinating structure of opposition'.[196] Understanding this dynamic, and the inherent violence of law, is crucial to understanding the division that exists over the past in Northern Ireland. Inverting the binaries reveals the oppositional nature of thought and the dominance of one particular way of conceptualising politics in Northern Ireland. This is true whether 'emergency' or 'transition' is the lens through which politics is refracted. Derrida is also clear, however, that the inversion of hierarchies is only the first step of deconstruction.[197] If we remain in this stage, then we remain within an oppositional structure, with the risk that the hierarchy will reassert itself. It is suggested that this is the point that has now been reached in Northern Ireland.

This chapter asked whether, in light of the inherent violence of law, a model of transitional justice rooted in law could effectively address political conflict. It has demonstrated that the legal framework of transition has itself exerted a form of (metaphysical) violence on politics in Northern Ireland. Whereas in the past the law had been used to delegitimise violence, and with it the political aspirations of those who engaged in or supported the use of violence, the acceptance of the 'normative' human rights arguments signified the beginning of a new phase marked by the metaphysical violence of law. As the issues of flags and parades demonstrate, the effect of law can be exclusionary. This exemplifies Derrida's theoretical point that violence and law are locked in a cycle of justification, whereby past violence is accepted as having been necessary in order to bring about the change that has been secured,[198] and the new legal order that relies for its authority on the way in which it guarantees that change. This represents a new form of (legal) violence that exerts its own force. The way in which the Agreement is framed represents the extent to which narratives that underlay the use of violence have been accepted. Their incorporation into the Agreement gave them legal form and dressed them in the cloak of legal legitimacy. Violence therefore remained at the heart of the new law.

This dynamic can be understood on two levels. The first, and more common, is that in accepting narratives of grievance that underpinned violence, the government has capitulated to violence. Here, violence and law are still seen as two

195 Positions (n. 164). This is discussed in Chapter 3.

196 Ibid. 41.

197 Ibid.

198 Douzinas (n. 95). This is discussed in Chapter 4.

separate phenomena. Violence, in the form of terrorism, has exerted an external force on law, and has managed to bend law to its will. This will result in a perception that the new order is fundamentally unjust. The other way of looking at it, and the one that is proposed here, is that violence was always present within the law. Rather than violence exerting an external pressure on law, violence comes from within law. As discussed in the previous chapter, the law itself was a form of violence. The concepts of emergency (violence) and human rights (law) existed in a state of violent hierarchy. The two existed not as separate and divisible concepts, but only with reference to each other.[199] Popular understandings of law and legality were constructed with reference to the interplay between the two. Whereas during the Troubles the discourse of terrorism and emergency conditioned attitudes towards violence and the legitimacy of legal responses to it, in the post-Troubles 'transition' phase, attitudes towards the legitimacy of the law are conditioned to a much greater extent by popular understandings of human rights. What has happened is simply that the violent hierarchy has been reversed. This is a cyclical rather than a linear movement. Law has not replaced violence. The twin concepts of human rights (law) and emergency (violence) are still present within the law, but human rights has now managed to establish itself as the dominant discourse, and with it the discourse of emergency has been violently subordinated. Our understanding of law and legality therefore continues to be constructed on the interplay between violence and law and will be determined largely on the basis of which narrative has managed to establish itself as dominant at any given time.[200]

What is important to recognise, therefore, is the interplay between the two. As violence is immanent to law, it cannot be transcended. We cannot move *from* violence *to* law. The violence continues in legal, rather than physical, form. It is the failure to acknowledge this violence, or to recognise its effects, that poses a risk for transitional justice. The dominance of the 'normative' approach to human rights and transitional justice has succeeded in excluding the 'political' view in which conflict-related issues are a matter for negotiation. The effect of this is to enclose the debate over the past within the 'theatrical space' of transitional justice. This inherently limits the possibilities for political compromise, and creates new sites of silence and exclusion. It creates a powerful barrier to those who wish to challenge the dominance of this discourse. The most recent violence on the streets of Northern Ireland represents the reassertion of that which has been suppressed. The excluded trace of politics is now challenging the dominance of the 'normative' order. In this way, in relying on law to achieve political reform, the model has reproduced the patterns of conflict that it sought to disarm.

It is suggested that, nearly twenty years after the Agreement, the hierarchy has reasserted itself, and that although the emergency/human rights hierarchy

199 Of Grammatology (n. 99). This is discussed in Chapter 3.

200 Jacques Derrida, *On Cosmopolitanism and Forgiveness*, Mark Dooley and Michael Hughes tr. (Routledge 2001).

has been inverted, we remain trapped within a conflictual opposition. No real structural change has been made that would allow politics in Northern Ireland to break free from oppositional modes of thinking. This is particularly true in respect of dealing with the past, where the antinomies of victim and perpetrator, and acknowledgement and denial, continue to dominate the debate. The fact that the violence of law cannot be transcended raises further questions for transitional justice. In particular, if law is the means by which justice is to be achieved, how can we avoid justice being tainted by the violence of the law? Does this element of mutual contamination between violence and law make justice impossible to achieve? These questions are explored in the following chapter, which examines the way in which the hierarchy has reasserted itself and how we might step outside the opposition in Northern Ireland.

Chapter 6

Justice

In its relatively short history, transitional justice as a field of inquiry has generated an impressive body of literature assessing, in abstract terms at least, the meaning of 'justice' in transition. From the early years that were dominated by the criminal justice response and the 'duty to prosecute',[1] through the introduction of the concept of 'truth as justice',[2] and via the 'local versus global' debates,[3] a range of different claims have been made in respect of how justice is to be both defined and achieved in the aftermath of violent conflict. And yet nobody is claiming to have found the one correct answer. While a range of transitional justice mechanisms are deemed 'necessary' steps towards dealing with a conflicted past, no one mechanism has yet managed to achieve the elusive goal of being the embodiment of justice. 'Justice' remains an essentially contested concept, despite the attention that has been paid to its pursuit in recent decades.

However, notwithstanding the absence of an agreed definition of justice, there has been considerable work undertaken in law and policy aimed at defining what justice might entail in transition. On a conceptual level, the meaning of 'justice' in transition has two aspects. The first is backward-looking accountability for abuses of the past. The second is the forward-looking guarantee of non-recurrence. The second aspect is guaranteed by the first. By ensuring accountability for the past, a new and more just future will be guaranteed.[4] Seen in these terms, justice is the goal towards which law and legal reform is oriented. It has also been treated as a concept with fixed meaning, whose achievement can be measured and evaluated.[5] The previous two chapters have explored in detail the relationship between violence

1 Diane Orentlicher, 'Settling Accounts: The Duty to Prosecute Human Rights Violations of Prior Regimes' (1991) 100 *Yale Law Journal* 2539.

2 Bronwyn Leebaw, 'The Irreconcilable Goals of Transitional Justice' (2008) 30 *Human Rights Quarterly* 95.

3 Kieran McEvoy and Lorna McGregor (eds), *Transitional Justice From Below: Grassroots Activism and the Struggle for Change* (Hart 2008).

4 United Nations, 'Report of the Secretary General on the Rule of Law and Transitional Justice in Conflict and Post Conflict Societies' (UN Doc. S/2004/616, United Nations 2004).

5 For discussion see Geoff Dancy, 'Impact Assessment, not Evaluation: Defining a Limited Role for Positivism in the Study of Transitional Justice' (2010) 4 *International Journal of Transitional Justice* 355.

and law that characterises transitional contexts. This chapter now seeks to explore the relationship between law and justice. This relationship is central to any analysis of transitional justice, but is one that has been largely overlooked in the literature. It will be suggested that, rather than interrogating the relationship *between* law and justice, transitional justice literature tends to equate justice *with* law. This is visible in the assumption upon which much policy and practice in the field is premised, namely that the outcome of legal reform will be justice.[6] This is the basic foundation on which the field of transitional justice is constructed. However, it also reflects the binary nature of transitional justice and the desire for determinate and present outcomes that a deconstructive reading seeks to destabilise.

Derrida's deconstruction of the relationship between law and justice provides valuable insight into the limitations of viewing justice as a determinate outcome to be achieved through law. Drawing primarily on his work in 'Force of Law', this chapter seeks to problematise the over-reliance on law as a means of both defining and pursuing justice. In so doing, it seeks to shed light on one of the most intractable problems that punctuates the 'transition' in Northern Ireland, namely the question of 'the Past'. The idea that we need to 'deal with the past' is one that is gaining traction. Whereas it was once seen as a specifically Republican political strategy,[7] there is now more widespread acknowledgement that some form of reckoning is required in order for Northern Ireland to move forward.[8] However, the purpose of such an exercise, and the terms on which it should be approached, remain sharply contested.[9] Reading justice through Derrida's deconstruction of law sheds new light on this debate. The previous two chapters have illustrated the immanence of violence to law. If justice is equated with law, then it stands to reason that justice will also then be contaminated by the violence of the law. This chapter therefore builds on the analysis of the violence of law presented in the previous two chapters to explore the implications of equating justice with law. It suggests that 'law as justice' keeps transitional justice trapped within an oppositional logic. It is only by recognising the violence of law, and resisting the urge towards closure, that justice, in a Derridean sense, becomes a possibility.

This chapter is divided into two sections. Section 6.1 provides a brief overview of key claims in respect to the relationship between law and justice in transition. It outlines the emergence of a new normative concept of the right to truth that underpins a range of transitional justice mechanisms. Using Northern Ireland as

6 See Ruti Teitel, *Transitional Justice* (Oxford University Press 2000).

7 See Bill Rolston, 'Dealing with the Past: Pro-State Paramilitaries, Truth and Transition in Northern Ireland' (2006) 28 *Human Rights Quarterly* 652; Patricia Lundy and Mark McGovern, 'A Trojan Horse? Unionism, Trust and Truth-Telling in Northern Ireland' (2008) 2 *International Journal of Transitional Justice* 42.

8 See the Stormont House Agreement 2014, in which all parties signed up to proposals for dealing with the past. This is discussed in more detail in section 6.2 below.

9 See most recently Sinn Fein's rejection of government proposals. V Kearney, 'Proposed Legislation on Past Unworkable, Says Sinn Féin' (BBC News Northern Ireland, 8 October 2015) www.bbc.co.uk/news/uk-northern-ireland-34481123, accessed 8 October 2015.

an example, the section considers the way in which truth has come to be linked to justice in transition, outlining the key component elements of truth and the way in which they are to be achieved in transitional contexts. It therefore highlights the connection made in law and policy between institutional mechanisms for dealing with the past and justice, and demonstrates the reliance placed on law as a means of achieving justice. Section 6.2 considers how deconstruction of the relationship between law and justice can contribute to our understanding of the possibility of transitional justice. It first examines the dominance of law in framing the debate over dealing with the past, suggesting that the debate remains trapped within an oppositional structure. The oppositional nature of the debate makes it contentious and perpetuates division over the purpose to be served by addressing the past. The section then moves on to address the distinction that Derrida draws between law and justice. It explores in detail Derrida's conception of justice, illustrating it with reference to transitional justice and the debate over dealing with the past in Northern Ireland. Finally, the chapter concludes by considering what Derrida's conception of justice 'to come' can contribute to our understanding of justice, and how ultimately it may provide a means of breaking free from the oppositional structure of law that has characterised the 'transition' in Northern Ireland to date.

6.1 What is transitional 'justice'?

Mapping an understanding of 'justice' in transition has been comparatively simplified in recent years. In the past such an exercise required a detailed review of the bodies of literature pertaining to, for example, criminal justice, truth recovery and victims, to name but a few, and an attempt to distil normative claims of general application from those.[10] However, the codification in recent years of the foundational principles of transitional justice has made this task much easier. As discussed in Chapter 2, the effect of the recent push towards codifying transitional justice in expert reports and toolkits has been to institute a significant new body of law and policy that brings together, in one coherent framework, the requirements of transitional justice.[11] As 'justice' constitutes the *logos* of this endeavour, it is therefore possible to trace, through analysis of this newly instituted framework, the perceived relationship between law, as the *means*, and justice, as the *end*, of transitional justice.[12]

The institution of a common definition of justice is significant not only in terms of international law, but also because of the influence that international norms

10 See Christine Bell, *Lex Pacificatoria: The Law of the Peacemaker* (Oxford University Press 2006) on the potential for drawing conclusions of general application.

11 See, most prominently, the updated Secretary General's Report. United Nations, 'The Rule of Law and Transitional Justice in Conflict and Post Conflict Societies: Report of the Secretary General to the Security Council' (UN Doc. S/2011/634, United Nations 2011).

12 It is of course acknowledged that there are many and various interpretations of 'justice' in this context, but this, it is suggested, is the dominant discourse, which is the subject of the current deconstruction. See Chapter 2 for more detailed discussion.

exert on domestic transitions. As discussed in Chapter 5, domestic transitions will be framed with reference to international standards. Demands in respect of transitional justice are buttressed by appeals to the higher authority of international law.[13] Further, governments can be called to account for their failure to adequately implement these international standards. Legal normativity is therefore a very powerful political weapon in post-conflict politics. Once particular rights in respect of transitional justice have achieved the status of law, they then become the subject of analysis in terms of whether or not the particular 'right' has been vindicated. The existence of this framework is therefore evident not only as abstract principles in international law and policy, but also in practice in how claims in respect of dealing with the past are articulated and evaluated in domestic contexts. In Northern Ireland, the question of how to deal with past violations and abuses is not commonly discussed in terms of 'transitional justice'. Rather it is the language of 'dealing with the past' that dominates political discourse.[14] However, while the terms of description may vary, the content of the debate is dominated by the architecture of transitional justice.[15] As discussed in Chapter 5, the language of transition is a relatively new import into law and politics in Northern Ireland. Absent from the Belfast Agreement 1998 itself, the terms transitional justice and also 'truth recovery' have gradually entered the legal landscape through the work of academics and NGOs that have helped to shape the debate in this area.[16] This has helped to focus the debate over what, if anything, should be done to address the legacy of the past. In this regard, the debate on dealing with the past that continues in Northern Ireland exemplifies the way in which the international framework on justice in transition founds and shapes domestic interactions. The next section will therefore discuss how justice has been defined in international law and policy, and how this definition has shaped approaches to dealing with the past in Northern Ireland.

6.1.1 How is 'justice' defined?

The Report of the Secretary General on the Rule of Law and Transitional Justice in Conflict and Post-Conflict Societies (the Report), which has underpinned much of the expansion of the field of transitional justice, explicitly articulates

13 See, for example, Amnesty International, *Northern Ireland: Time to Deal with the Past* (Belfast, 2013), which highlights the binding nature of international law and standards on the UK government. This is discussed in more detail in section 6.1.2 below.

14 However, see the recent Northern Ireland Human Rights Commission (NIHRC) report advocating a 'transitional justice approach' that suggests an attempt to mainstream the language of transitional justice into dealing with the past debate. Northern Ireland Human Rights Commission, *Dealing with Northern Ireland's Past: Towards a Transitional Justice Approach* (Belfast, 2013).

15 Kieran McEvoy, 'Making Peace with the Past: Options for Truth Recovery Regarding the Conflict In and About Northern Ireland' (Healing Through Remembering 2006); Amnesty International (n. 13).

16 This alliance is common in transitional societies. See Jelena Obradović-Wochnik, 'The "Silent Dilemma" of Transitional Justice: Silencing and Coming to Terms with the Past in Serbia' (2013) 7 *International Journal of Transitional Justice* 328.

a 'common language for justice' that underpins the United Nations' activities in the field of transitional justice. The definition provided casts justice as 'an ideal of accountability and fairness in the protection and vindication of rights and the prevention and punishment of wrongs'.[17] The way in which this is to be achieved is explicitly linked to the protection of individual rights, as articulated in both procedural and substantive terms in international law. This linking of justice with rights reveals a clear, causal connection between law (in the form of human rights law) and the justice that is sought. This connection between law and justice has also developed with specific reference to the exigencies of justice in transition.[18] While the emphasis on accountability and the vindication of rights already speaks to a legalistic approach to justice, the content of the law has also evolved significantly to encompass the particular context of transition. In this way, as discussed in Chapter 5, the law provides a common language in which demands in respect of transitional justice can be made. Most notably for current purposes, an updated version of the Report, published in 2011, highlighted how the 'normative framework supporting transitional justice' had been strengthened[19] and now includes a 'right to justice, truth and guarantees of non-recurrence'.[20] The most notable development in this context is the evolution of a 'right to truth' that acts as a focal point for the pursuit of justice.[21] The emergence of this particular legal construct brings increased coherence to the debate over how to achieve 'justice' in transition. Linked both to the duty to investigate (sometimes referred to as the right to justice) and to the right to an effective remedy, the right to truth is a central link in the 'justice' chain.[22] It provides a more clearly articulated basis from which both theory and activism can proceed.[23] The dominance of this particular model of

17 Secretary General's Report 2011 (n. 11) para. 7.

18 For more detailed discussion, see Chapter 2.

19 Secretary General's Report 2011 (n. 11) para. 17.

20 Ibid. para. 19.

21 The 'Right to Truth' was recognised by the Human Rights Council in 2005. UN Commission on Human Rights, Human Rights Resolution 2005/66: Right to the Truth (E/CN.4/RES/2005/66, United Nations 2005). It was further characterised as an inalienable and autonomous right in 'Report of the Office of the High Commissioner for Human Rights, Implementation of General Assembly Resolution 60/251 Entitled Human Rights Council' (UN Doc. A/HRC/5/7, United Nations 2007). For more detail on the origins of this right, see Eduardo González and Howard Varney (eds), *Truth Seeking: Elements of Creating an Effective Truth Commission* (International Center for Transitional Justice 2013).

22 According to the Office of the High Commissioner for Human Rights, 'From the conceptual viewpoint, this right therefore occupies a central and fundamental position in action to combat impunity and in the quest for justice.' United Nations (n. 21) para. 3.

23 The seminal work in this regard is that of Priscilla Hayner. Hayner first documented the work of truth commissions internationally, before bringing her findings together into a coherent conceptual framework for analysing the contribution of truth to justice in transition. This conceptual framework then allowed for the construction of a normative regime, and continues to underpin work in both theory and practice. Priscilla Hayner, 'Fifteen Truth Commissions – 1974–1994' (1994) 16 *Human Rights Quarterly* 597.

justice is evident in the way in which it has come to frame the debate over dealing with the past in Northern Ireland.

The right to truth is regarded as an autonomous and imprescriptible right of victims of human rights abuse.[24] As such, it places a legal obligation on the state to ensure that the right is vindicated.[25] There are a number of different justifications given for placing obligations on states in respect of truth. These include the suggestion that truth is necessary for the consolidation of peace or for achieving reconciliation, which are often cited as the basis for establishing a truth commission in the aftermath of conflict.[26] Truth, it is argued, can help to establish facts and promote accountability,[27] thereby contributing to the establishment of a credible historical record. It can ensure that victims' needs are met, and contribute to justice, thereby preventing recurrence of the abuse.[28] It is therefore a central pillar of the framework of transitional justice. This centrality is evident in the Northern Ireland context where reports by NGOs continue to highlight the role that truth-telling plays in dealing with the past. In 2006, in a report that pre-dates the articulation by the UN of a 'right to truth', the cross-community initiative Healing Through Remembering published a range of different options for dealing with the past.[29] Each of these was rooted in a different vision of 'truth' and the role that it could play. This report, as the first of its kind, was influential in opening up the debate over what 'truth' entailed in Northern Ireland's transition, but also in making the statement that truth was important. This was again highlighted by the Consultative Group on the Past (CGP), established by the government in 2007 to consult on how best to deal with the past. In its report, published in 2009, the CGP emphasised that truth was 'crucial to the prospect of reconciliation'.[30] Most recently, a report by Amnesty International, published in 2014, has again highlighted the importance of truth as an 'essential element of the duty to investigate human rights violations'.[31] Truth therefore underpins calls to deal with the past in Northern Ireland.

In the transitional context, the right to truth has been interpreted as including a number of different composite elements, all of which may contribute to justice in the aftermath of conflict. The first of these is the right to an investigation. This is an essential aspect of being able to secure access to justice and ensure that victims,

24 United Nations, 'Updated Set of Principles for the Protection and Promotion of Human Rights Through Action to Combat Impunity (UN Doc. E/CN.4/2005/102/Add.1, United Nations 2005).

25 Ibid.

26 UN Commission on Human Rights Resolution 2005/66 (n. 21).

27 Secretary General's Report 2011 (n. 11).

28 For the most detailed account of claims made in respect of truth-seeking in transition, see Priscilla Hayner, *Unspeakable Truths: Transitional Justice and the Challenge of Truth Commissions* (Routledge 2010).

29 McEvoy (n. 15).

30 Consultative Group on the Past, 'Report of the Consultative Group on the Past' (HC 2009–10, UK Parliament 2009) 25, http://cain.ulst.ac.uk/victims/docs/consultative_group/cgp_230109_report.pdf, accessed 17 November 2015 (hereinafter 'CGP').

31 Amnesty International (n. 13).

and society at large, have access to the relevant information necessary to pursue the truth about the violations that they have suffered. The most notable development in this regard is the elaboration by the ECHR in the context of Article 2 of a procedural element of the right to life, which places an obligation on the state to conduct an effective investigation into any death that occurs as a result of the use of force by the state. The development of this procedural requirement has been driven largely as a result of cases emanating from Northern Ireland, in which the actions of the state in respect to the lethal use of force have been challenged.[32] In this regard, Article 2 of the ECHR has provided a pivotal reference point from which claims in respect of accountability for past deaths resulting from state action can proceed.[33] The procedural element of the right to life under Article 2 has been interpreted as requiring that the investigation be independent,[34] its findings must be made publicly available[35] and it must be effective in determining responsibility for the death.[36] Therefore, on a fundamental level the right to an investigation engages the right of victims to know what happened. It also speaks to the need to ensure that victims have effective access to justice in order to pursue their cases. This right to an investigation, and access to justice, forms part of the long-established 'right to an effective remedy', defined as 'equal and effective access to justice', as well as access to information concerning violations, and adequate, effective and prompt reparation for harm suffered.[37] The existence of such rights for victims places a corresponding duty on the state to ensure that the laws and procedures are in place to meet those requirements.[38]

From a transitional justice perspective, it has been argued that the incorporation of the provisions of the ECHR, including Article 2, into domestic law in the UK through the Human Rights Act 1998 brought with it a particular responsibility in respect of facilitating Northern Ireland's transition from conflict to peace.[39] Termed a 'litigation strategy',[40] effective use has been made of the jurisprudence

32 The procedural aspect of Art. 2 was first set out in the case of *McKerr v United Kingdom* [2002] 34 EHRR 20.

33 Marny Requa and Gordon Anthony, 'Coroners, Controversial Deaths, and Northern Ireland's Past Conflict' [2008] *Public Law* 443, 444.

34 *Jordan v United Kingdom* [2003] EHRR 2; *McKerr v United Kingdom* [2002] 34 EHRR 20; *Kelly v United Kingdom* App, no. 17579/90 (ECHR, 4 May 2001).

35 *Kaya v Turkey* [1998] 28 EHRR 1.

36 *McCann, Farrell and Savage v United Kingdom* [1996] 21 EHRR 97.

37 United Nations, 'Basic Principles and Guidelines on the Right to a Remedy and Reparation for Victims of Gross Violations of International Human Rights Law and Serious Violations of International Humanitarian Law': GA Res. 60/147 (UN Doc. A/RES/60/147, United Nations 2006) para. 11 (hereinafter 'Guidelines').

38 The existence of these obligations is confirmed in the Guidelines (ibid.). The scope of the obligation includes the duty to 'investigate violations effectively, promptly, thoroughly and impartially'. Ibid. para. 3b.

39 Christine Bell and Johanna Keenan, 'Lost on the Way Home? The Right to Life in Northern Ireland' (2005) 32(1) *Journal of Law and Society* 68.

40 Ibid.

of the ECHR in respect of the procedural obligation contained in Article 2 to put pressure on the state to reform key structures within the criminal justice system.[41] In particular, the requirement of an effective investigation has been interpreted as holding at least the possibility of redressing the previous difficulties in countering arguments on the part of the state that its use of force was legitimate.[42] It therefore redresses past illegitimacy through a programme of 'legal institutional transformation', encompassing the structures of policing and criminal justice.[43]

The final link in the justice chain is the right to reparation. According to the UN Guidelines, reparations are intended to 'promote justice by redressing gross violations of international human rights law'.[44] Reparation is a broadly defined concept in transitional justice and includes aspects of restitution, compensation, rehabilitation, satisfaction and guarantees of non-recurrence.[45] It requires not only the verification of facts, but also full public disclosure of the truth of what happened. As a result of this broad and holistic definition of reparation, it has been held to encompass less legal and more social outcomes, such as the preservation of historical memory, for example, or the provision of social and health services aimed at social rehabilitation in the wake of human rights abuse. However, of particular note in this context is the guarantee of non-recurrence that requires the review and reform of law so as to prevent future conflict. In the Northern Ireland context, Amnesty International emphasised how establishing the truth about the past will make it 'less likely that past violations and abuses would be repeated'.[46] This guarantee of non-recurrence in many ways is the underpinning foundation of the right to truth, and provides a legitimating discourse. 'Truth' is the way in which the future is insured against a recurrence of the past.

This comprehensive institution of a law and policy of transitional justice, evidenced in the increasing body of international law and its application in the domestic context, brings claims in respect of accountability and reparation within the scope of the legal framework.[47] This lends them the authority of law and legitimates them as demands in a transitional context. As Subotić suggests, transitional justice advocacy relies on a 'legalistic frame to portray [its] claims as universally objective and uncontroversial because [it relies] on human rights standards'.[48] They are no longer simply political or moral demands, but are rather a source of international legal obligation on the part of the state.[49] This provides a crucial focal point for advocacy and campaigning in respect of

41 In particular: coronial law; police ombudsman; inquiries.

42 Bell and Keenan (n. 39) 73.

43 Ibid. 70.

44 Guidelines (n. 37) 15.

45 For more detailed definitions of each of these elements, see ibid. paras 15–23.

46 Amnesty International (n. 13) 15.

47 See Jelena Subotić, 'The Transformation of International Transitional Justice Advocacy' (2012) 6 *International Journal of Transitional Justice* 106.

48 Ibid. 118.

49 Guidelines (n. 37).

accountability for the past.[50] Further, in addition to the articulation of the substantive content of justice in transition, international law increasingly provides a clear framework for achieving those requirements. This is evidenced in the menu of options available to states for dealing with the past. The next section will discuss how the existence of this menu of options is reflected in debate in Northern Ireland, and the effect that it has had on the articulation of political claims in respect of the past.

6.1.2 How is 'justice' achieved?

Chapter 2 discussed how, in transitional justice, theory has often followed practice. The establishment of trials and truth commissions did not arise at first as a result of a normative framework for transition that included the 'right to truth'.[51] Rather, claims for normativity in respect of truth have followed from the experiences of transitional societies that have established such mechanisms.[52] The two now dovetail, with a range of institutional options available for the pursuit of justice. These centre primarily on the requirement of an effective investigation into abuses. As suggested, there is no one institutional mechanism that is regarded as being *the* correct way to achieve truth and justice in transition. However, just as the various requirements of truth and justice have been elaborated in a more or less coherent legal framework, there is now also broad convergence of opinion over the ways in which the rights themselves can be addressed.

There are a number of well-established mechanisms that have been used and promoted internationally as a means of meeting transitional justice requirements, as demonstrated by the 'toolkits' that provide practical guides to these mechanisms, including prosecutions, truth commissions, vetting and reparations.[53] These mechanisms are also reflected in the debate over dealing with the past in Northern Ireland. Termed the 'landscape of legal processes' by the CGP,[54] there are a range of mechanisms that already exist, and a number that do not currently exist but whose establishment now appears imminent.[55] What is striking, however, is that this 'landscape' identified by the CGP is largely reflective of the *visible* debate over dealing with the past.[56]

50 For a detailed analysis of how the international law framework has shaped domestic advocacy, see Subotić (n. 47).

51 See Ruti Teitel, 'Transitional Justice Genealogy' (2003) 16 *Harvard Human Rights Law Journal* 69 on the origins of these mechanisms and their place within the conceptual and legal development of transitional justice.

52 Hayner (n. 23).

53 For discussion, see Chapter 2.2.

54 CGP (n. 30) 106.

55 Stormont House Agreement (n. 8).

56 It is also largely consistent with the international 'package' composed of truth, justice and reparations. See Subotić (n. 47) 120.

These mechanisms form the common basis of analysis presented in NGO reports and academic commentary on the subject of dealing with the past.[57] As such there is a clearly demarcated intellectual space within which the debate over dealing with the past is being conducted. This debate occurs within the 'theatrical space' created by the international model of transitional justice.[58] The existence of legal obligations that are regarded as 'imprescriptible' rights and guaranteed as a matter of international law serve to 'insure' claims in respect of the need to deal with the past in the domestic context.[59] This is a good example of the displacement of political questions into the legal realm, where particular claims can be 'insured' with reference to the higher authority of international law, thereby guaranteeing their status as legal obligation in the domestic transitional context. It is also another example of the way in which 'normative' understandings of human rights have subordinated 'political' understandings.[60]

In 2015 there were significant developments in relation to dealing with the past in Northern Ireland. In December 2014 the main political parties reached agreement on, among other issues, the creation of a number of bodies to address the legacy of the past.[61] The Stormont House Agreement (SHA) has effectively moved the debate from disagreement over whether there should be any form of reckoning with the past on to the terrain of the detail of how it should be addressed.[62] This agreement is explicitly framed as contributing towards the 'transition to long term peace and stability'[63] and attempts to create a more holistic process for dealing with the past to replace the piecemeal approach that has dominated efforts to date.[64] It has also made the prospect of progress on the past a more immediate reality, in that a commitment has been made that the legacy mechanisms

57 See, for example, Kieran McEvoy and Louise Mallinder, 'Truth, Amnesty and Prosecutions: Models for Dealing with the Past': 2nd Submission to Haas-O'Sullivan Talks (Belfast, 2013). The authors were asked to provide a report on applicable 'models' to be considered.

58 Jacques Derrida, *On Cosmopolitanism and Forgiveness*, Mark Dooley and Michael Hughes tr. (Routledge 2001). See also Subotić (n. 47).

59 Jacques Derrida, 'Force of Law: The Mystical Foundation of Authority' in Drucilla Cornell *et al.* (eds), *Deconstruction and the Possibility of Justice* (Routledge 1992) (hereinafter 'Force of Law') on 'insuring' international law in this context is used to insure the role of law against challenges either in respect of its origin or its dominant interpretation.

60 This is equally true in both the international and domestic contexts. Dube highlights how the emphasis on the 'packaged' version of justice 'has ostracized those who harbor different feelings, emotions, views and perspectives on transitional justice'. Siphwe Ignatius Dube, 'Transitional Justice Beyond the Normative: Towards a Literary Theory of Political Transitions' (2011) 5 *International Journal of Transitional Justice* 177, 183.

61 Stormont House Agreement (n. 8).

62 See Committee on the Administration of Justice, 'Dealing with the Past in Northern Ireland: Implementing the Stormont House Agreement' (2015) Conference Report and Papers www.caj.org.uk/contents/1289, accessed 9 March 2016.

63 Stormont House Agreement (n. 8) 21.

64 See Christine Bell, 'Dealing With the Past in Northern Ireland' (2002) 26 *Fordham International Law Journal* 1095 on the 'piecemeal' approach to dealing with the past. This term has come to be the accepted shorthand for the failure to adequately deal with the past to date.

envisaged by the SHA will be created by 2016, and that their work will be completed within five years of that date. The SHA reflects two distinct aspects of truth recovery – namely the pursuit of factual or 'forensic' truth, reflected in the commitment to facilitating the pursuit of justice and information recovery in a manner that is human rights compliant,[65] as well as addressing the more broadly defined goal of 'narrative' truth reflected in the commitment to promote reconciliation and acknowledge and address the suffering of victims and survivors.[66] To this end, the SHA makes a commitment to establish four separate legacy mechanisms for dealing with the past. These can be divided roughly along the individual/collective axis of those pursuing forensic truth, namely the investigation of historic cases with a view to providing information to victims and their families, and those that are oriented towards the narrative function of truth, in terms of broader social benefit.

The first of these legacy mechanisms to address forensic truth is a Historical Investigations Unit (HIU). The primary purpose of this unit will be to 'take forward investigations into outstanding Troubles-related deaths'.[67] This mechanism is most closely associated with criminal justice and with the human rights obligations of the state in terms of conducting effective investigations into controversial deaths. If established, it will replace the range of mechanisms that currently exist to comply with the Article 2 ECHR obligations.[68] The existing package of measures includes public inquiries,[69] investigations by the Police Ombudsman and ongoing criminal investigations of historic cases by the Historical Enquiries Team (HET) of the Police Service of Northern Ireland (PSNI).[70] The purpose of this unit is first and foremost to investigate historic cases and to bring new prosecutions where evidence allows.[71] The work of the HIU will be complemented by an Independent Commission for Information Retrieval (ICIR).[72] The purpose of this body will be to 'enable victims and survivors to seek and privately receive information about the (Troubles-related) deaths of their next of kin'.[73] This body

65 Stormont House Agreement (n. 8) 21. There is also specific commitment that the approach to dealing with the past will be balanced, proportionate, transparent, fair and equitable.

66 In drawing this distinction between two different aspects of truth recovery, I draw on the work of McEvoy (n. 15) in mapping the different approaches to truth.

67 Stormont House Agreement (n. 8) 30.

68 With the exception of legacy inquests, which will continue to operate as a separate process to the HIU. Ibid. 31. For discussion of the role and significance of inquests, see Requa and Anthony (n. 33).

69 See Marny Requa, 'Keeping Up with Strasbourg: Article 2 Obligations and Northern Ireland's Pending Inquests' [2012] 4 *Public Law* 610 on how these meet transitional justice requirements.

70 The Stormont House Agreement (n. 8) 34 provides that the Historical Investigations Unit will consider all cases in respect of which the Historical Inquiries Team and the Police Ombudsman NI have not completed their work, including HET cases which have already been identified as requiring re-examination.

71 Ibid. 35. The decision whether to prosecute or not lies with the Director of Public Prosecutions.

72 This model builds on the existing Independent Commission on the Location of Victim's Remains that allows information on the whereabouts of the 'disappeared' to be passed to the authorities in confidence.

73 Stormont House Agreement (n. 8) 41.

will remain entirely separate from the justice system[74] and information passed to it will not be admissible in criminal or civil proceedings.[75] For victims, this means that while they may be provided with information by this body, that information alone will not lead to a prosecution. While this may appear to compromise justice for victims, it is nevertheless an important feature in light of the aim of the Commission to retrieve information that might not be forthcoming where a threat of criminal or civil proceedings remains.[76] While information provided in this context cannot be passed on to the HIU and will not contribute towards the pursuit of criminal justice, the Commission nevertheless contributes towards truth recovery through the collection of information that can be passed to victims, thereby satisfying the needs of victims to know what happened to their loved ones and why.[77] Information received by the ICIR may also contribute to thematic analysis of the conflict, thereby also contributing to broader narrative goals. These two bodies specifically address the need to investigate past crimes and to provide as much information as possible to victims. As such they are victim-centred and individually oriented.

The other two bodies address more explicitly the social function of truth recovery. The first of these is an oral history archive that will 'provide a central place for people from all backgrounds ... to share experiences and narratives related to the Troubles'.[78] The value of oral history projects is well recognised in transitional justice scholarship, and indeed a number of such projects already operate in Northern Ireland.[79] The key contribution that such a body makes to truth and dealing with the past is in providing a forum for victims and survivors to have their story heard. It thus speaks clearly to the overarching principle of acknowledging and addressing the suffering of victims and survivors. Such an archive potentially broadens the pursuit of truth beyond individual cases and refocuses attention on broader social and personal issues. It is also an important source of information from which the proposed Implementation and Reconciliation Group (IRG) will draw. This group is to be established to 'oversee themes, archives and information recovery'.[80] Information may be drawn from

74 Ibid. 45.

75 Ibid. 46. The Commission would also be exempted from judicial review, freedom of information, Data Protection and National Archives legislation in both the UK and Ireland as a means of safeguarding the confidentiality of the process. Ibid. 47.

76 While information provided to the ICIR will be inadmissible in criminal or civil proceedings, the simple act of providing information to the ICIR does not guarantee immunity from suit, nor does it constitute an amnesty for those providing information. Where evidence or information comes to light from other sources, such as an HIU investigation, the individual may still face prosecution. Ibid. 49.

77 This in itself is an important goal of truth recovery in transitional justice. See Hayner (n. 28).

78 Stormont House Agreement (n. 8) 22.

79 Ardoyne Commemoration Project, *Ardoyne: The Untold Truth* (Belfast, 2002). For analysis of such participatory processes, see Patricia Lundy and Mark McGovern, 'Whose Justice: Rethinking Transitional Justice from the Bottom Up' (2008) 35 *Journal of Law and Society* 265.

80 Stormont House Agreement (n. 8) 51.

any of the legacy mechanisms, and the function of this body will be to oversee the production of a thematic report or reports that highlight key themes and patterns emerging from the other legacy mechanisms. This body is the one explicitly charged with 'contribut[ing] to reconciliation, better understanding of the past and reducing sectarianism'.[81] Its function is therefore the production of the narrative truths of the conflict, contributing to the overarching goal of justice through truth, acknowledgement and reconciliation. Expressly noted in the context of the work of the IRG is the fact that the 'UK and Irish governments will consider statements of acknowledgement'.[82]

What unites the different options proposed by different bodies is the influence that law exerts on their design. The requirements of justice in transition are determined by reference to legal rules and standards, which in turn constrain what is and is not considered to be a legitimate response to past conflict.[83] This is summed up in the assertion that any initiative to deal with the past must be 'human rights compliant'.[84] Arguably this approach follows naturally from the conceptualisation of transitional justice that has cast law not only as a means of achieving justice, but also as incorporating values of justice.[85] In the context of entrenched social conflict, the model of transitional justice intentionally attempts to displace difficult political issues, such as dealing with the past, from the realm of politics and into the realm of law as a means of depoliticising truth and justice.[86] The aim of this strategy is to provide objective standards that can frame the debate, thereby keeping it within the parameters of law and away from physical violence. This is done with reference to the overarching *logos* of justice, a transcendental, or natural, standard which is to be achieved through legal means. The risk with this approach, however, is that it reduces the pursuit of justice in transition to a calculation where efforts are concentrated on ensuring that initiatives comply with law and with legal standards, rather than on deeper inquiry as to what justice really means.[87] Deconstructive reading begins to destabilise the certainties associated with the determinate 'means' and 'ends' of law and justice. Derrida suggests that the concepts of law and justice cannot be regarded as fully distinct from each other.[88] For Derrida, justice does not exist as an objective or transcendent standard that can

81 Ibid. 52.

82 Ibid. 53.

83 For example, the 2006 Healing Through Remembering Report (n. 15) included the option of 'Drawing a Line Under the Past'. This option has ceased to appear in policy documents on the past, and in fact now represents the excluded 'other' of the dealing with the past debate, in that it is no longer considered a legitimate option.

84 Stormont House Agreement (n. 8).

85 Teitel (n. 6) (see Chapter 2.1 for discussion). In the context of truth recovery, see Leebaw (n. 2).

86 Teitel (n. 6), as discussed in Chapter 2.1.

87 See Alejandro Castillejo-Cuéllar, 'Historical Injuries, Temporality and the Law: Articulations of a Violent Past in Two Transitional Scenarios' (2014) 25 *Law and Critique* 47.

88 Indeed, he states that 'Everything would be simple if this distinction between justice and *droit* were a true distinction, an opposition whose functioning was logically regulated and permitted mastery'. 'Force of Law' (n. 59) 22.

be achieved through law.[89] But nor is justice the same thing as law. Rather, the two exist in a relationship of interdependence. In 'Force of Law', Derrida identifies how law, or 'right', 'claims to exercise itself in the name of justice, and that justice is required to establish itself in the name of a law that must be "enforced"'.[90] It is this interrelationship between law and justice that both opens up the possibility of deconstruction and makes it necessary.[91] Crucially, what deconstruction reveals is the way in which equating justice with law undermines the possibility of justice. If law is violent, then treating justice as the same as law will inscribe the same oppositional structure into the concept of justice.

Central to calls for truth recovery in transitional contexts is the rationale that truth will lead to a shared understanding of the conflict that will in turn foster reconciliation and the creation of a new political community.[92] As Bankowski suggests, the project of reconciliation that drives much of the 'truth' work in transitional justice 'assumes that a perfected past can perform reintegration'.[93] This is rooted in a linearity whereby a conflicted past is replaced with a new legal order that in turn guarantees the future.[94] A normative framework of transition therefore sets a specific outcome to be achieved – namely justice.[95] The means by which this is to be achieved is through the vindication of the right to truth, with the attendant calculations and compromises that it entails. Therefore, under this model justice is measured by reference to whether or not law and legal standards pertaining to the right to truth have been properly implemented. This is a linear progression, from violence to law, and ultimately to justice. This can be seen in the way in which Northern Ireland's 'transition' is narrated. In the beginning there was conflict, violence, murder, injustice. This is the contested *past*, the legacy of which transitional justice aims to address. In the case of Northern Ireland, the most commonly accepted temporal scope of the problematic 'past' is the period of the Troubles, dating from 1969 until the Belfast Agreement of 1998.[96] Transitional justice operates in the *present*. In 2015 we grapple with how best to deal with the contested past.

The aim of the various mechanisms proposed in the Stormont House Agreement is to attempt to come to some sort of resolution of the past. This

89 See discussion in Chapter 3.1 on *Différance*.

90 'Force of Law' (n. 59) 22.

91 Ibid.

92 Amnesty International (n. 13); McEvoy (n. 15); Hayner (n. 28).

93 Zenon Bankowski, 'The Risk of Reconciliation' in Scott Veitch (ed.), *Law and the Politics of Reconciliation* (Ashgate 2007) 49.

94 This is the guarantee of non-recurrence that chracterises transitional justice, and the 'forward-looking' element of justice in transition. Teitel (n. 6).

95 Increasingly, justice is being interpreted instrumentally, as a means towards the broader goal of reconciliation and reconstruction. Nevertheless, the pursuit of 'justice' remains significant. See, e.g., Leebaw (n. 2); Dube (n. 60); Subotić (n. 47).

96 Although it should be acknowledged that this 'definition' of the temporal scope of the conflict is in itself a form of violence in that it obliterates broader historic narratives of injustice and dates the existence of 'conflict' only from the emergence of anti-state political violence. See Castillejo-Cuéllar (n. 87).

reflects the foundational assumption of transitional justice that the past must be addressed. Society, it has been suggested, has a 'right to the truth about the past'.[97] Crucially, the purpose of this exercise, the end towards which the means of truth recovery aims, is to arrive at a 'shared understanding' of the past. This involves challenging what are seen as 'obstacles to laying bare the truth'[98] and the 'failure to develop a shared public understanding and recognition of the abuses committed by all sides'.[99] It also places an emphasis on concepts such as acknowledgement and reconciliation as a means of achieving this end.[100] In turn, the goal of achieving a shared public understanding of the conflict is not just an imperative for the present, but also for the *future*. Knowing the truth, it has been suggested, is essential to ensure that lessons can be learned, making it less likely that the past will be repeated.[101] It is thus clear how the debate over dealing with the past is structured along a temporally linear spectrum in which the means of truth are oriented towards a determined end of justice. The next section will consider Derrida's deconstruction of the relationship between law and justice and what it reveals about both the linearity of the model and also the possibility of arriving at a determined end to transition.

6.2 Law and justice

'Force of Law' presents Derrida's first explicit engagement with the relationship between law and justice. Whereas his earlier work had articulated the interplay of violence and law,[102] it was not until 'Force of Law' that he explicitly addressed the implications of this immanence of violence to the law for our understanding of justice. In this regard, the definition of justice is important, because if justice is regarded as the same thing as law, or alternatively if law is viewed as a means to justice, then justice will similarly be tainted by the violence of the law. When seen in this light, 'justice' becomes a problematic endpoint of transition. Law, for Derrida, is 'essentially deconstructible'. As discussed in Chapter 3, a concept is 'essentially deconstructible' where it is founded on interpretable textual strata (i.e. it exists in codified form), or where its ultimate foundation is by definition unfounded.[103] Put simply, deconstruction of law entails interrogating its claims to legality or to legitimacy.[104] This means that we do not accept at face value claims of self-evidence, impartiality or objectivity in transitional justice. Rather, a constantly questioning attitude towards the law must be maintained. Recent

97 Healing Through Remembering, *Dealing with the Past? An Overview of Legal and Political Approaches Relating to the Conflict in and about Northern Ireland* (Belfast, 2013).
98 Amnesty International (n. 13) 5.
99 Ibid. 7.
100 See most notably CGP (n. 30) 54.
101 Amnesty International (n. 13) 15.
102 See Chapter 4.
103 'Force of Law' (n. 59) 14. See Chapter 3 for more detailed discussion.
104 Ibid. For detailed discussion, see Chapter 3 and Chapter 4.

developments in transitional justice at the levels of both scholarship and policy have focused on articulating the relationship between law and justice in transition. The institution of the *logos* of justice into the written text of law and policy in this context therefore makes deconstruction of claims to legitimacy possible. It also reveals the distinction between law and justice that underpins Derrida's understanding of justice. Whereas law for Derrida is 'essentially deconstructible', justice cannot be deconstructed.[105] Rather, the *distinction* between law and justice is what makes deconstruction possible.[106] For Derrida, 'deconstruction takes place in the interval that separates the undeconstructibility of justice from the deconstructibility of [law] (authority, legitimacy etc.)'.[107] Derrida terms this interval in which deconstruction takes place an *aporia* – a brief space in time before a legal decision is made.[108]

For Derrida, justice is not a fixed and quantifiable standard whose achievement can be measured. Justice exists in 'aporetic experiences', in 'moments in which the decision between just and unjust is never insured by a rule'.[109] What does this mean in practice? Where justice is treated as the endpoint of law, it becomes a fixed destination, something towards which law and legal decision-making is oriented. However, while law may be oriented towards justice, to say that the correct interpretation or application of law can achieve justice is a different proposition.[110] Addressing the distinction between law and justice, Derrida suggests that law is a calculation. It is a process whereby an outcome is achieved by reference to existing rules and standards, and the outcome is guaranteed or 'insured' by those rules. It therefore deals in certainties, and the balancing of competing positions with reference to existing rules and conventions. In contrast, a Derridean concept of justice rejects the certainty associated with law in favour of an open-ended approach in which justice is never fully present but remains locked in a continual process of negotiation and renegotiation.[111]

In order to understand this point, it is necessary to return for a moment to Derrida's early work on violence and the construction of meaning. For Derrida, meaning is constructed on the interplay between oppositional concepts that exist in a state of hierarchy.[112] Meaning rests on the ability of one particular concept or interpretation to dominate others. Similarly, the authority of law guarantees the interpretation privileged by law through the act of legal decision-making.

105 However, Derrida distinguishes justice from law: 'nor is it a transcendent standard that exists outside or beyond the law and can as such be achieved through law.' Ibid. 14.

106 Ibid. 15.

107 Ibid. 15.

108 Ibid. 15.

109 Ibid. 16.

110 Derrida states that 'law is the element of calculation; and it is just that there be law, but justice is incalculable'. Ibid. 16.

111 This is the element of deferral that underpins the structure of *différance* upon which all meaning is constructed. Jacques Derrida, *Of Grammatology*, Gayatri Chakravorty Spivak tr. (Johns Hopkins University Press 1976).

112 Ibid. This is the essential structure of *différance* upon which all meaning is constructed.

Whereas prior to the decision being made there may be many competing interpretations of what justice would entail, the act of decision-making privileges one 'dominant' interpretation and violently subordinates and excludes all others. At this moment the exercise of law is reduced to a calculation – to the application of the objective law – and the possibility of justice is thereby lost. Derrida further elaborates on this dynamic with reference to the purported universality of law. He highlights how 'justice, as law, seems always to suppose the generality of a rule, a norm or a universal imperative'.[113] This creates a clear tension between the application of an apparently universal rule and the experience of that rule by the individual. Even where the general rule requires consideration of its effect in singular or individual cases, to act simply in accordance with objective law is not doing justice.[114] Therefore, for Derrida, justice exists in the moment just before the decision is made. In this moment there remains the *possibility* that any of the competing interpretations may be chosen as the correct one. All compete on equal terms, none being able to rely on law to guarantee its dominance. This is the moment in which 'the decision between just and unjust is never insured by a rule'.[115] Once the decision has been made, that possibility disappears. To speak of justice as a *possibility* is therefore to speak of justice as residing in the moment, no matter how brief, before the violence of the law intervenes. This, for Derrida, is the *aporia* in which justice resides, and it is characterised by its openness to the 'other'.[116] Where deconstruction becomes relevant is in how it encourages a relentless pursuit of justice.[117] Law as justice encourages the moment of decision. It prioritises the present certainty of legal determination over the inherent risk of leaving disagreements unresolved.[118] However, deconstruction, rather than accepting dominant or given narratives of what the law is and how it can resolve conflict in an impartial manner, requires ongoing deconstruction of the law itself, to ensure that its dominance does not bury the possibility of justice. For this reason, for Derrida, deconstruction is justice.[119]

Having explained his understanding of justice, Derrida goes on to provide a number of examples of how and where these *aporias* between law and justice arise. For Derrida, it is in these spaces that deconstruction finds its privileged place.[120] Each of these examples, it is suggested, casts light on some of the limitations of relying too heavily on law as a means of ensuring justice in transition. They also provide useful

113 'Force of Law' (n. 59) 17.

114 Ibid.

115 Ibid. 16.

116 Ibid.

117 Derrida suggests that 'constantly to maintain an interrogation of the origin, grounds and limits of our conceptual, theoretical or normative surrounding justice is on deconstruction's part anything but a neutralization of the interests of justice'. Ibid. 20.

118 See Emilios Christodoulidis, 'Truth and Reconciliation and Risks' (2000) 9 *Social and Legal Studies* 179.

119 'Force of Law' (n. 59) 15.

120 Ibid. 21.

tools through which to deconstruct attitudes towards dealing with the past. In the case of Northern Ireland, the debate over dealing with the past is often represented as a clash between those who call for a comprehensive process to investigate the past and those who resist such calls.[121] This is the classic antinomy of 'acknowledgement' versus 'denial' that is characteristic of transitional justice.[122] Because of the dominance of the transitional narrative, and the ability of its advocates to appeal to the higher normative authority of international law to back up their claims, there is a quality of self-evidence about the assertion that an overarching mechanism for dealing with the past is necessary.[123] This is further supported by the fact of the concrete political proposals, soon to achieve legal status, as to how this is to be achieved.[124] The following section will therefore use Derrida's exemplars to illustrate the applicability of deconstruction to the Northern Ireland context.

6.2.1 First aporia: the rule

> '[I]f the act simply consists of applying a rule, of enacting a program or effecting a calculation, we might say that it is legal, that it conforms to law … but we would be wrong to say that the decision was just.'[125]

The first *aporia*, and the most straightforward, builds on the distinction drawn above between law and justice. For Derrida, law is not the same thing as justice. Rather, the ability to distinguish between on the one hand the calculated application of a legal rule and the pursuit of justice on the other is key. The very fact that a right to justice, to truth or to a remedy have been instituted in law and policy makes them 'essentially deconstructible'. This is particularly clear in the context of the instituted definition of justice in transition. As discussed in section 6.1, the right to truth, including the right to justice, has been interpreted as incorporating a number of elements, most of which are also evidenced in practice in the case of Northern Ireland. These include, most notably, efforts at satisfying the procedural requirement of Article 2 ECHR. Given the ongoing pertinence of questions over accountability for state actions during the Troubles, it has been suggested that these cases 'form part of the transitional legal landscape in Northern Ireland' and that 'any response to them must be conceptualised in that frame of reference'.[126]

121 In broad terms this division is drawn along political lines, with nationalists and Republicans more likely to be in favour of 'dealing with the past' than Unionists or Loyalists. For discussion, see Lundy and McGovern (n. 7).

122 Colm Campbell and Fionnuala Ní Aoláin, 'The Paradox of Transitions in Liberal Democracies' (2005) 27 *Human Rights Quarterly* 172.

123 This is the prevailing political and legal context discussed in detail in Chapter 5. See also Jacques Derrida, 'Spectres of Marx' (1994) 15 *New Political Science* 7 on self-evidence.

124 Stormont House Agreement (n. 8).

125 'Force of Law' (n. 59) 23.

126 Fionnuala Ní Aoláin, 'Truth Telling, Accountability and the Right to Life in Northern Ireland' (2002) 5 *European Human Rights Law Review* 572, 573.

Indeed, Article 2 has been used both to frame demands for justice, and also to critique efforts by the state to satisfy its obligations thereunder. This particular debate therefore encapsulates well what Derrida refers to as the 'element of calculation' inherent in the enforcement of law.

As discussed, Article 2 has been used effectively to require the state to engage with the requirements of transitional justice in Northern Ireland. By pursuing a 'litigation strategy', lawyers for the families of those killed by the state during the course of the Troubles have managed to force the state to provide mechanisms for providing information on historic cases.[127] In this regard, Article 2 has been explicitly characterised as requiring transitional justice,[128] in the form of effective investigations and access to justice. It has also managed to move particularly contentious issues, such as collusion between state forces and paramilitary organisations, from the political into the legal realm, thereby making them visible to the law and forcing a response from the state.[129] However, there have also been limitations to this mechanism as a means of 'dealing with the past'. The most pertinent of these, and that which best illustrates Derrida's concern with rules, is that framing 'justice' as a matter of compliance with the requirements of Article 2 has allowed for a technical response to historic cases. This is what Derrida refers to as the 'conservative and reproductive activity of judgment'.[130] Where a legal decision consists of simply applying a generic rule, Derrida highlights how 'we might say it is legal, that it conforms to law ... but we would be wrong to say that the decision was just'.[131] This dynamic has formed the basis of considerable critique of efforts to deal with the past to date in Northern Ireland.

A good example of this reductive capacity of law and legalism is seen in respect of what are known as 'legacy inquests'.[132] Whereas the coronial court has been widely regarded as one among the package of measures designed to ensure Article 2 compliance, and therefore contribute towards the 'right to truth', its potential in respect of historic cases has been significantly curtailed in practice.[133] In 2004 the House of Lords, when asked to rule on whether or not the procedural obligations contained in Article 2 applied to investigations into controversial deaths that occurred before the Human Rights Act came into force in 2000, decided that it did not. This confirmation of the principle of non-retroactivity effectively prevented Article 2 from being used to require new investigation into historic cases, thereby limiting its use as a mechanism for dealing with the past. The principle of non-retroactivity was modified in the 2011 case of *Re McGaughey*, in which the Court confirmed that there might be certain circumstances in which Article 2 may

127 Bell and Keenan (n. 39).

128 Ibid.

129 Ní Aoláin (n. 126).

130 'Force of Law' (n. 59) 23.

131 Ibid. 23.

132 These are inquests into controversial deaths that occurred before the Human Rights Act came into effect in 2000. For discussion, see Requa (n. 69).

133 This fact has been officially acknowledged in the Stormont House Agreement (n. 8) 31.

bind a state in respect of a death that occurred post-2000.[134] Specifically any *new* investigation into a death occurring prior to 2000 must be Article 2-compliant. This ruling led to a number of requests being lodged with the Attorney General for Northern Ireland for inquests to be established.[135] However, the ruling does not apply to all deaths and the decision has caused uncertainty in the respect that is likely to reduce the question of to which cases *McGaughey* applies to an ever more detailed 'calculation' as to what the law requires.[136] The very detailed technical nature of the deliberation on this issue arguably stands at odds with a more holistic approach to dealing with the past, of which inquests are simply one element.

The second example of legalism constraining the pursuit of truth relates to public inquiries. Inquiries have been used as a high-profile mechanism for investigating particularly controversial deaths, including those that occurred on Bloody Sunday. While such inquiries ostensibly fall within the bounds of transitional justice as 'one source of truth among other legalistic mechanisms of transitional justice',[137] there is a strong vein of critique that highlights the risk that the terms of reference upon which inquiries are founded may be unduly restricted, and as such be used by governments to 'deflect criticism and avoid blame'.[138] Seen in this light, where the terms of reference are designed in such a way as to satisfy narrowly defined legal obligations, but do not address broader truth or justice concerns, there is a risk that the inquiry impedes, rather than advances, justice.[139] Similarly the work of the Historical Enquiries Team has been critiqued as falling short of the requirements of Article 2, both procedurally, in terms of how it has conducted its investigations,[140] but also on a broader level in terms of how its approach to securing apologies for families can in fact deny the possibility of justice.[141] Lundy and Rolston highlight the risk that issuing apologies as a result of HET investigations into killings by soldiers may be used by the state to 'insulate itself from further probing that might eventually yield more telling results',[142] and in this way 'establish a narrative of the past that resonates with the state's self image'.[143] They stress that apology

134 Specifically this applies to cases where, although the death occurred before 2000, no effective investigation took place before that date. Such cases are thereby distinguished from those that were investigated prior to 2000, to which Article 2 does not apply. For detailed discussion of the McGaughey decision, see Requa (n. 69).

135 Ibid. 619.

136 Ibid. 619.

137 Ibid. 406.

138 Angela Hegarty, 'The Government of Memory: Public Inquiries and the Limits of Justice in Northern Ireland' (2002) 26 *Fordham International Law Journal* 1148,1159.

139 See Requa (n. 69) for discussion of this dynamic.

140 Patricia Lundy, 'Can the Past be Policed? Lessons from the Historical Enquiries Team in Northern Ireland' (2009) 11 *Journal of Law and Social Challenges* 109.

141 Patricia Lundy and Bill Rolston, 'Redress for Past Harms? Official Apologies in Northern Ireland' (2015) *International Journal of Human Rights* http://dx.doi.org/10.1080/13642987.2015.1050235, accessed 19 October 2015.

142 Ibid. 13.

143 Ibid. 5.

taken alone cannot obviate the need for the state to comply with its human rights obligations, nor be regarded as a sufficient form of reparation.

What unites these critiques is the perceived failure to adequately take into account the specific context created by transitional justice when interpreting the purpose of such bodies. By treating 'justice' as a matter of compliance with law and legal terms of reference, the possibility of deeper transformation is buried. Justice becomes reduced to the calculation of whether or not law has been properly implemented. It also arguably allows the 'emergency' narrative to re-establish itself against that of 'human rights'. Indeed, it has been suggested that this 'context' itself has constrained progress on using Article 2 as a means of addressing cases related to the past. Bell and Keenan suggest that in this case the context of Northern Ireland actually impedes the progressive development of Article 2 because of fear of 'past'-related cases and the risk of opening the floodgates to a large number of historic cases.[144] In addition, and more broadly speaking, the risk of relying too heavily on a normative model of what dealing with the past *should* look like constrains the potential of critique to shape the debate in new directions.[145] What the preceding discussion reveals is that, while there is a robust debate being conducted with respect to the requirements of the law, this engages only a narrow definition of justice.

It has been argued that such mechanisms must be located within the broader framework of transitional justice, making justice a 'consequentialist yardstick' by which they can be judged.[146] A restrictive reading of the requirements of Article 2 effectively prevents it from being used as vehicle for a systemic process for addressing the past. Each of these critiques focuses on the way in which law narrows the terms on how the government will deal with the past.[147] The decision being made is a calculation, a balancing of a calculated and reductive reading of the requirements of the law that protects the interest of the state, and a more expansive reading that would confirm the 'transitional justice' elements of the case. A common criticism that unites them is that, by taking an unduly restrictive approach to investigation of the past, the opportunity is lost to address broader goals of truth recovery. In contrast to this element of calculation, Derrida does not suggest that legal decision-making can be avoided, but rather highlights the responsibility that the judge bears for making 'fresh judgment'. At the heart of this *aporia* is the violence of the law. A decision that consists simply of conformity with the law cannot be justice because the law upon which it rests is itself a moment of violence. Therefore, to justify a legal decision with reference to prior conventions and laws simply defers the possibility of justice.[148] As discussed in

144 Bell and Keenan (n. 39) 82.

145 See, for an example of the limits of normative critique, Aoife Duffy, 'A Truth Commission for Northern Ireland' (2010) 4 *International Journal of Transitional Justice* 26, using human rights law to critique the CGP proposals.

146 Lundy and Rolston (n. 141) 6.

147 For a more general critique of this trend, see Colm Campbell and Catherine Turner, 'Utopia and the Doubters: Truth, Transition and the Law' (2008) 23 *Legal Studies* 374.

148 'Force of Law' (n. 59) 14.

Chapter 4, the moment of founding of all law will be a moment of violence. In this moment, 'in the founding of law or in its institution, the same problem of justice will have been posed and violently resolved'.[149] Therefore, all decisions that are justified or 'insured' by reference to law and specific legal orders will themselves bear that violence.[150] The judge therefore has an obligation to consider the singularity of each case and to be guided by the call for justice, rather than simply the formulaic application of law. This leads us to the second *aporia*, in which Derrida discusses the implications of the violence of law for the possibility of making a just decision.

6.2.2 *Second aporia: 'the ghost of the undecidable'*

> 'Justice as law is never exercised without a decision that *cuts*, that divides.'[151]

This *aporia* follows on from the first, in that it relates to the process through which a legal decision must pass. As outlined above, for Derrida, justice exists in the moment before the decision is made, where an infinite number of possibilities remain. As this moment precedes every legal decision, every decision should therefore pass through this phase of what Derrida terms the 'undecidable'.[152] This undecidability does not consist simply of the balancing of two clearly defined and competing positions. It is not concerned with 'two contradictory and very determinate rules, each equally imperative'.[153] Such form of balancing is simply a calculation in which predetermined rules are applied. Rather, the experience of 'undecidability' refers to the openness to infinite possibilities that exceeds the exercise of calculation. This moment of 'undecidability' itself represents an *aporia* in that it is a fleeting moment before a decision is made, in which there are no set or determinate outcomes. It is a moment in which no one authoritative law can determine what a 'just' outcome would be. The significance of the concept of 'undecidability' therefore lies in the way in which it requires us to remain open to divergent interpretations of justice, and to resist the temptation to shape experiences and testimonies to fit preconceived criteria.

This point is particularly important with respect to the distinction between factual or forensic truth, and the broader goals of acknowledgement and reconciliation that are often promoted as flowing from truth recovery processes.[154] Whereas forensic truth can be pursued on an individual or case-by-case basis, acknowledgement and reconciliation translates this demand for truth, and for

149 Ibid. 23.

150 For example, the 'violence' of the origin of the ECHR and the legal order that it created will also be brought to bear on the decision. For more detailed discussion, see Chapter 4.

151 'Force of Law' (n. 59) 24 (emphasis in original).

152 Ibid. 24.

153 Ibid.

154 See Jeremy Sarkin and Erin Daly, 'Too Many Questions, Too Few Answers: Reconciliation in Transitional Societies' (2004) 35(3) *Columbia Human Rights Law Review* 101.

acknowledgement, into a political demand that will be more easily shaped by law.[155] As the CGP highlighted, the two versions of the past that dominate debate in Northern Ireland differ not so much in the facts of what happened, but in the moral assessment of the rightness and wrongness of what was done by opposing sides.[156] From this flows myriad other divisions, including most prominently the disagreement over who is legitimately entitled to call themselves a 'victim'.[157] Competing accounts of the legal and moral justification of violence on both sides leads to particularly acute disagreement over victimhood and allegations on both sides that a problematic hierarchy of victimhood exists.[158] This division persists, notwithstanding the codification of the definition of a 'victim' in legislation,[159] thus demonstrating the practical limitations of law as a means of transcending politics. This, it is suggested, is where law and its claims to impartiality, rather than transcending difficult political issues, is complicit in creating and sustaining polarised and oppositional models. The existence of a specific legal framework created by transitional justice introduces an element of violence into legal decision-making. What this means is that where a decision is made with reference to the imperatives of transitional justice, it will recreate the violence of that legal order. Inevitably, therefore, the decision will be divisive.

The interpretive context that has been created by the Agreement has cast Northern Ireland as being in 'transition' from a state of conflict to that of peace. Integral to the 'transitional' context is the assumption that law has in the past 'failed' to deal with conflict.[160] This stands in stark contrast to Unionist memories and understandings of the conflict.[161] Therefore, one of the reasons most often expressed for Unionist resistance to dealing with the past is that it will be used as a vehicle for historical revisionism.[162] The fear is often expressed that Republicans will use such processes as a means of legitimating their own actions while simultaneously blaming Unionists for causing the conflict.[163] When read through the lens of transitional justice, this position appears to be rooted in a political intransigence

155 As McEvoy and McConnachie suggest, 'law formalizes blame, both practically and symbolically'. Kieran McEvoy and Kerstin McConnachie, 'Victims and Transitional Justice: Voice, Agency and Blame' (2013) 22 *Social and Legal Studies* 489, 504.

156 CGP (n. 30) 53.

157 For a good example of the divisive nature of this debate, see Hansard, 'Daily Debates' (2013) Col. 234 onwards, in which the Democratic Unionist Party address the definition of a victim.

158 See Cheryl Lawther, *Truth, Denial and Transition: Northern Ireland and the Contested Past* (Routledge 2014).

159 S 3 of the Victims and Survivors (Northern Ireland) Order 2006 defines a victim as 'someone who has been … injured as a result of or in consequence of a conflict related incident'. It therefore incorporates a broad interpretation of victimhood. It further includes those bereaved in such incidents, or who care for those injured as a result of such incidents: s 3(b) and 3(c).

160 Campbell and Ní Aoláin (n. 122).

161 See Kirk Simpson, *Unionist Voices and the Politics of Remembering the Past in Northern Ireland* (Palgrave 2009).

162 Ibid.

163 Rolston (n. 7); Lawther (n. 158).

borne of the loss of a previously privileged political position.[164] Unionist unwillingness to engage is interpreted as a form of denial over their culpability for the conflict.[165] What a Derridean perspective reveals, however, is that far from arriving from outside law, this position flows quite logically from the relationship between violence, law and justice.[166]

The orientation of transitional justice towards past redress for failings of the law creates a perception that 'justice' in this context relates only to justice for abuses committed by the state.[167] Demands for truth are further advanced on the Republican side.[168] Having effectively mobilised around the transitional model and the legal imperatives of investigation, successful campaigns for inquiries to date have tended to focus on allegations of state wrongdoing.[169] This is a not unexpected consequence of the fact that both human rights law and transitional justice are state-centric models. They are founded on the need to hold the state to account for its treatment of its citizens. However, this feeds into a broader fear that any process of 'truth recovery' will inevitably focus on wrongdoing by the state, and will as such be inherently biased in favour of Republican meta-narratives of the conflict.[170] The effect of relying on law as a means of addressing justice in transition is to attempt to 'fit' complex and competing narratives of violence and suffering into a neat and formulaic framework.

Transitional justice as a legal order prescribes a body of rules and criteria that sets the terms of contestation. Its binary structure requires that we be able to distinguish between the competing positions. In this way law will 'cut, and divide'.[171] It works within an oppositional structure in which there will be two 'sides' that adopt competing positions and shapes the way resistance to dealing with the past is analysed. For example, transitional justice takes as its starting point that there have been failures of law in the past. The antinomy that this creates

164 See Kirk Simpson, 'Political Strategies of Engagement: Unionists and Dealing with the Past in Northern Ireland' (2013) 8 *British Politics* 2.

165 Lawther (n. 158).

166 For Derrida, recognising this violence is the condition for critique. 'For a critique of violence – that is to say an interpretive, meaningful evaluation of it – to be possible, one must first recognize meaning in a violence that is not an accident arriving from outside law.' 'Force of Law' (n. 59) 35.

167 For example, the CGP highlighted a fatalistic attitude among Unionists that any process of dealing with the past would inevitably find the state to be at fault. CGP (n. 30) 68. This leaves ordinary Unionists doubly vulnerable in that they fear a Republican strategy that seeks to place blame for the conflict on the state, but also an 'Ulsterisation' of the blame on the part of the state, displacing responsibility away from the British government and on to the locally recruited security forces, thereby placing the blame almost entirely on the Northern Ireland Unionist community.

168 Unionists, in contrast, continue to express preference for a criminal justice response to historic cases whereby crimes would be investigated and perpetrators punished. See, for example, Ulster Unionist Party, Proposals for Flags, Parades and Dealing with the Past (March 2014) http://uup.org/assets/images/featured/proposals%20on%20parades%20protests%20flags%20and%20dealing%20with%20the%20past.pdf, accessed 16 November 2015.

169 See Requa (n. 69).

170 Rolston (n. 7); Lundy and McGovern (n. 7).

171 'Force of Law' (n. 59) 24.

is that between acknowledgement and denial.[172] *Either* one 'acknowledges' these past failures, and implicitly accepts the narrative of past injustice that has given rise to it, *or* one 'denies' it, rejecting the narrative of injustice in favour of a competing interpretation of the causes and legitimacy of political violence. This opposition, and the way in which it shapes analysis of transitional justice, flows naturally from the oppositional structure of law. It also bears on our capacity to recognise the other side. The 'context' of transitional justice creates a particular lens through which stories of the conflict are refracted. Their significance is interpreted in light of the desired outcome of transition – namely the 'acknowledgement' of past abuses. This in itself represents a form of violence, in that these stories are not heard on their own terms, but rather their validity is judged on the extent to which they conform to transitional justice imperatives of truth and acknowledgement.[173] The acceptance of one narrative *necessarily* entails the violent subordination of the other. This element of violence is integral to the law. Therefore, the debate on dealing with the past will always be trapped within an oppositional structure whereby one side will 'win' and the other will 'lose'.[174] In this way reliance on law can result in our efforts at transcending violence and conflict remaining trapped within an oppositional structure and as such trapped within a cycle of metaphysical violence.

The practical result of this oppositional structure of law, and its dominance in framing the debate on dealing with the past in Northern Ireland, is that the debate on the adequacy of the mechanisms proposed by the Stormont House Agreement continues to be conducted, for the most part, from the trenches. Both sides have their own narratives, and both have their own dead.[175] Collective memory is shaped on both sides by emblematic instances of violence that embody collective suffering.[176] On both sides are stories of human suffering, and the desire to know the truth of what happened. Yet these remain inextricably, and problematically, linked to the struggle for the macro-narrative of the conflict.[177] This is what Derrida refers to as the oscillation between two determinate positions. There are two competing and equally compelling stories of victimhood for which there are demands for truth and acknowledgement of wrongdoing. And

172 Campbell and Ní Aoláin (n. 122). For detailed discussion of the significance of the concept of denial in transitional justice, see Lawther (n. 158).

173 See Jill Stauffer, *Ethical Loneliness: The Injustice of Not Being Heard* (Columbia University Press 2015).

174 This dynamic in turn gives rise to the unwillingness of some to participate in a process where the terms are viewed as being set in advance in a way that favours one side at the expense of the other. See Simpson (n. 164).

175 For significance, see Jacques Derrida, *Politics of Friendship*, George Collins tr. (Verso 1997).

176 On the significance of collective memory for transitional justice in the Northern Ireland context, see Kris Brown, 'What It Was Like to Live Through a Day: Transitional Justice and the Memory of the Everyday in a Divided Society' (2012) 6 *International Journal of Transitional Justice* 444.

177 As Weinstein highlights, the toolkit approach to transitional justice can result in painful debate about whose views have priority. Harvey Weinstein, 'Editorial Note: The Myth of Closure, the Illusion of Reconciliation: Final Thoughts on Five Years as Co-Editor-in-Chief' (2011) 6 *International Journal of Transitional Justice* 1, 4.

yet in this case justice, in a Derridean sense, cannot be achieved through the application of law.[178] Any decision made in these circumstances will be a moment of violence because it will necessarily privilege one narrative at the expense of the other. This reveals the divisive nature of any attempt to deal with the past, where questions of suffering and victimhood are bound up with contested narratives of the past.[179] Indeed, to take the analysis a step further, the application of law to adjudicate between these two competing positions does not even allow for the experience of 'undecidability' that is a necessary element of justice for Derrida. The effect of channelling debates about dealing with the past into the binary structure of law is to effectively exclude or suppress the myriad alternate stories and experiences that do not fit neatly into these dominant narratives.[180] For example, an oppositional model does not easily accommodate stories of non-state or intra-community violence, such as the torture and execution of suspected informers by the IRA.[181] Nor does it accommodate stories of Unionist victims of state violence for whom criticising the state risks appearing to accept Republican versions of history.[182] It does not allow for broader interrogation of complex relationships between the state, political leadership and grass-roots communities that could help to destabilise the boundaries of this opposition, particularly on the Unionist side.[183] More problematically, the binary nature of the Republican versus Unionist opposition effectively excludes other alternative means of analysing the causes of the conflict. For example, a gender perspective is notably absent from all official discourse on dealing with the past,[184] as is a broader socio-economic analysis of violence.[185]

178 Although of course justice, in the retributive, criminal justice sense, can still be pursued.

179 This dynamic is not unique to Northern Ireland but rather plays out across transitional societies. See McEvoy and McConnachie (n. 155).

180 This is a common theme in transitional justice. See, e.g., Fiona Ross, *Bearing Witness: Women in the Truth and Reconciliation Commission in South Africa* (Pluto 2003); Claire Moon, 'Narrating Political Reconciliation: Truth and Reconciliation in South Africa' (2006) 15 *Social and Legal Studies* 257; Fionnuala Ní Aoláin and Catherine Turner, 'Gender, Truth and Transition' (2007) 16 *UCLA Women's Law Journal* 229.

181 For discussion, see Campbell and Turner (n. 147).

182 Kirk Simpson, *Truth Recovery in Northern Ireland: Critically Interpreting the Past* (Manchester University Press 2009) 28; Lundy and McGovern (n. 7).

183 Contrast, for example, Lawther's work on Unionist political elites and the official discourse on dealing with the past with Simpson's ethnographic and oral history work with grass-roots Unionist communities. Each views Unionist positions on truth recovery through a different lens and comes out with differing perspectives on Unionist attitudes in this regard. Lawther (n. 158); Simpson (n. 161).

184 Legacy Gender Integration Group, *Gender Principles for Dealing with the Legacy of the Past* (Belfast, 2015).

185 In fact, despite the articulation of a strong concept of equality in the Agreement, the discourses of transitional justice and equality do not really 'speak' to each other. Tim Cunningham, 'Monitoring Equality – Reflexive Regulation, Planning Systems, and the Role of Discrimination Law: Lessons from Northern Ireland' (2015) 14 *Equal Rights Review* 119. See also Paul Nolan, 'Northern Ireland Peace Monitoring Report No. 3' (Community Relations Council 2014); Committee on the Administration of Justice, *Equality in Northern Ireland: The Rhetoric and the Reality* (Belfast, 2006).

The dominance of the transitional justice narrative and its emphasis on the benefits of truth recovery also effectively silences those who question the underlying value of truth,[186] or who question the capacity of 'transitional justice' to achieve justice at all. The very existence of these competing versions of justice is what constitutes the 'undecidability' through which any decision must pass. It is also what ceases to exist at the moment the decision is made. And yet these alternative voices do not simply disappear at the moment of decision. Rather, they remain trapped within the law itself,[187] the dangerous trace of the excluded that threatens the dominance of the law. The excluded presence of these alternative conceptions of justice, those that are suppressed at the moment of decision, prevents any decision from being absolutely just.[188] As Derrida writes: 'its ghostliness deconstructs from within any assurance of presence, any certitude or any supposed criteriology that would assure us of the justice of a decision, in truth of the event of a decision'.[189] The fact that there are many and competing visions of what justice should entail means that we can never say that the correct application of the law has achieved, in objective terms, justice. It is only by recognising the complexity of the debate and the way in which it has marginalised those accounts that do not fit neatly into the oppositional structure that undecidability, and justice, can be experienced. For this to be achieved, the urge must be resisted to reduce complex testimonies to a binary opposition between two competing versions of 'truth'.

The fact that any legal decision will be a moment of violence leads to the third and final *aporia*. Law in times of transition is valued for its certainty, for the closure it brings and for the way in which it can signal a new beginning. However, Derrida's third *aporia* specifically addresses the limitations of this drive for certainty and for determinate presence that characterises transitional justice.

6.2.3 Third aporia: 'the urgency that obstructs the horizon of knowledge'

> 'But justice, however unpresentable it may be, doesn't wait … a just decision is always required *immediately*, "right away."'[190]

The previous two *aporias* have addressed how Derrida sees justice as residing in the moment before a legal decision that reasserts the authority of law is made.

186 See for example Cheryl Lawther, 'Denial, Silence and the Politics of the Past: Unpicking Opposition to Truth Recovery in Northern Ireland' (2013) 7 *International Journal of Transitional Justice* 157, quoting a prominent Unionist political leader who questions how knowing the truth will help.

187 This is the structure of *différance* within which all meaning operates. See Chapter 3 for discussion.

188 Derrida writes that there is 'no moment in which a decision can be called presently and fully just; either it has not yet been made according to a rule, and nothing allows us to call it just, or it has already followed a rule – whether received, confirmed, conserved or reinvented – which in its turn is not absolutely guaranteed by anything; and moreover if it were guaranteed, the decision would be reduced to calculation and we couldn't call it just.' 'Force of Law' (n. 59) 24.

189 Ibid. 25.

190 Ibid. 26.

What has been demonstrated is how deconstruction challenges legal determinacy and the 'certitude of a present justice'.[191] It does so, according to Derrida, in the name of an infinite justice, based not on calculation and exchange, but rather as something that is owed as a 'gift without exchange … without calculation and without rules'.[192] Here Derrida is suggesting that 'justice' requires recognition of the individual rather than the application of general rules. Where any determination on the 'past' is made with reference to the legal framework of transitional justice, it will 'always maintain within itself some irruptive violence'[193] in which the singular is subordinated to the general. Justice consists in the recognition of the singularity of each particular case. This is contrasted with the generality of a rule, which is insured by law or prior convention. The application of a general rule is no more than a calculation and therefore cannot be called 'justice'.

In the context of dealing with the past, the 'singular' represents the voice of each individual victim and their experience of suffering.[194] The 'general' represents the desire for a shared understanding of conflict that insures the future against a recurrence of the past.[195] The 'singular' needs of the victim are therefore juxtaposed with the 'general' aim of social reconstruction. Attempts to institute public engagement on the subject of the past ignores singularity in favour of a generalised model of how best to address truth and justice.[196] However, the fundamental premise of Derrida's work is that we cannot rely on fixed binaries to guarantee meaning. Deconstruction requires us to work between the two poles of the singular and the general and to recognise the ongoing negotiation between them. While an ideal of justice would require a judge to consider the full singularity of each particular case, there will never be enough time available to do this.[197] Justice requires a decision, and therefore some element of legal violence will be inevitable.[198] What is necessary is to recognise this element of violence.

This returns us to the idea of justice as an endpoint to be achieved, a definite point towards which law can carry us. The desire for a determinate presence of justice demands that a decision be made and that an endpoint be reached.[199] This is a philosophical incarnation of what Weinstein has more recently identified as

191 Ibid. 25.

192 Ibid. 25.

193 Ibid. 27.

194 Hastings Donnan and Kirk Simpson, 'Silence and Violence among Northern Ireland Border Protestants' (2007) 72 *Ethnos* 5.

195 The effect of this 'general' conception of justice is to subordinate individual experiences to the general, to mould them to fit the desired narrative of justice.

196 See Brandon Hamber and Richard Wilson, 'Symbolic Closure through Memory, Reparation and Revenge in Post Conflict Societies' (2002) Research Papers: Paper 5 http://digitalcommons.uconn.edu/hri_papers/5, accessed 19 October 2015. See also Weinstein (n. 177); Dube (n. 60).

197 'Force of Law' (n. 59) 26. For Derrida, the court 'cannot furnish itself with infinite information and the unlimited knowledge of conditions, rules or hypothetical imperatives that could justify it'.

198 Ibid. 26.

199 Derrida describes this as a 'structural urgency and precipitation of justice'. Ibid. 27.

the 'myth of closure' that drives much work in the field of transitional justice.[200] Reconciliation, achieved through narrative truth, is the goal. This speaks directly to the calculations that are made in respect of truth and justice in transition – namely, what is the price of peace? The paradigmatic examples in this regard include the exchange of truth in return for immunity from prosecution or the receipt of information or apology in exchange for forgiveness. In each case a calculated transaction is conducted, during which political considerations intervene in the relationship between the victim and the perpetrator.[201] In this context there is an underlying assumption that truth will further understanding and will therefore combat partial narratives and myths that prevent any collective understanding from emerging.[202] While on the personal level this form of engagement with the 'other' can help to improve relationships, at the political level it is complicated by the macro-struggle that continues to play out over the conflict and the relationship between violence, law and consequently justice that underpins it.[203] In these terms justice becomes trapped between an ideal standard, whereby truth recovery, acknowledgement and forgiveness lead to justice and a reconciled future, and the empirical reality of ongoing challenge to the ends and means of dealing with the past.[204]

This is a theme that Derrida explores further in his essay *On Cosmopolitanism and Forgiveness*. Here, addressing specifically the question of forgiveness in the wake of mass atrocity, Derrida distinguishes between genuine interpersonal reconciliation on the one hand, and the 'calculated transaction' required when politics intervenes in the victim/perpetrator relationship on the other. At the interpersonal level, Derrida suggests that 'as soon as the victim "understands" the criminal, as soon as she exchanges, speaks, agrees with him, the scene of reconciliation has commenced'.[205] This is true even where the victim cannot forgive; for, in recognising the other, reconciliation has begun.[206] However, where this form of exchange is 'required' as a means towards a predetermined end, it is no longer possible to speak of true reconciliation, for the encounter has been reduced to a transaction, calculated to adhere to rules.[207] This is particularly true when speaking of

200 For Weinstein, this reflects a broadening of the goals of transitional justice to encompass the 'elusive ideas of reconciliation and closure in order to move countries towards a broader vision of reconstituted societies based upon democratic principles, rule of law and observance of human rights norms'. Weinstein (n. 177).
201 On Cosmopolitanism and Forgiveness (n. 58).
202 Healing Through Remembering (n. 97). This theme is well explored in Lawrence McKeown's play *Those You Meet on the Street*, reviewed by Catherine Turner, 'The Art(s) of Dealing with the Past' (RightsNI, 1 April 2015) http://rightsni.org/2015/04/the-arts-of-dealing-with-the-past/, accessed 19 October 2015.
203 On Cosmopolitanism and Forgiveness (n. 58).
204 Ibid; Spectres of Marx (n. 123).
205 On Cosmopolitanism and Forgiveness (n. 58) 49.
206 Ibid.
207 Ibid. 50. 'A "finalized" forgiveness is not forgiveness; it is only a political strategy or a psychotherapeutic economy.'

forgiveness in the context of truth recovery.[208] The emphasis placed on acknowledgement, or on the idea of atonement for a wrong committed, for Derrida reduces the idea of apology and forgiveness to a conditional exchange,[209] in which forgiveness is invoked in pursuit of a definite political goal behind which 'all sorts of strategic ruses can hide themselves abusively behind a "rhetoric" or a "comedy" of forgiveness'.[210] The singular experience of the victim is subordinated to the general goal of reconciliation, and in this process the responsibility for reconciliation is shifted onto the victim.[211] The personal and the political (or the singular and the general) therefore represent opposite poles in terms of reconciliation as well as justice. Personal reconciliation, which is the prerogative of the victim alone, resides in the sphere of pure forgiveness, made without condition.[212] In contrast, political reconciliation exists as a calculated strategy, as a means towards an end. Rather than collapsing the distinction between the two and speaking of a generalised concept of 'reconciliation', the challenge is to find a way to work between the two.[213] In practical terms this speaks to the distinction between 'forensic' truth and 'narrative' truth and the difficulty of reconciling the pursuit of the two.

Working between personal and political reconciliation without a determined endpoint of unity allows for the possibility of acknowledging the other without necessarily accepting the legitimacy of their position in respect of the macro-causes of violence. This refocuses attention on the personal rather than the political, allowing the debate over the past to move beyond the stalemate caused by the rigidity of law. This requires a willingness to abandon the ideal of 'closure' or of a temporally bounded space within which transitional justice will be achieved. In short, it requires the creation of a political space 'in the middle' within which these processes can occur.[214] In contrast to the drive for certainty that law embodies – the need to have 'dealt' with the past – a political space requires that the past remain the subject of an ongoing and open conversation.[215] This is not to suggest that there should be no official processes or mechanisms to support this conversation. Nor does it deny that there may be difficult truths that need to be heard on both sides. Rather, these processes should be based on a 'narrative

208 While the relationship between truth, forgiveness and reconciliation is far from clear or agreed in transitional justice, there is nevertheless a tendency to conflate the three. See Rebecca Saunders, 'Questionable Associations: The Role of Forgiveness in Transitional Justice' (2011) 5 *International Journal of Transitional Justice* 119. This is discussed in more detail in Chapter 2.

209 On Cosmopolitanism and Forgiveness (n. 58) 34.

210 Ibid. 50.

211 Dube (n. 60); Panu Minkinnen, 'Ressentiment as Suffering: On Transitional Justice and the Impossibility of Forgiveness' (2007) 19 *Law and Literature* 513. For an example of this dynamic in context, see Lundy and Rolston (n. 141).

212 In particular, pure forgiveness does not require repentance on the part of the perpetrator.

213 On Cosmopolitanism and Forgiveness (n. 58) 45. 'It is between these two poles, irreconcilable and indissociable, that decisions and responsibilities are to be taken.'

214 Bankowski (n. 93); Andrew Schapp, 'The Time of Reconciliation and the Space of Politics' in Scott Veitch (ed.), *Law and the Politics of Reconciliation* (Ashgate 2007) 9, 14.

215 Christodoulidis (n. 118) 189.

of inclusion whereby participants open themselves to others and learn from them and are changed by them'.[216] Rather than viewing justice as the outcome of a process in which two previously oppositional positions are reconciled, it must be seen as the continual process of negotiation between these two positions. Seen in these terms, the conflict and the past will not be 'resolved' – it is unlikely that an agreed account of rights and wrongs of the conflict will be reached – but nor will politics remain trapped in an oppositional cycle of violence (physical or metaphysical) whereby opposing sides jostle to assert their dominance and necessarily silence their opposition. This approach can be summed up, in the words of Derrida, as justice '*to come*'.

Law as the means of achieving justice in transition risks emphasising victory, and a 'completion where one will be the winner and one the loser'.[217] Where dealing with the past, and the questions of victimhood, recognition and acknowledgement that it entails, is framed predominantly with reference to law, the ability to rely on law to assert the 'rightness' of one's own position, and the righteousness of one's own actions absolves each person, individually and collectively, from the obligation to listen to the other.[218] Reliance on a legal discourse of 'rights' risks entrenching differences and turning victims into 'competitors not collaborators' in the pursuit of justice.[219] Where there is a chance that a legal determination can be achieved that confirms that one side was right and the other was wrong, there is no incentive for either side to listen to the other, to hear their experiences as anything other than politically manipulated half-truths, nor to recognise that, although they may differ in their opinions, behind each story is a personal tragedy.[220] The desire to achieve a shared narrative of conflict undermines the possibility of listening and recognition at the political level through the emphasis it places on the need to resolve disagreement.[221] Where rights are asserted, they rely on the force of law for their authority.[222]

The metaphysical violence of the law therefore permeates all levels of the debate over law and justice in transition. The violence of law means that relying on law as a means to justice keeps politics trapped within a 'moral economy of exchange and power'[223] defined by the oppositional concepts of victim and perpetrator, winner and loser and trapped within a cycle of violence. The violence of the law cannot be transcended; therefore, what is necessary is to recognise its existence and try to find ways to break free from the oppositional model created by law. One way of

216 Bankowski (n. 93) 63.

217 Ibid. 59.

218 Bankowski suggests that 'resting secure in your victimhood defines your identity as timeless and unwilling to engage'. Ibid. 51.

219 Ibid. 51.

220 This is a risk inherent in any legal institution, namely that it will 'support hegemonic collective memories to the suppression of others'. Christodoulidis (n. 118) 193.

221 Ibid. 194.

222 Bankowski (n. 93) 57.

223 Ibid. 60.

doing this, facilitated by Derrida's philosophy of justice, is by adopting an approach based on justice as recognition of the other.[224] This has particular resonance for the pursuit of 'narrative' truth in Northern Ireland. The work of the proposed Oral History Project and the Implementation and Reconciliation Group in particular can be guided by a more open-ended approach that recognises rather than denies the ongoing contestation over the past. In particular, this would require engagement with the possibility that no agreed narrative of the past is possible. This does not mean that pursuing 'truth' is futile. It may be possible to establish some objective truths, particularly 'forensic' truths. However, the purpose of such an exercise should not be to eliminate differences of opinion through the articulation of a unified account of the conflict, but rather to provide a forum within which a democratic conversation can take place, where views on both sides are openly challenged rather than suppressed or excluded by the violence of the law.[225]

6.3 Conclusion: justice 'to come'

It will never be possible to say that 'justice' in the Derridean sense has been achieved. Rather, Derrida sees justice as a possibility, as something that is always '*to come*'.[226] This represents an injunction to view justice as an open-ended process that requires continual deconstruction. It also requires an acknowledgement that justice means different things to different people, and that any model that seeks to comprehensively deal with the past must be able to accommodate not just multifaceted but also competing views.[227] Justice '*to come*' is not simply the reproduction of the present, but rather 'opens up for *l'avenir* the transformation, the recasting or refounding of law and politics'.[228] It thus speaks of the need to break free from existing structures, from rules, calculations and anticipations.[229]

Derrida takes care to distinguish his conception of justice 'to come' from the idea of a regulative ideal that sets a horizon on the possibility of achieving justice.[230] In this regard he is distinguishing his concept of justice from that of Kant, and in particular from the idea of a transcendent standard of justice that can be achieved through law or right.[231] For Derrida, for reasons already discussed, the pursuit of

224 Mathias Mahlmann, 'Law and Force: 20th Century Radical Legal Philosophy, Post Modernism and the Foundations of Law' (2003) 9 *Res Publica* 19, 31. 'Respect for the Other is the means of escaping this violence.'

225 See also Campbell and Turner (n. 147).

226 'Force of Law' (n. 59) 27.

227 See Noa Vaisman, 'Variations on Justice: Argentina's Pre- and Post- Transitional Justice and the Justice to Come' (2015) Ethnos http://dx.doi.org/10.1080/00141844.2015.1080746, accessed 19 October 2015.

228 'Force of Law' (n. 59) 27.

229 Ibid.

230 Ibid.

231 See Jacques Derrida, 'Autoimmunity: Real and Symbolic Suicides' in Giovanna Borradori (ed.), *Philosophy in a Time of Terror: Dialogues with Jurgen Habermas and Jacques Derrida* (University of Chicago Press 2003) 85 on the critique of a regulatory ideal.

justice through law will always involve some 'dissymmetry and some quality of violence'.[232] This is because of the desire to be able to say that justice has been achieved in the here and now.[233] In contrast, Derrida's vision of justice is open-ended – it is always 'to come'.[234] This conception of justice offers an alternative to the conceptualisation of law as justice that dominates transitional justice. It enjoins us to conceive of justice as something that requires the ongoing recognition of the singularity of the other and their experiences of suffering as well as our own.[235] Bankowski sums up what it means to act 'in the middle', to reject the certainties of law in favour of a more open-ended concept of justice 'to come': 'The middle is an anxious place – it is risky and unsettled, and therefore the place of vulnerability (i.e. far removed from established certainties); there is no end, no safe haven which, risky though the journey is, we can ultimately aim for.'[236]

Justice, in the Derridean sense, therefore requires that we recognise the singularity of each experience, and be open to learn from it. This will not happen within a set five-year time frame. Justice, in this sense, cannot be achieved in the present. It will always exist some time in the future. This sentiment is summarised in the context of transitional justice by Weinstein, where he suggests that rather than seeking closure through transitional justice, we accept that forgiveness and reconciliation are projects of the future. In the meantime, living together without physical violence may be enough.[237] Justice 'to come' in this regard consists not of set endpoints and time frames specified in law, but of a wwillingness to listen to each other in the hope that change will eventually happen. It may also involve stepping outside the 'theatrical space' of transitional justice that has dominated the debate so far. Conceiving justice in these terms encourages a more realistic assessment of the objectives of legacy mechanisms and the extent to which they can achieve those goals.

232 'Force of Law' (n. 59) 27.

233 This is the metaphysics of presence that Derrida sees as characterising classical philosophy, and which deconstruction seeks to destabilise. See Chapter 3 for discussion.

234 'Force of Law' (n. 59).

235 Mahlmann sums this dynamic up well when he states that 'justice amounts, in Derrida's view … to a unilateral relation with a person, to the obligation to respect and appreciate her uniqueness, her otherness'. Mahlmann (n. 224) 30.

236 Bankowski (n. 93) 56.

237 Weinstein (n. 177) 5.

Conclusion

The impossibility of transitional justice?

It has been argued that from the beginning of the twenty-first century a new juridical concept of transitional justice has emerged. The emergence of this concept represents a performative event of considerable force in international law, the effect of which has been to create a 'theatrical space' within which efforts at peace-making play out.[1] Chapter 2 outlined how diverse legal and political responses to war and conflict gave rise to the 'concept' of transitional justice that has been gradually instituted in law and policy. This new body of rules has created a bounded space within which transitional justice is implemented and evaluated. The creation of this 'theatrical space', it has been argued, represents a 'coup de force'[2] in which the role of politics, which had been the dominant force both nationally and internationally, was usurped by that of law.[3] 'Transitional justice' represented a new system that could be contrasted with the corrupt or immoral system it replaced,[4] a new way of thinking about justice in the aftermath or war or repression. In this way, the field of transitional justice holds itself apart from earlier (failed) models that were found wanting in terms of their compliance with set standards of justice.[5] The exceptional nature of transitional justice was legitimised by the promise of a new beginning.[6] Under the new normative model it would no longer be necessary to trade justice against peace. Rather, what was promised was a future in which peace would be based on justice and the rule of law.[7] This book has explored the dominance of this new normative model of transitional justice,

1 Jacques Derrida, *On Cosmopolitanism and Forgiveness*, Mark Dooley and Michael Hughes tr. (Routledge 2001) 29.

2 Jacques Derrida, 'Force of Law: The Mystical Foundation of Authority' in Drucilla Cornell *et al.* (eds), *Deconstruction and the Possibility of Justice* (Routledge 1992).

3 Ruti Teitel, 'Transitional Justice Genealogy' (2003) 16 *Harvard Human Rights Law Journal* 69 (hereinafter 'Genealogy').

4 Ibid. See also Costas Douzinas, 'Violence, Justice and Deconstruction' (2005) 6 *German Law Journal* 171.

5 Genealogy (n. 3). This is the third stage of Teitel's genealogy.

6 This is discussed in more detail in Chapter 2.

7 United Nations, 'Report of the Secretary General on the Rule of Law and Transitional Justice in Conflict and Post Conflict Societies' (UN Doc. S/2004/616, United Nations 2004).

and its ability to deliver lasting change. Ultimately, what is now suggested is that while lawyers must grapple with these questions of justice, if the model is to avoid becoming overly reliant on law and legal standards, critical engagement with that law is also essential.

The conclusion presents three reflections arising from the process of deconstructing transitional justice. The first is a reflection on the merits of adopting a critical approach to a field dominated by doctrine. It is argued that theory can open up new insights that can feed into policy and practice in this area. The second reflection concerns the circularity of violence and law, highlighting how this circularity undermines some of the core goals of transitional justice. Finally, the third reflection speaks to the title, namely the idea that transitional justice is 'impossible'. It clarifies Derrida's understanding of impossible, and calls for greater openness in how 'justice' is conceptualised.

1. The importance of critique in transitional justice research

It has been argued that existing mainstream approaches to transitional justice represent a desire for a determinate standard of justice against which the success of transitional justice can be measured.[8] However, this approach, it is suggested, introduces a polarised system of thinking about questions of justice in transition.[9] The field itself is constructed around a number of binary oppositions, the most obvious of which is that of war and peace. This is the central organising binary around which transitional justice discourses are constructed. The assumption inherent in this is that we are moving from a state of war (violence) to a state of peace (law), and that these are two distinct states that can be easily distinguished from each other. This encourages rigid distinctions in how we think about transitional justice. It dictates how and where the boundaries of the transitional space are drawn, thereby determining, for example, who is to be considered a victim, who should face prosecution and what mechanisms can be legitimately used to pursue transitional justice.[10] Therefore, while we can measure objective indicators of reform, doctrinal and empirical methods are less able to account for the complexity of transitional politics. This is where critical engagement can help to encourage a more nuanced engagement with the concept of transitional justice and its goals that complements the task of evaluating claims. Deconstruction, it has been argued, can help expose the dynamics of how we think about these questions. It challenges us to think beyond existing structures of thought rather than simply inverting them.

In transitional justice literature, the role of law has been reconceptualised to recognise the distinct role played by law in times of political upheaval.[11] For

8 See Chapter 2.

9 See Chapter 2. See also Colm Campbell and Fionnuala Ní Aoláin, 'The Paradox of Transitions in Liberal Democracies' (2005) 27 *Human Rights Quarterly* 172.

10 See Chapter 6.

11 Ruti Teitel, *Transitional Justice* (Oxford University Press 2000).

example, Teitel's original conceptualisation of the role of law in transition was deliberately intended to replace the rigidity of traditional legalism with a more flexible and responsive model that recognised the necessary negotiation between law and politics in transition.[12] Yet in recent years the field of transitional justice has been dominated by a toolkit approach that subjects the singular demands of justice in transition to generalised rules, norms and imperatives. The assumption of this model is that the application of rules and programmes for action is a means for achieving justice. It allows for the consistent opposition of violence with law, thereby providing the foundation for a reliance on law as a tool of transition. What remains, therefore, is a binary structure of war and peace that assumes that the two are distinct and identifiable ways of being, and that movement from one to the other is possible.

Law, under this conceptualisation, is the means by which we move from violence towards justice. However, deconstructing the nature of the relationship between violence and law reveals an altogether different dynamic, and one that casts considerable new light on some of the perennial problems of transitional justice. In particular, it helps to provide a coherent framework for analysing *why* opposition to transitional justice arises. This is important because opposition and challenge arises for diverse reasons and in diverse geographical and political contexts. This work has discussed the example of Northern Ireland, where the opposition arises largely along party political lines. However, there are other examples of challenge to the success of transitional justice. For example, in South Africa challenge arises around ongoing socio-economic divisions.[13] In Rwanda tensions remain over local versus national and international responses to violence,[14] and in Argentina the 'calculated' nature of efforts at transitional justice continues to engender resistance.[15] Rather than viewing each instance of opposition as a discrete obstacle to be overcome, analysing the structural conditions of transitional justice enables a deeper understanding of what connects these sites of opposition and how they could be addressed.

Rather than representing the relationship between violence and law as a linear progression from one to the other, in which success is measured by the extent to which we can demonstrate the opposition between violence and law, what emerges is a circular logic. Rather than viewing transitional justice as a linear progression from war to peace, with the peace agreement marking the break that enables that

12 Genealogy (n. 3).

13 Tsepo Madlingozi, 'Good Victim, Bad Victim: Apartheid's Beneficiaries, Victims and the Struggle for Social Justice' in Wessel Le Roux and Karin Van Marle (eds), *Law, Memory and the Legacy of Apartheid: Ten Years after AZAPO v President of South Africa* (Pretoria University Law Press 2007).

14 Phil Clark, 'Negotiating Reconciliation in Rwanda: Popular Challenges to the Official Discourse of Post-Genocide National Unity' (2014) 8 *Journal of Intervention and State Building* 303.

15 Claire Moon, 'Who'll Pay Reparations on my Soul? Social Control and Social Suffering in Argentina' (2012) 21 *Social and Legal Studies* 187; Noa Vaisman, 'Variations on Justice: Argentina's Pre- and Post- Transitional Justice and the Justice to Come' (2015) Ethnos http://dx.doi.org/10.1080/00141844.2015.1080746, accessed 19 October 2015.

progression, the circular model reveals the immanence of violence to law. As discussed in Chapter 4, the success of political violence will lie in the extent to which it succeeds in securing *post hoc* legitimation through law.[16] In this way the peace agreement also plays an important symbolic role. The peace agreement will make an implicit statement on the legitimacy of the violence, reflected in the extent to which the language of the agreement adopts particular narratives of the causes of conflict. As this is the moment from which the authority of law will derive, it is also the moment in which violence, both political and metaphysical, becomes inscribed into the heart of the legal regime that is created.[17]

Law is therefore not an impartial and objective arbiter of justice and cannot be clearly distinguished from violence. The act of naming a process as 'transitional justice' makes a clear statement that will set the terms on which transitional politics must be conducted.[18] It sets limits on what can and cannot legitimately be contested. This raises significant questions over who decides, and according to what criteria, the content or narrative of transitional justice. Who sets the priorities? And what effect does this have on competing narratives? These questions are not just of rhetorical interest. Derrida highlights how the dominant power will be the one that manages to impose, and thus legitimate (or legalise), on a national or world stage the terminology, and thus the interpretation, that best suits it in a given situation.[19] As discussed in Chapter 5, this gives rise to practical difficulties with establishing a normative regime, such as transitional justice, that has the power to define and shape processes of social reform. Rather than maintaining a presence that is independent of politics or morality, the distinction between the legal field of transitional justice and the politics that it aims to transcend is revealed to be an illusion. Far from existing independently from history, politics and morality, transitional justice bears within it traces of all of these influences, each of which haunts it from within, and each of which has the potential to reassert its presence.[20]

The presence of these excluded traces within transitional justice speaks to the second reflection on the relationship between law and justice. A key goal of transitional justice is the guarantee of non-recurrence. By addressing the past, it is argued that transitional justice helps prevent a recurrence of violence in the future. However, as discussed in the following section, an over-reliance on law may undermine this goal.

16 See Chapter 5.

17 'Force of Law' (n. 2).

18 Jacques Derrida, 'Devant La Loi' in Alan Udof (ed.), *Kafka and the Contemporary Critical Performance* (Indiana University Press 1987) 128 (hereinafter 'Before the Law').

19 Jacques Derrida, 'Autoimmunity: Real and Symbolic Suicides' in Giovanna Borradori (ed.), *Philosophy in a Time of Terror: Dialogues with Jurgen Habermas and Jacques Derrida* (University of Chicago Press 2003) 85, 105.

20 Jacques Derrida, 'Spectres of Marx' (1994) 15 *New Political Science* 7 (hereinafter 'Spectres of Marx'). This is demonstrated through ongoing contestation of 'normative' claims in respect of dealing with the past, for example, whereby political interpretations of transitional justice continue to 'haunt' legal approaches. See Chapter 6 for discussion.

2. Transitional justice as autoimmunity

The next question to be addressed is why deconstructing the relationship between law and politics in transitional justice is important. Of course law is political, and of course war will be continued by other means. What has been proposed is that deconstructing this dynamic allows us to consider the deeper structures that transitional justice is built upon. To complete the cycle, what has happened is that, in telling the story of the conflict, one side comes to be privileged over the other. The boundaries of what is acceptable thought and action in transitional contexts has been set by the act of instituting law. This means that there will inevitably be those who are left outside the boundaries of acceptable opinion – those who reject the authority of the law and see themselves as oppressed within the new order. This dynamic was discussed in Chapter 5, with the example of the most recent wave of protest against decisions relating to flags and parades in Northern Ireland. However, this dynamic applies not only to those who find themselves on the wrong side of history, but also to those who believe that transitional justice is not enough – that it is a means to diffuse more radical demands for justice.[21] If rigid boundaries are imposed on how we discuss questions of transition, then access to the debate itself will be restricted to those who are able or willing to speak the language of transitional justice.[22] As highlighted in Chapter 5, this potentially sets the scene for a recurrence of physical violence as a manifestation of disillusionment with the state.[23]

Ironically, therefore, in relying on law to achieve political reform, the model of transitional justice risks reproducing and regenerating the patterns of conflict that it seeks to disarm. This is evident in the case of Northern Ireland, where attitudes towards the 'dealing with the past' agenda continue to be divided along the Unionist/nationalist political divide. Despite the attempt by the Belfast Agreement to create unity from diversity,[24] attitudes remain divided along traditional lines. These attitudes are perpetuated by the structure of transitional justice.[25] Ironically, in the quest to immunise society against a recurrence of violence, transitional justice adopts rigid structures that themselves are founded in violence. Derrida refers to this phenomenon as 'auto-immunity', whereby the structures adopted to address violence ultimately destroy the capacity of society to effectively respond to conflict by peaceful means.[26] The desire to achieve closure on past events, to reach

21 Rosemary Nagy, 'Transitional Justice as Global Project: Critical Reflections' (2008) 29 *Third World Quarterly* 275.

22 This in itself is a form of injustice for 'Force of Law' (n. 2).

23 This occurs as that which is excluded remains trapped within the opposition, returning to haunt the dominant political community. See Spectres of Marx (n. 20).

24 See John Hume, 'Ireland – The Healing Process' (1998) 22 *Fordham International Law Journal* 1171.

25 Curtis also notes this dynamic in the context of human rights in Northern Ireland. She highlights how rights talk 'incorporated the logic and language of the local conflict rather than resituating local understandings of the conflict in terms of international law and norms'. Jennifer Curtis, *Human Rights as War by other Means: Peace Politics in Northern Ireland* (University of Pennsylvania Press 2014) 67.

26 Autoimmunity (n. 19).

a solution in the present that will safeguard the future, places boundaries or limits on the possibility of justice in these circumstances. Once the desired outcome of law becomes fixed and determinate, any responsiveness that would allow law to pursue alternative conceptions of justice is lost.[27]

However, there is a risk in critiquing the use of law as a means of pursuing social change. If taken to its logical conclusion, a critique of the violence of law would entail a rejection of the idea of law as a means *towards* justice. Mahlmann identifies this as a paradox in Derrida's work. He suggests that while deconstruction intends 'radically to criticise violence', it may in the process delegitimate 'one of the more promising tools for curbing violence in the real world'.[28] For this reason, Derrida himself is clear that the 'impossibility' of justice is not a reason to eschew the use of law as a means of pursuing just ends.[29] In 'Force of Law' he states, 'That justice exceeds law and calculation, that the unpresentable exceeds the determinable cannot and should not serve as an alibi for staying out of juridico-political battles'.[30] Therefore, it can be seen that Derrida does not reject the idea of law altogether. Indeed, it has been highlighted how deconstruction is an affirmative rather than a destructive force.[31] It does not consist of dismantling institutions themselves, but rather 'structures within institutions that have become too rigid, or are dogmatic or which work as an obstacle to future research'.[32] Deconstruction therefore opens up possibilities that have been suppressed by virtue of the dominance of one particular way of conceptualising transitional justice.

What is central is the ability to recognise the potentially coercive effects of law. Relying too heavily, or without question, on law and the inviolability of law can reduce it to an ultimately arbitrary standard. Where any particular concept, such as 'transitional justice', comes to be regarded as fixed, the risk is that the concept itself ceases to be subjected to scrutiny.[33] The unquestioning acceptance of norms becomes not only possible but commonplace. Looking beyond the opposition of violence and law, towards a more nuanced engagement with the relationship between the two, therefore helps us to avoid some of the risks inherent in relying too heavily on purely normative frameworks. Why deconstruction is useful, therefore, is that it provides a means by which to articulate some of these difficult issues in transitional justice – it provides an alternative framework for analysis that encourages ongoing questioning of our methods and interrogation

27 Jacques De Ville, 'Sovereignty without Sovereignty: Derrida's Declarations of Independence' (2008) 19 *Law and Critique* 87, 105.

28 Mathias Mahlmann, 'Law and Force: 20th Century Radical Legal Philosophy, Post Modernism and the Foundations of Law' (2003) 9 *Res Publica* 19, 33.

29 Jacques Derrida, 'The Laws of Reflection: Nelson Mandela, In Admiration' in Jacques Derrida and Mustafa Tlili (eds), *For Nelson Mandela* (Seaver Books 1987) 18.

30 'Force of Law' (n. 2) 28.

31 Discussed in Chapter 3

32 Jacques Derrida and John D Caputo, *Deconstruction in a Nutshell: A Conversation with Jacques Derrida* (Fordham 1997) (hereinafter 'Villanova Roundtable') 8.

33 William Sokoloff, 'Between Justice and Legality: Derrida on Decision' (2005) 58 *Political Research Quarterly* 341.

of the deeper assumptions on which the field is premised. It helps to explain the existence of dissent to seemingly universal goods, such as human rights and justice, and to engage with this dissent in a more productive manner. It also highlights the importance of an ethic of respect and recognition that can be used to ground practice. This is important if transitional justice as a field is to avoid becoming rigid and unresponsive.

Importantly, it is not suggested that we can break the circular logic of law. Rather, critical engagement with transitional justice research enables us to recognise this logic and to ask bigger questions about how we measure the success of transitional justice. The failure to acknowledge the political nature of the law is a form of metaphysical violence. However, this is the violence that is immanent to the law. Any critique of violence must therefore 'recognise meaning in a violence that is not an accident arriving from outside the law'.[34] For Derrida, 'That which threatens law already belongs to it'.[35] Therefore, the debate to be had is not how to avoid politicisation, but how to acknowledge the contested and ultimately violent nature of law. Derrida suggests that 'each advance in politicisation obliges one to reconsider, and so to reinterpret, the very foundations of law such as they had previously been calculated or delimited'.[36] In these terms, questioning the assumptions of law itself helps to reveal the hierarchical nature of meaning and the oppositional structure upon which law in transition is constructed. Exposing this opposition and the way in which it shapes our understanding of transitional justice is the crucial first step of deconstruction.[37] Rather than entrenching patterns of conflict by perpetuating a false distinction between violence and law, we should be thinking about ways of managing this tension in a way that does not simply repeat the circular logic of violence. This may ultimately mean being more open to non-legal strategies, and to expanding our definitions of 'justice' in transition. This leads to the final reflection on the relationship between law and justice in transition, namely that justice is only possible by eschewing legal certainty and embracing the undecidable.

3. 'Impossible' is not the opposite of 'possible'

Despite the meteoric rise of transitional justice, it remains a relatively new concept. The implications of the performative force by which it emerged therefore remain unclear. Derrida acknowledges that the force of the emergence of related concepts such as 'crimes against humanity' or even 'human rights' can be seen either as 'an immense progress, an historic transformation' or alternatively as 'a concept still obscure in its limits, fragile in its foundations'.[38] This means that no

34 'Force of Law' (n. 2) 35.
35 Ibid.
36 Ibid. 28.
37 Jacques Derrida, *Positions* (The Athlone Press 1981) 41.
38 On Cosmopolitanism and Forgiveness (n. 1) 30.

authoritative judgment can be made one way or the other on the success of transitional justice. This judgment will come only with time. This therefore begs the question of why the title speaks of the 'impossibility' of transitional justice. The 'impossible' for Derrida is not the opposite of possible.[39] They do not denote two separate and fixed positions. Rather, the structure of *différance* upon which meaning is constructed creates the conditions for the possible.[40] While we may never reach a determined outcome, an agreed 'truth' or a pure concept of 'justice', we nevertheless, through ongoing deconstruction, strive towards justice, and in this *process* we make justice possible.

In situations defined by political conflict and by competing narratives, placing too great an emphasis on the application of norms also absolves responsibility for openness to the 'other'. What this means for transitional justice is that, rather than emphasising legal certainty and avoiding the undecidable, justice requires ongoing openness to the 'other'. The 'other' might be alternative political views of the merits of transitional justice. It might be conflicting interpretations of the morality of violence. It might be the victim from the opposing political community. However it manifests itself, we must remain open to the 'other' in the hope that one day there will be reconciliation. This is made possible through ongoing negotiation between competing and oppositional narratives. In this way, when speaking of 'justice', an analogy can be drawn with hope. Hope keeps us moving forward. We cannot exorcise the past. It will always remain trapped as the excluded trace that must be suppressed. Its return is the spectre that haunts the present and the future.[41] What we can and must do is to find a way to live with that past in a way that keeps us moving forward. This is only possible through ongoing critique and recognition of the inherently political nature of the choices being made with respect to the contested past.

For Derrida, justice represents a call for more consequential change, 'not simply in the naïve sense of calculated, deliberate and strategically controlled intervention, but in the sense of a maximum intensification in progress, in the name of neither a simple symptom nor simple cause'.[42] Therefore, while justice can be used to orient juristic efforts,[43] it is not the fixed endpoint of law. Derrida suggested in 'Force of Law' that it was 'foreseeable and desirable that studies of deconstructive style should culminate in the problematic of law and justice'.[44] It seems equally foreseeable and desirable that studies of transitional justice should culminate in deconstruction of the concepts of law and justice on which the field is founded. Deconstruction itself is a problematisation of the foundations of law, politics and

39 See Jacques Derrida, *Monolingualism of the Other: or, The Prosthesis of Origin*, Patrick Mensah tr. (Stanford University Press 1998).

40 See Richard Beardsworth, *Derrida and the Political* (Routledge 1996) 26.

41 Spectres of Marx (n. 20).

42 'Force of Law' (n. 2) 9.

43 Petra Gehring, 'The Jurisprudence of the "Force of Law"' in Peter Goodrich *et al.* (eds), *Derrida and Legal Philosophy* (Palgrave Macmillan 2008) 55, 64.

44 'Force of Law' (n. 2) 7.

morality. It has been demonstrated how questions of law, politics and morality are intimately linked in the context of transitional justice, to the extent that a rigid distinction between the concepts themselves can no longer withstand scrutiny. In transitional justice, the urge must be resisted to rely exclusively upon determinate frameworks of justice. Law should not be instrumentally subordinated to a determined outcome, but rather must remain open to the possibility of justice. Justice for Derrida is not simply a juridical or political concept, but opens up for the future the possibility of transformation, of re-casting or re-founding law and politics. The challenge to remain open to critical engagement is rooted in the idea of an infinite version of justice that is irreducible to law. It is in this ongoing process of questioning that justice lies – in the openness to the other, the existence of whom is immanent to the idea of transition. In this way deconstruction is transitional justice.

Bibliography

Abou-El-Fadl R, 'Beyond Conventional Transitional Justice: Egypt's 2011 Revolution and the Absence of Political Will' (2012) 6 *International Journal of Transitional Justice* 318

Adams G, 'To Cherish a Just and Lasting Peace' (1998) 22 *Fordham International Law Journal* 1179

Akhavan P, 'Justice in The Hague, Peace in the Former Yugoslavia? A Commentary on the United Nations War Crimes Tribunal' (1998) 20 *Human Rights Quarterly* 737

Amnesty International, *Northern Ireland: Time to Deal with the Past* (Belfast, 2013)

—— *United Kingdom: Killings by Security Forces in Northern Ireland* (New York, 1986)

An Na'im A, 'Editorial Note: From the Neo-colonial "Transitional" to Indigenous Formations of Justice' (2013) 7 *International Journal of Transitional Justice* 197

Anthony G, 'Judicial Review in Northern Ireland – A Guide to the "Real" Devolution Issues' (2009) 14(3) *Judicial Review* 230

—— and Mageean P, 'Habits of Mind and "Truth Telling": Article 2 ECHR in Post-Conflict Northern Ireland' in K McEvoy *et al.* (eds), *Judges, Transition and Human Rights* (Oxford University Press 2007)

Arbour L, 'Economic and Social Justice for Societies in Transition' (2007) 40(1) *International Law and Politics* 1

Ardoyne Commemoration Project, *Ardoyne: The Untold Truth* (Belfast, 2002)

Arthur P, 'How "Transitions" Reshaped Human Rights: A Conceptual History of Transitional Justice' (2009) 31 *Human Rights Quarterly* 321

Asmal K, 'Truth, Reconciliation and Justice: The South African Experience in Perspective' (2000) 63 *Modern Law Review* 1

Atria F, 'Reconciliation and Reconstruction' in Scott Veitch (ed.), *Law and the Politics of Reconciliation* (Ashgate 2007)

Bankowski Z, 'The Risk of Reconciliation' in Scott Veitch (ed.), *Law and the Politics of Reconciliation* (Ashgate 2007)

Beardsworth R, *Derrida and the Political* (Routledge 1996)

Bell C, 'Dealing With the Past in Northern Ireland' (2002) 26 *Fordham International Law Journal* 1095

—— *Lex Pacificatoria: The Law of the Peacemaker* (Oxford University Press 2006)

—— *Peace Agreements and Human Rights* (Oxford University Press 2000)

—— 'Peace Agreements: Their Nature and Legal Status' (2006) 100 *American Journal of International Law* 373

—— 'Transitional Justice, Interdisciplinarity and the State of the "Field" or "Non-Field"' (2009) 3 *International Journal of Transitional Justice* 5

—— and Kavanaugh K, 'Constructive Ambiguity, or Internal Self Determination? Self Determination, Group Accommodation and the Belfast Agreement' (1998) 22 *Fordham International Law Journal* 1345

—— and Keenan J, 'Lost on the Way Home? The Right to Life in Northern Ireland' (2005) 32(1) *Journal of Law and Society* 68

—— and O'Rourke C, 'Does Feminism Need a Theory of Transitional Justice?' (2007) 1 *International Journal of Transitional Justice* 23

—— Campbell C and Ní Aoláin F, 'Justice Discourses in Transition' (2004) 13 *Social and Legal Studies* 305

Benjamin W, 'Critique of Violence' in Edmund Jephcott tr., *Reflections: Essays, Aphorisms, Autobiographical Writings* (Random House 1995)

Bennington G and Derrida J, *Jacques Derrida*, Geoffrey Bennington tr. (University of Chicago Press 1993)

Bickford L *et al.*, *Documenting Truth* (International Centre for Transitional Justice 2009)

Boraine A, *A Country Unmasked: Inside South Africa's Truth and Reconciliation Commission* (Oxford University Press 2000)

Boyle K, Hadden T and Hillyard P, *Law and State: The Case of Northern Ireland* (University of Massachusetts Press 1975)

—— *Ten Years on in Northern Ireland: The Legal Control of Political Violence* (The Cobden Trust 1980)

Brown K, 'Rights and Victims, Martyrs and Memories: The European Court of Human Rights and Political Transition in Northern Ireland' in Antoine Buyse and Michael Hamilton (eds), *Transitional Jurisprudence and the ECHR: Justice, Politics and Rights* (Cambridge University Press 2011)

—— 'What It Was Like to Live Through a Day: Transitional Justice and the Memory of the Everyday in a Divided Society' (2012) 6 *International Journal of Transitional Justice* 444

Buonamono R, 'The Economy of Violence: Derrida on Law and Justice' (1998) 11(2) *Ratio Juris* 168

Campaign for Social Justice in Northern Ireland, *Northern Ireland: The Plain Truth* (Dungannon, 1964)

Campbell C and Connolly I, 'A Model for the "War Against Terrorism"? Military Intervention in Northern Ireland and the Falls Curfew' (2003) 30 *Journal of Law and Society* 341

—— and Ní Aoláin F, 'The Paradox of Transitions in Liberal Democracies' (2005) 27 *Human Rights Quarterly* 172

—— and Turner C, 'Utopia and the Doubters: Truth, Transition and the Law' (2008) 23 *Legal Studies* 374

—— Ní Aoláin F and Harvey C, 'The Frontiers of Analysis: Re-framing the Transition in Northern Ireland' (2003) 66 *Modern Law Review* 317

Campbell G, 'The Peace Process and the Protestants' in Dominic Murray (ed.), *Protestant Perceptions of the Peace Process in Northern Ireland* (Cain 2000)

Castillejo-Cuéllar A, 'Historical Injuries, Temporality and the Law: Articulations of a Violent Past in Two Transitional Scenarios' (2014) 25 *Law and Critique* 47

Charlesworth H and Chinkin C, *The Boundaries of International Law: A Feminist Analysis* (Manchester University Press 2000)

Chinkin C, 'Rape and Sexual Abuse of Women in International Law' (1994) 5 *European Journal of International Law* 326

Christodoulidis E, 'Truth and Reconciliation and Risks' (2000) 9 *Social and Legal Studies* 179

Clark P, *The Gacaca Courts and Post-Genocide Justice and Reconciliation in Rwanda: Justice Without Lawyers* (Cambridge University Press 2010)

—— 'Negotiating Reconciliation in Rwanda: Popular Challenges to the Official Discourse of Post-Genocide National Unity' (2014) 8 *Journal of Intervention and State Building* 303

Collins B, 'The Belfast Agreement and the Nation that "Always Arrives at Its Destination"' (2002) 20 *Penn State International Law Review* 385

Committee on the Administration of Justice, 'Dealing with the Past in Northern Ireland: Implementing the Stormont House Agreement' (2015) Conference Report and Papers, www.caj.org.uk/contents/1289, accessed 21 March 2016

—— *Equality in Northern Ireland: The Rhetoric and the Reality* (Belfast, 2006)

—— *Mapping the Rollback: Human Rights Provisions of the Belfast/Good Friday Agreement 15 Years On* (Belfast, 2013)

Consultative Group on the Past, 'Report of the Consultative Group on the Past' (HC 2009–10, UK Parliament 2009) http://cain.ulst.ac.uk/victims/docs/consultative_group/cgp_230109_report.pdf, accessed 17 November 2015

Cornell D, 'The Violence of the Masquerade: Law Dressed Up as Justice' (1990) 11 *Cardozo Law Review* 1047

Corson B, 'Transcending Violence in Derrida: A Reply to John McCormick' (2001) 29 *Political Theory* 866

Critchley S, 'An Ethos of Reading' (2005) 129 *Radical Philosophy* 26

Cunningham T, 'Monitoring Equality – Reflexive Regulation, Planning Systems, and the Role of Discrimination Law: Lessons from Northern Ireland' (2015) 14 *Equal Rights Review* 119

Curtis J, *Human Rights as War by other Means: Peace Politics in Northern Ireland* (University of Pennsylvania Press 2014)

Daly E, 'Truth Skepticism: An Inquiry into the Value of Truth in Times of Transition' (2008) 2 *International Journal of Transitional Justice* 23

Dancy G, 'Impact Assessment, not Evaluation: Defining a Limited Role for Positivism in the Study of Transitional Justice' (2010) 4 *International Journal of Transitional Justice* 355

Davies M, 'Derrida and Law: Legitimate Fictions' in Tom Cohen (ed.), *Jacques Derrida and the Humanities: A Critical Reader* (Cambridge University Press 2002)

Democratic Dialogue, *Politics in Public – Freedom of Assembly and the Right to Protest* (Belfast, 1998)

Derby J, 'Conflict in Northern Ireland: A Background Essay' in Seamus Dunn (ed.), *Facets of the Conflict in Northern Ireland* (Macmillan Press 1995)

Derrida J, 'Autoimmunity: Real and Symbolic Suicides' in Giovanna Borradori (ed.), *Philosophy in a Time of Terror: Dialogues with Jurgen Habermas and Jacques Derrida* (University of Chicago Press 2003)

—— *The Death Penalty, Volume 1*, Peggy Kamuf tr. (University of Chicago Press 2014)

—— 'Declarations of Independence' in Elizabeth Rottenberg (ed.), *Negotiations: Interventions and Interviews, 1971–2001* (Stanford University Press 2002)

—— 'Devant La Loi' in Alan Udof (ed.), *Kafka and the Contemporary Critical Performance* (Indiana University Press 1987)

—— 'Force of Law: The Mystical Foundation of Authority' in Drucilla Cornell *et al.* (eds), *Deconstruction and the Possibility of Justice* (Routledge 1992)

—— 'The Laws of Reflection: Nelson Mandela, In Admiration' in Jacques Derrida and Mustafa Tlili (eds), *For Nelson Mandela* (Seaver Books 1987)

—— 'Letter to a Japanese Friend' in Peggy Kamuf and Elizabeth G Rottenberg (eds), *Psyche: Interventions of the Other Volume III* (Stanford University Press 2008)
—— *Monolingualism of the Other: or, The Prosthesis of Origin*, Patrick Mensah tr. (Stanford University Press 1998)
—— *Of Grammatology*, Gayatri Chakravorty Spivak tr. (Johns Hopkins University Press 1976)
—— *On Cosmopolitanism and Forgiveness*, Mark Dooley and Michael Hughes tr. (Routledge 2001)
—— *Politics of Friendship*, George Collins tr. (Verso 1997)
—— *Positions* (The Athlone Press 1981)
—— 'Signature, Event, Context' in Alan Bass tr., *Margins of Philosophy* (The Harvester Press 1982)
—— 'Spectres of Marx' (1994) 15 *New Political Science* 7
—— 'Violence and Metaphysics' in Alan Bass tr., *Writing and Difference* (Routledge 1978)
—— and Caputo JD, *Deconstruction in a Nutshell: A Conversation with Jacques Derrida* (Fordham 1997)
De Ville J, 'Sovereignty without Sovereignty: Derrida's Declarations of Independence' (2008) 19 *Law and Critique* 87
Dhawan N, 'Transitions to Justice' in Susanne Buckley-Zistel and Ruth Stanley (eds), *Gender in Transitional Justice* (Palgrave MacMillan 2011)
Dickson B, 'The House of Lords and the Northern Ireland Conflict – A Sequel' (2006) 69 *Modern Law Review* 383
Dingley J and Morgan J, 'Job Discrimination in Northern Ireland in Relation to the Theory of Ethnic Nationalism' (2005) 7 *National Identities* 51
Donnan H and Simpson K, 'Silence and Violence among Northern Ireland Border Protestants' (2007) 72 *Ethnos* 5
Douzinas C, 'Violence, Justice and Deconstruction' (2005) 6 *German Law Journal* 171
—— and Geary A, *Critical Jurisprudence: The Political Philosophy of Justice* (Hart 2005)
Dube S, 'Transitional Justice Beyond the Normative: Towards a Literary Theory of Political Transitions' (2011) 5 *International Journal of Transitional Justice* 177
Duffy A, 'A Truth Commission for Northern Ireland' (2010) 4 *International Journal of Transitional Justice* 26
Dugard J, 'Retrospective Justice: International Law and the South African Model' in A James McAdams (ed.), *Transitional Justice and the Rule of Law in New Democracies* (University of Notre Dame Press 1997)
Dworkin R, 'Hard Cases' (1975) 88 *Harvard Law Review* 1057
—— *Law's Empire* (Fontana 1986)
Ellison G and Martin G, 'Policing, Collective Action and Social Movement Theory: The Case of the Northern Ireland Civil Rights Campaign' (2000) 51 *British Journal of Sociology* 681
Engle K, 'International Human Rights and Feminism: Where Discourses Meet' (1992) 13 *Michigan Journal of International Law* 517
Fearon K and McWilliams M, 'The Good Friday Agreement: A Triumph of Substance over Style' (1998) 22 *Fordham International Law Journal* 1250
Fraser N, 'The Force of Law: Metaphysical or Political?' (1991) 13 *Cardozo Law Review* 1325
Frazer E and Hutchings K, 'Remnants and Revenants: Politics and Violence in the Work of Agamben and Derrida' (2011) 13 *British Journal of Politics and International Relations* 127
Gearty C, 'Terrorism and Morality' (2003) 4 *European Human Rights Law Review* 377

Gehring P, 'The Jurisprudence of the "Force of Law"' in Peter Goodrich *et al.* (eds), *Derrida and Legal Philosophy* (Palgrave Macmillan 2008)

González E and Varney H (eds), *Truth Seeking: Elements of Creating an Effective Truth Commission* (International Center for Transitional Justice 2013)

Goodrich P *et al.*, 'Introduction: A Philosophy of Legal Enigmas' in P Goodrich *et al.* (eds), *Derrida and Legal Philosophy* (Palgrave Macmillan 2008)

Gready P and Robbins S, 'From Transitional to Transformative Justice: A New Agenda for Practice' (2014) 8 *International Journal of Transitional Justice* 344

Griffiths JAG, *The Politics of the Judiciary* (Manchester University Press 1977)

Gross O and Ní Aoláin F, *Law in Times of Crisis: Emergency Powers in Theory and Practice* (Cambridge 2006)

—— 'To Know Where We Are Going, We Need to Know Where We Are: Revisiting States of Emergency' in Angela Hegarty and Siobhan Leonard (eds), *Human Rights: An Agenda for the Twenty First Century* (Cavendish 1998)

Hamber B and Wilson R, 'Symbolic Closure through Memory, Reparation and Revenge in Post Conflict Societies' (2002) Research Papers: Paper 5 http://digitalcommons.uconn.edu/hri_papers/5, accessed 19 October 2015

Hamilton M, 'Freedom of Assembly, Consequential Harms and the Rule of Law: Liberty Limiting Principles in the Context of Transition' (2007) 27 *Oxford Journal of Legal Studies* 75

—— and Buyse A, 'Introduction' in Antoine Buyse and Michael Hamilton (eds), *Transitional Jurisprudence and the European Convention on Human Rights* (Cambridge University Press 2011)

Hart HLA, *The Concept of Law* (Clarendon Press 1961)

—— 'Legal Positivism', *Encyclopaedia of Philosophy* (1967)

Hayner P, 'Fifteen Truth Commissions – 1974–1994' (1994) 16 *Human Rights Quarterly* 597

—— *Unspeakable Truths: Transitional Justice and the Challenge of Truth Commissions* (Routledge 2010)

Healing Through Remembering, *Dealing with the Past? An Overview of Legal and Political Approaches Relating to the Conflict in and about Northern Ireland* (Belfast, 2013)

Hearty K, 'A Shared Narrative? A Case Study of the Contested Legacy of Policing in the North of Ireland' (2014) 54 *British Journal of Criminology* 1047

Hegarty A, 'The Government of Memory: Public Inquiries and the Limits of Justice in Northern Ireland' (2002) 26 *Fordham International Law Journal* 1148

Hennessy T, *A History of Northern Ireland 1920–1996* (Gill and Macmillan 1997)

Her Majesty's Stationery Office, 'Disturbances in Northern Ireland: Report of the Commission Appointed by the Governor of Northern Ireland' (Belfast, 1969) (Cameron Report)

—— 'Report of a Committee to Consider, in the Context of Civil Liberties and Human Rights, Measures to Deal with Terrorism in Northern Ireland' (London, 1975) (Gardiner Report)

—— 'Report of the Tribunal of Inquiry on Violence and Civil Disturbances in Northern Ireland in 1969' (Belfast, 1972) (Scarman Report)

Hillyard P, *Suspect Community: People's Experience of the Prevention of Terrorism Act in Britain* (Pluto Press 1993)

Hume J, 'Ireland – The Healing Process' (1998) 22 *Fordham International Law Journal* 1171

Independent Commission on Policing for Northern Ireland, 'A New Beginning: Policing in Northern Ireland' (Belfast, 1999) (Patten Report)

International Institute for Democracy and Electoral Assistance, *Reconciliation After Violent Conflict: A Handbook* (Stockholm, 2003)

Kant I, *To Perpetual Peace* (1795)

Kearney V, 'Proposed Legislation on Past Unworkable, Says Sinn Féin' (BBC News Northern Ireland, 8 October 2015) www.bbc.co.uk/news/uk-northern-ireland-34481123, accessed 8 October 2015

Khatib S, 'Towards a Politics of "Pure Means": Walter Benjamin and the Question of Violence' (2015) Anthropological Materialism http://anthropologicalmaterialism.hypotheses.org/1040, accessed 19 October 2015

Kingsbury B, 'Legal Positivism as Normative Politics: International Society, Balance of Power and Lassa Oppenheim's Positive International Law' (2002) 13 *European Journal of International Law* 401

Koskenniemi M, *From Apology to Utopia: The Structure of International Legal Argument* (Cambridge University Press 2005)

Kritz NJ (ed.), *Transitional Justice: How Emerging Democracies Reckon with Former Regimes* (United States Institute of Peace 1996) vols 1–3

Kuovo S, 'Review Essay: Feminism, Gender and International (Criminal) Law: From Asking the "Woman Question" in Law to Moving Beyond Law' (2014) 16 *International Feminist Journal of Politics* 669

—— and Pearson Z, 'Introduction' in Sari Kuovo and Zoe Pearson (eds), *Feminist Perspectives on Contemporary International Law: Between Resistance and Compliance* (Hart 2011)

LaCapra D, 'Violence, Justice and the Force of Law' (1990) 11 *Cardozo Law Review* 1065

Lacey N, 'Modern Positivism: H.L.A. Hart and Analytical Jurisprudence' in James Penner *et al.* (eds), *Jurisprudence and Legal Theory* (Oxford University Press 2005)

Lai C, 'On Violence, Justice and Deconstruction' (2003) 29 *Concentric: Studies in English Literature and Linguistics* 23

Laplante L, 'Transitional Justice and Peacebuilding: Diagnosing and Addressing the Socioeconomic Roots of Violence through a Human Rights Framework' (2008) 2 *International Journal of Transitional Justice* 331

Lawlor L, 'From the Trace to the Law: Derridean Politics' (1989) 15 *Philosophy and Social Criticism* 1

Lawther C, 'Denial, Silence and the Politics of the Past: Unpicking Opposition to Truth Recovery in Northern Ireland' (2013) 7 *International Journal of Transitional Justice* 157

—— 'Securing the Past: Policing and the Contest over Truth in Northern Ireland' (2010) 50 *British Journal of Criminology* 455

—— *Truth, Denial and Transition: Northern Ireland and the Contested Past* (Routledge 2014)

Leebaw B, 'The Irreconcilable Goals of Transitional Justice' (2008) 30 *Human Rights Quarterly* 95

—— *Judging State Sponsored Violence, Imagining Political Change* (Cambridge University Press 2011)

Legacy Gender Integration Group, *Gender Principles for Dealing with the Legacy of the Past* (Belfast, 2015)

Livingstone S, 'The House of Lords and the Northern Ireland Conflict' (1994) 57 *Modern Law Review* 333

Lundy P, 'Can the Past Be Policed? Lessons from the Historical Enquiries Team in Northern Ireland' (2009) 11 *Journal of Law and Social Challenges* 109

Lundy P, and McGovern M, 'A Trojan Horse? Unionism, Trust and Truth-Telling in Northern Ireland' (2008) 2 *International Journal of Transitional Justice* 42

—— 'Whose Justice: Rethinking Transitional Justice from the Bottom Up' (2008) 35 *Journal of Law and Society* 265

—— and Rolston B, 'Redress for Past Harms? Official Apologies in Northern Ireland' (2015) *International Journal of Human Rights* http://dx.doi.org/10.1080/13642987.2015.1050235, accessed 19 October 2015

McCormick JP, 'Derrida on Law: or, Poststructuralism Gets Serious' (2001) 29 *Political Theory* 395

McDonald H, 'Government Creates Northern Ireland Ceasefire Monitor after IRA Claims' *The Guardian* (London, 18 September 2015) www.theguardian.com/uk-news/2015/sep/18/government-northern-ireland-ceasefire-monitor-ira-claims, accessed 19 October 2015

McEvoy K, 'Beyond Legalism: Towards a Thicker Understanding of Transitional Justice' (2007) 34 *Journal of Law and Society* 411

—— 'Human Rights, Humanitarian Interventions and Paramilitary Activities in Northern Ireland' in Colin Harvey (ed.), *Human Rights, Equality and Democratic Renewal in Northern Ireland* (Hart 2001)

—— 'Law, Struggle and Political Transformation in Northern Ireland' (2000) 27(4) *Journal of Law and Society* 542

—— 'Making Peace with the Past: Options for Truth Recovery Regarding the Conflict In and About Northern Ireland' (Healing Through Remembering 2006)

—— 'What Did Lawyers Do During the War? Neutrality, Conflict and the Culture of Quietism' (2011) 74 *Modern Law Review* 350

—— and McConnachie, K, 'Victims and Transitional Justice: Voice, Agency and Blame' (2013) 22 *Social and Legal Studies* 489

—— and McGregor L (eds), *Transitional Justice From Below: Grassroots Activism and the Struggle for Change* (Hart 2008)

—— and Mallinder L, 'Truth, Amnesty and Prosecutions: Models for Dealing with the Past': 2nd Submission to Haas-O'Sullivan Talks (Belfast, 2013)

—— and Morison J, 'Beyond the Constitutional Moment: Law, Transition and Peacemaking in Northern Ireland' (2003) 24 *Fordham International Law Journal* 961

—— and White C, 'Security Vetting in Northern Ireland: Loyalty, Redress and Citizenship' (1999) 61 *Modern Law Review* 341

—— *et al.*, 'Dealing with the Past in Northern Ireland: Amnesties, Prosecutions and the Public Interest': Written Submission to Dr Richard Haass and Dr Meaghan O'Sullivan and the Panel of Parties in the Northern Ireland Executive (Belfast, 2013) http://blogs.qub.ac.uk/amnesties/files/2013/11/Amnesties-Prosecutions-and-Public-Interest-Submission-to-Haass-talks.pdf, accessed 19 October 2015

McEvoy L, McEvoy K and McConnachie K, 'Reconciliation Is a Dirty Word: Conflict, Community Relations and Education in Northern Ireland' (2006) 60 *Journal of International Affairs* 81

MacGinty R and Du Toit P, 'A Disparity of Esteem: Relative Group Status in Northern Ireland after the Belfast Agreement' (2007) 28 *Political Psychology* 13

McHugh M and McKeown L, 'DUP MP Nigel Dodds Hit by Brick During North Belfast Twelfth Riot' (*Belfast Telegraph*, 13 July 2013) www.belfasttelegraph.co.uk/news/northern-ireland/dup-mp-nigel-dodds-hit-by-brick-during-north-belfast-twelfth-riot-29417638.html, accessed 19 October 2015

McKittrick D *et al.*, *Lost Lives: The Stories of the Men, Women and Children Who Died as a Result of the Northern Ireland Troubles* (Mainstream Publishing 1999)
Madlingozi T, 'Good Victim, Bad Victim: Apartheid's Beneficiaries, Victims and the Struggle for Social Justice' in Wessel Le Roux and Karin Van Marle (eds), *Law, Memory and the Legacy of Apartheid: Ten Years after AZAPO v President of South Africa* (Pretoria University Law Press 2007)
Mageean P and O'Brien M, 'From the Margins to the Mainstream: Human Rights and the Good Friday Agreement' (1998) 22 *Fordham International Law Journal* 1498
Mahlmann M, 'Law and Force: 20th Century Radical Legal Philosophy, Post Modernism and the Foundations of Law' (2003) 9 *Res Publica* 19
Maley W, 'Beyond the Law? The Justice of Deconstruction' (1999) 10 *Law and Critique* 49
Mallinder L, *Amnesty, Human Rights and Political Transitions: Bridging the Peace and Justice Divide* (Hart 2008)
—— *Belfast Guidelines on Amnesty and Accountability* (Transitional Justice Institute 2014)
Mamdani M, 'From Justice to Reconciliation: Making Sense of the African Experience' in Colin Leys and Mahmood Mamdani (eds), *Crisis and Reconstruction: African Perspectives* (Nordisk Afrikainstitut 1997)
Mani R, 'Dilemmas of Expanding Transitional Justice, or Forging the Nexus between Transitional Justice and Development' (2008) 2 *International Journal of Transitional Justice* 253
Manseragh N, 'The Influence of the Past' in David Watt (ed.), *The Constitution of Northern Ireland: Problems and Prospects* (Heinemann 1981)
Matthews B, 'Why Deconstruction Is Beneficial' (2000) 4 *Flinders Journal of Law Reform* 105
Matua M, 'What Is the Future of Transitional Justice?' (2015) 9 *International Journal of Transitional Justice* 1
Miller Z, 'Effects of Invisibility: In Search of the "Economic" in Transitional Justice' (2008) 2 *International Journal of Transitional Justice* 266
Minkinnen P, 'Ressentiment as Suffering: On Transitional Justice and the Impossibility of Forgiveness' (2007) 19 *Law and Literature* 513
Mitchell D, 'Cooking the Fudge: Constructive Ambiguity and the Implementation of the Northern Ireland Agreement, 1998–2007' (2009) 24 *Irish Political Studies* 321.
Moon, C, 'Narrating Political Reconciliation: Truth and Reconciliation in South Africa' (2006) 15 *Social and Legal Studies* 257
—— 'Prelapsarian State: Forgiveness and Reconciliation in Transitional Justice' (2004) 17 *International Journal for the Semiotics of Law* 185
—— 'Who'll Pay Reparations on my Soul? Social Control and Social Suffering in Argentina' (2012) 21 *Social and Legal Studies* 187
Morrison J and Lynch M, 'Litigating the Agreement: Towards a New Judicial Constitutionalism for the UK from Northern Ireland' in Kieran McEvoy *et al.* (eds), *Judges, Transition and Human Rights: Essays in Memory of Stephen Livingstone* (Oxford University Press 2007) 105
Moyo K, 'Mimicry, Transitional Justice and the Land Question in Racially Divided Former Settler Colonies' (2015) 9 *International Journal of Transitional Justice* 70
Muvingi I, 'Sitting on Powder Kegs: Socioeconomic Rights in Transitional Societies' (2009) 3 *International Journal of Transitional Justice* 163
Nagy R, 'Transitional Justice as Global Project: Critical Reflections' (2008) 29 *Third World Quarterly* 275

Nesiah V, 'Missionary Zeal for a Secular Mission: Bringing Gender to Transitional Justice and Redemption to Feminism' in Sari Kuovo and Zoe Pearson (eds), *Feminist Perspectives on Contemporary International Law: Between Resistance and Compliance* (Hart 2011)

Ní Aoláin F, 'Advancing Feminist Positioning in the Field of Transitional Justice' (2012) 6 *International Journal of Transitional Justice* 205

—— *The Politics of Force: Conflict Management and State Violence in Northern Ireland* (Blackstaff Press 2000)

—— 'Transitional Emergency Jurisprudence: Derogation and Transition' in Antoine Buyse and Michael Hamilton (eds), *Transitional Jurisprudence: Transitional Justice and the ECHR* (Cambridge 2011)

—— 'Truth Telling, Accountability and the Right to Life in Northern Ireland' (2002) 5 *European Human Rights Law Review* 572

—— and Turner C, 'Gender, Truth and Transition' (2007) 16 *UCLA Women's Law Journal* 229

Nolan P, 'Northern Ireland Peace Monitoring Report No. 3' (Community Relations Council 2014)

—— *et al.*, *The Flag Dispute: Anatomy of a Protest* (Queens University Belfast 2014)

Northern Ireland Civil Rights Association, *We Shall Overcome: The History of the Northern Ireland Civil Rights Association 1968–1978* (Belfast, 1978)

Northern Ireland Human Rights Commission 'A Bill of Rights for Northern Ireland: Advice to the Secretary of State for Northern Ireland' (Belfast, 2003) www.nihrc.org/uploads/publications/bill-of-rights-for-northern-ireland-advice-to-secretary-state-2008.pdf, accessed 19 October 2015

——, *Dealing with Northern Ireland's Past: Towards a Transitional Justice Approach* (Belfast, 2013)

Obel Hansen T, "The vertical and horizontal expansion of transitional justice: Explanations and implications for a contested field' in Susanne Buckley-Zistel *et al.* (eds) *Transitional Justice Theories* (Routledge 2014) 105

Obradović-Wochnik J, 'The "Silent Dilemma" of Transitional Justice: Silencing and Coming to Terms with the Past in Serbia' (2013) 7 *International Journal of Transitional Justice* 328

Office of the High Commissioner for Human Rights, *Transitional Justice and Economic, Social and Cultural Rights* (UN Doc. HR/PUB13/5, United Nations 2014)

O'Leary, Brendan and John McGarry, *The Politics of Antagonism: Understanding Northern Ireland* (Athlone Press, 1993)

Olsen T, Payne L and Reiter A, *Transitional Justice in Balance: Comparing Processes, Weighing Efficacy* (United States Institute of Peace 2010)

Orentlicher D, 'Settling Accounts: The Duty to Prosecute Human Rights Violations of Prior Regimes' (1991) 100 *Yale Law Journal* 2539

Orford A, 'Commissioning the Truth' (2006) 15 *Columbia Journal of Gender and Law* 851

O'Rourke, Catherine 'Feminist Scholarship in Transitional Justice: A De-Politicising Impulse?' (2014) 51 *Women's Studies International Forum* 118

—— *Gender Politics in Transitional Justice* (Routledge 2013)

—— 'International Law and Domestic Gender Justice, or Why Case Studies Matter' in Martha Fineman and Estelle Zinsstag (eds), *Feminist Perspectives on Transitional Justice: From International and Criminal to Alternative Forms of Justice* (Intersentia 2013)

Paisley I, 'Peace Agreement – or Last Piece in a Sellout Agreement?' (1998) 22 *Fordham International Law Journal* 1273

Parades Commission, Determination Made in Relation to the Ligoniel True Blues LOL 1932 Parade Notified to Take Place in Belfast on Friday, 12 July 2013, www.paradescommission.org/fs/files/det-ligoniel-true-blues-lol-1932-12july-2013.pdf, accessed 16 March 2016

Primoratz I, 'What Is Terrorism?' (1990) 7 *Journal of Applied Philosophy* 129

Quinn J (ed.), *Reconciliation(s): Transitional Justice in Postconflict Societies* (McGill-Queen's University Press 2009)

Ramshaw S, 'Deconstructing Jazz Improvisation: Derrida and the Law of the Singular Event' (2006) 2 *Critical Studies in Improvisation* 1

Raz J, *The Authority of Law* (Clarendon Press 1979)

Reilly N, *Women's Human Rights: Seeking Gender Justice in a Globalising Age* (Polity 2009)

Requa M, 'Keeping Up with Strasbourg: Article 2 Obligations and Northern Ireland's Pending Inquests' [2012] 4 *Public Law* 610

—— 'Truth, Transition and the Inquiries Act 2005' (2007) 12(4) *European Human Rights Law Review* 404

—— and Anthony G, 'Coroners, Controversial Deaths, and Northern Ireland's Past Conflict' [2008] *Public Law* 443

Robbins S, 'Mapping a Future for Transitional Justice by Learning from its Past' (2015) 9 *International Journal of Transitional Justice* 181

Rolston B, 'Dealing with the Past: Pro-State Paramilitaries, Truth and Transition in Northern Ireland' (2006) 28 *Human Rights Quarterly* 652

Rooney E, 'Intersectionality: A Feminist Theory for Transitional Justice' in Martha Fineman and Estelle Zinsstag (eds), *Feminist Perspectives on Transitional Justice: From International and Criminal to Alternative Forms of Justice* (Intersentia 2013)

Rosenfeld M, 'Deconstruction and Legal Interpretation: Conflict, Indeterminacy and the Temptations of the New Legal Formalism' in Drucilla Cornell *et al.* (eds), *Deconstruction and the Possibility of Justice* (Routledge 1992)

Ross F, *Bearing Witness: Women in the Truth and Reconciliation Commission in South Africa* (Pluto 2003)

Sankey D, 'Towards the Recognition of Subsistence Harms: Reassessing Current Approaches to Socio-Economic Forms of Violence in Transitional Justice' (2013) 8 *International Journal of Transitional Justice* 121

Sarkin J, 'The Tension Between Justice and Reconciliation in Rwanda: Politics, Human Rights, Due Process and the Role of Gacaca Courts in Dealing with the Genocide' (2001) 45 *Journal of African Law* 143

—— and Daly E, 'Too Many Questions, Too Few Answers: Reconciliation in Transitional Societies' (2004) 35(3) *Columbia Human Rights Law Review* 101

Saunders R, 'Questionable Associations: The Role of Forgiveness in Transitional Justice' (2011) 5 *International Journal of Transitional Justice* 119

Schapp A, 'The Time of Reconciliation and the Space of Politics' in Scott Veitch (ed.), *Law and the Politics of Reconciliation* (Ashgate 2007)

Schmid E and Nolan E, 'Do No Harm? Exploring the Scope of Economic and Social Rights in Transitional Justice' (2014) 8 *International Journal of Transitional Justice* 362

Sharp D, 'Emancipating Transitional Justice from the Bonds of the Paradigmatic Transition' (2014) 9 *International Journal of Transitional Justice* 150

Simpson K, 'Political Strategies of Engagement: Unionists and Dealing with the Past in Northern Ireland' (2013) 8 *British Politics* 2

—— *Truth Recovery in Northern Ireland: Critically Interpreting the Past* (Manchester University Press 2009)
—— *Unionist Voices and the Politics of Remembering the Past in Northern Ireland* (Palgrave 2009)
—— 'Untold Stories: Unionist Remembrance of Political Violence and Suffering in Northern Ireland' (2008) 3 *British Politics* 465
—— 'Voices Silenced, Voices Re-discovered: Victims of Violence and the Reclamation of Language in Transitional Societies' (2007) 3 *International Journal of Law in Context* 89
Sinn Fein, *Towards a Lasting Peace in Ireland: Sinn Fein Manifesto for the Westminster Election* (Belfast, 1992)
Sinnerbrink R, 'Deconstructive Justice and the "Critique of Violence": On Derrida and Benjamin' (2006) 16 *Social Semiotics* 485
Sokoloff W, 'Between Justice and Legality: Derrida on Decision' (2005) 58 *Political Research Quarterly* 341
Stauffer J, *Ethical Loneliness: The Injustice of Not Being Heard* (Columbia University Press 2015)
—— 'Speaking Truth to Reconciliation: Political Transition, Recovery and the Work of Time' (2013) 4 *Humanity* 27
Subotić J, 'The Transformation of International Transitional Justice Advocacy' (2012) 6 *International Journal of Transitional Justice* 106
Teichman J, 'How to Define Terrorism' (1989) 64 *Philosophy* 505
Teitel R, *Transitional Justice* (Oxford University Press 2000)
—— 'Transitional Justice Genealogy' (2003) 16 *Harvard Human Rights Law Journal* 69
The Holy Bible, King James Version (Cambridge University Press 1611)
Tremlett G, 'Human Rights Groups are Complicit in Murder, Says Trimble', *The Guardian* (London, 29 January 2004) www.theguardian.com/uk/2004/jan/29/northernireland.humanrights, accessed 19 October 2015
Trimble D, 'The Belfast Agreement' (1998) 22 *Fordham International Law Journal* 1145
Turner C, 'The Art(s) of Dealing with the Past' (RightsNI, 1 April 2015) http://rightsni.org/2015/04/the-arts-of-dealing-with-the-past/, accessed 19 October 2015
—— 'Deconstructing Transitional Justice' (2013) 24 *Law and Critique* 193
—— 'Delivering Lasting Peace, Democracy and Human Rights in Transition: The Role of International Law' (2008) 2 *International Journal of Transitional Justice* 126
—— 'Flag Protests, Politics and Transition in Northern Ireland' (Critical Legal Thinking 2013) http://criticallegalthinking.com/2013/02/04/flag-protests-politics-and-transition-in-northern-ireland/, accessed 6 August 2015
—— 'Human Rights and the Empire of (International) Law' (2011) 29 *Law and Inequality* 313
—— 'Political Representations of Law in Northern Ireland' [2010] *Public Law* 451
—— 'The "Right" to Protest on Northern Ireland's Streets' (Human Rights in Ireland, 20 January 2013) http://humanrights.ie/civil-liberties/turnerresponse/, accessed 14 August 2015
—— 'Transitional Constitutionalism and the Case of the Arab Spring' (2015) 64 *International and Comparative Law Quarterly* 267
—— and Houghton R, 'Constitution Making and Post-Conflict Reconstruction' in Matthew Saul and James Sweeney (eds), *International Law and Post-Conflict Reconstruction* (Routledge 2015)
Ulster Unionist Party, Proposals for Flags, Parades and Dealing with the Past (March 2014) http://uup.org/assets/images/featured/proposals%20on%20parades%20protests%20flags%20and%20dealing%20with%20the%20past.pdf, accessed 16 November 2015

United Nations, 'Basic Principles and Guidelines on the Right to a Remedy and Reparation for Victims of Gross Violations of International Human Rights Law and Serious Violations of International Humanitarian Law': GA Res. 60/147 (UN Doc. A/RES/60/147, United Nations 2006)

—— 'Guidance Note of the Secretary General: United Nations Approach to Transitional Justice' (United Nations 2010)

—— 'Guidance Note on Gender and Transitional Justice' (United Nations 2010)

—— 'Human Rights and Transitional Justice: Report of the United Nations High Commissioner for Human Rights' (UN Doc. A/HRC/4/87, United Nations 2006)

—— 'Mandate of the UN Rapporteur on the Promotion of Truth, Justice, Reparation and Guarantees of Non-Recurrence' (UN Doc. A/HRC/RES/18.7, United Nations 2011)

—— 'Report of the Office of the High Commissioner for Human Rights, Implementation of General Assembly Resolution 60/251 Entitled Human Rights Council' (UN Doc. A/HRC/5/7, United Nations 2007)

—— 'Report of the Secretary General on the Rule of Law and Transitional Justice in Conflict and Post Conflict Societies' (UN Doc. S/2004/616, United Nations 2004)

—— 'The Rule of Law and Transitional Justice in Conflict and Post Conflict Societies: Report of the Secretary General to the Security Council' (UN Doc. S/2011/634, United Nations 2011)

—— 'Rule of Law Tools for Post Conflict States: Amnesties' (UN Doc. HR/PUB/09/1, United Nations 2009)

—— 'Rule of Law Tools for Post Conflict States: Prosecution Initiatives' (UN Doc. HR/PUB/06/4, United Nations 2006)

—— 'Rule of Law Tools for Post Conflict States: Reparations Programmes' (UN Doc. HR/PUB/08/1, United Nations 2008)

—— 'Rule of Law Tools for Post Conflict States: Truth Commissions' (UN Doc. HR/PUB/06/1, United Nations 2006)

—— 'Rule of Law Tools for Post Conflict States: Vetting: An Operational Framework' (UN Doc. HR/PUB/06/5, United Nations 2006)

—— 'Updated Set of Principles for the Protection and Promotion of Human Rights Through Action to Combat Impunity' (UN Doc. E/CN.4/2005/102/Add.1, United Nations 2005)

UN Commission on Human Rights, Human Rights Resolution 2005/66: Right to the Truth (E/CN.4/RES/2005/66, United Nations 2005)

UN Women, *A Window of Opportunity: Making Transitional Justice Work for Women*, 2nd edn (United Nations 2010)

Vaisman N, 'Variations on Justice: Argentina's Pre- and Post- Transitional Justice and the Justice to Come' (2015) Ethnos http://dx.doi.org/10.1080/00141844.2015.1080746, accessed 19 October 2015

Walsh D, *The Use and Abuse of Emergency Legislation in Northern Ireland* (The Cobden Trust 1983)

Weinstein H, 'Editorial Note: The Myth of Closure, the Illusion of Reconciliation: Final Thoughts on Five Years as Co-Editor-in-Chief' (2011) 6 *International Journal of Transitional Justice* 1

—— *et al.*, 'Editorial Note' (2007) 1(1) *International Journal of Transitional Justice* 1

Wilke C, 'Enter Ghost: Haunted Courts and Haunting Judgments in Transitional Justice' (2010) 21 *Law and Critique* 73

Wilson R, *The Politics of Truth and Reconciliation in South Africa: Legitimising the Post-Apartheid State* (Cambridge University Press 2001)
Whyte J, 'How Much Discrimination Was There under the Unionist Regime 1921–1968?' in Tom Gallagher and James O'Connell (eds), *Contemporary Irish Studies* (Manchester University Press 1983)

Cases

Brannigan and McBride v United Kingdom [1993] 17 EHRR 539
Brogan and Others v United Kingdom [1988] 11 EHRR 177
Ex Parte Lynch [1980] NI 126
In the Matter of an Application by Colaiste Feirste for Judicial Review of a Decision of the Department of Education Relating to School Transport [2011] NIQB 98
In the Matter of an Application by Damien McComb for Judicial Review [2003] NIQB 47
In Re Northern Ireland Human Rights Commission (Northern Ireland) [2002] UKHL 25
In Re Treacy's and Another's Application for Judicial Review [2000] NI 330
Jordan v United Kingdom [2003] EHRR 2
Kaya v Turkey [1998] 28 EHRR 1
Kelly v United Kingdom App. no. 17579/90 (ECHR, 4 May 2001)
McCann and Others v United Kingdom [1995] 21 EHRR
McCann, Farrell and Savage v United Kingdom [1996] 21 EHRR 97
McKerr v United Kingdom [2002] 34 EHRR 20
Prosecutor v Kallon SCSL-04-15-A
Re Committee on the Administration of Justice (CAJ) and Another's Application for Judicial Review [2015] NIQB 59
Re Downes' Application [2009] NICA 26
Re Duffy's Application [2008] UKHL 4
Re Parsons [2004] NI 38
Robinson v Secretary of State for Northern Ireland [2002] UKHL 32
Stewart v United Kingdom App. No. 10044/82 (ECHR, 1984)

Legislation

United Kingdom

Civil Authorities (Special Powers) Act (Northern Ireland) 1922
Education (Northern Ireland) Order 1998
Government of Ireland Act 1920
Justice (Northern Ireland) Act 2002
Magistrates Court (Northern Ireland) Order 1981
Northern Ireland Act 1998
Northern Ireland (Emergency Provisions) Act 1973
Northern Ireland (Emergency Provisions) (Amendment) Act 1975
Northern Ireland (Emergency Provisions) Act 1978
Northern Ireland (Emergency Provisions) Act 1987
Northern Ireland (Sentences) Act 1998
Police (Northern Ireland) Act 2000

Prevention of Terrorism (Temporary Provisions) Act 1984
Public Order Act (Northern Ireland) 1951
Public Processions (Northern Ireland) Act 1998
Victims and Survivors (Northern Ireland) Order 2006

Republic of Ireland

Nineteenth Amendment to the Constitution Act 1998

Treaties

Agreement Between the Government of the United Kingdom of Great Britain and Northern Ireland and the Government of the Republic of Ireland (Cmnd.9657, 1985)
A New Framework for Agreement [1994] 34 ILM 946
Beijing Declaration and Platform for Action (1995) www.un.org/womenwatch/daw/beijing/, accessed 16 March 2016
Belfast (Good Friday) Agreement 1998
St Andrews Agreement 2006
Stormont House Agreement 2014
The Joint Declaration by An Taoiseach Mr Albert Reynolds, TD and the British Prime Minister, The Rt Hon. John Major, MP (Cm. 2442, 1993)

Index

www.ingramcontent.com/pod-product-compliance
Ingram Content Group UK Ltd.
Pitfield, Milton Keynes, MK11 3LW, UK
UKHW011013180926
475701UK00004B/711
* 9 7 8 1 1 3 8 4 8 1 8 7 9 *